Thank You for Asking

Thank You for Asking

Conversing with Young Adults About the Future Church

Sara Wenger Shenk

with Deborah Good, Bethany Spicher,
Aram DiGennaro, Annie Lengacher,
Melody King, Nate Barker,
Allan Reesor-McDowell,
and Chet Denlinger

Herald
Press

Scottdale, Pennsylvania
Waterloo, Ontario

Library of Congress Cataloging-in-Publication Data

Thank you for asking : conversing with young adults about the future church /
edited by Sara Wenger Shenk ; with Deborah Good ... [et al.].
    p. cm.
 ISBN 0-8361-9305-9 (pbk. : alk. paper)
 1. Mennonites. 2. Young adults—Religious life. 3. Christian life—Mennonite
authors. I. Shenk, Sara Wenger, 1953- II. Good, Deborah.
 BX8121.3.T43 2005
 289.7'73'0842—dc22
                                        2005010551

Unless otherwise indicated, the Bible text is from the *New Revised Standard
Version Bible,* Copyright ©1989, by the Division of Christian Education of the
National Council of the Churches of Christ in the USA, and is used by permission.

To Deborah, Aram, Bethany, Annie, Melody, Nate, Allan, and Chet,
and all the young adults who so freely shared their stories.

Contents

Part 1
Introduction

Part 2
Narratives

Part 3
Practices

Part 4
Vision for the Future Church

Part 5
Conclusions

Foreword

It should be no surprise that many of the most innovative leaders in the church over the last few decades have come to pastoral and theological leadership from youth and college ministry. That's not to say that youth ministry is a stepping-stone to "real" ministry. I have often said that if I could have had two careers, my other would have been in lifelong youth ministry. But it is to say that working with young adults is a lot like emergency-room medicine: you probably learn more there in a month than you might learn in a more traditional medical practice in five years. You are exposed to unpredictable trauma, undiagnosed illness, and raw unedited symptoms at a pace and with an intensity that throws you into the deep end of life.

That's the feeling I had as I read these pages. They represent a gritty, honest, unedited, blood-sweat-and-tears immersion into the spiritual, social, emotional, and sexual lives of young adults. In all their beauty and chaos, integration and disintegration, they provide a window into the realities of ministry to people of all ages.

I say that because my years of ministry have taught me that, in a real sense, we never truly grow up. As the work of human-development researchers like William Perry and journalists like Gail Sheehy makes clear, there never is a plateau at which human adults stop changing. Their identities may go from liquid to Jell-O, but they don't go, in this life at least, to hard cement.

The stories and interviews you are about to dive into will give you a feel for the dynamic of identity formation, the deep challenge of faith formation, the struggle for intellectual integration of faith and life and community, and the unending search for meaning, grounding, and hope. You will see people you know, and no doubt you will see yourself—because we never outgrow these growing experiences as long as we're alive.

Stories become universal by being personal and particular. In that way, the Mennonite particularities of these stories are not an obstacle, but rather a bridge to connection with others who did not have the good fortune of being born in an Anabaptist setting. Believing as I do that the Anabaptist heritage has treasures desperately needed by the church (and the world) in these emerging postmodern times, I am glad that the Mennonite-ness of these stories will be accessible beyond parochial borders. A wide array of readers will gain a taste and feel for what "Mennos" are about. But because I have the great honor of visiting and speaking with the widest range of Christian denominations, I am also aware that Presbyterians, Catholics, Pentecostals, Episcopalians, and others will feel that these Mennonite stories, with a few small adjustments, could be their own. We're more alike than we usually realize.

There's pain in these pages, honest pain and messy pain. As Sara Wenger Shenk quotes at the end of chapter 23, "A community needs to reflect reality; we have to have communities in the church that talk about God, but we also have to have communities that talk about not God." She's right. In the Bible we have Job and Lamentations and Ecclesiastes, and often it is our young voices who best carry on their tradition of honesty, questioning, doubt, disillusionment. That is a gift.

One of the gifts of this book is not only to hear the voices of young adults, but also to hear from a fifty-year-old woman of faith and reflection. In all of this, Sara doesn't pretend to be a detached observer. She offers her personal insights and analysis in response, and she weaves the voices of these young adults together with the voice of her own grandfather, from his travelogue published in 1902. In this way, we are given something here that is timely, rooted in the middle of the first decade of the twenty-first century, but also something that is not faddish and stuck in a narrow band of time. That shouldn't surprise us, since this collection of voices in many ways echoes the collection of voices we have in Scripture—voices at once rooted in their own time and place and yet also relevant to us, whatever our age, whatever our location.

We aren't used to slowing down long enough to listen well to anybody, especially the youngest among us. Many will be tempted to skip ahead to chapter 27, which offers Sara's concluding reflections. If they do so, they'll find some great insights there, but they'll be bypassing the wholesome meal and rushing to dessert. Each reader would be wise, like Sara and her research team, to pay these young adults one of the most valuable currencies of all: attention.

—Brian D. McLaren

Preface

This is a book of stories—the stories of young adults as told to their peers. Perhaps better than many of us, these young adults are sensing the shape the future church will need to take to be real, down-to-earth, and life-giving for their generation in the twenty-first century.

Young adults, writes Sharon Daloz Parks, do many things.[1] They work, party, play, earn degrees, travel, protest, create art, explore, establish long-term relationships, form households, volunteer, become parents, initiate projects, serve internships, become financially independent, deal with major physical and emotional challenges, die young. However, the central work of the young adult, Parks writes, isn't located in any of these. Rather, the promise and vulnerability of young adulthood lie in the birth of critical awareness, and the dismantling and reconstruction of the meaning of self, other, world, and "God."

In *The Fabric of Faithfulness*, Steven Garber describes the period between adolescence and adulthood as "crucible" years, when basic integrity between belief and behavior is forged. How, he wonders, do young adults learn to coherently connect what they believe about the world with how they live in the world? In other words, how does a worldview composed in large part by formative stories from our childhood become a chosen way of life? This work has enormous consequences for the years of adulthood that follow.

The extent to which young adults make sense of their lives by reflecting on, and intentionally choosing, stories and concrete practices to shape a worldview and a way of life is of great interest to me. In my book *Anabaptist Ways of Knowing: A Conversation About Tradition-Based, Critical Education* (Telford, PA: Cascadia, 2003), I supply a philosophical, theological basis for an approach to educational formation that involves "indwelling narratives" and "revitalizing core practices." Now, however, along with a team of young adults, I explore the practical, real-life dimensions of formative stories and practices as described by young adults. I learn from young adults every day where I work, at Eastern Mennonite Seminary. I am endlessly curious about why people are the way they are. Growing up as a middle child in a big family and in multiple cultures necessitated that I learn ethnographic observation skills—for reasons of basic survival.

---

1. I take my definition of young adulthood from Sharon Daloz Parks, *Big Questions, Worthy Dreams: Mentoring Young Adults in Their Search for Meaning, Purpose, and Faith* (San Francisco: Jossey-Bass, 2000), 3: "Young people typically between seventeen and thirty—the 'twenty-somethings.'"

How, I've wondered, are young adults negotiating the tremendous challenges facing them? We live in a time of massive cultural change. Some have called it the end of one age and the beginning of another. Change in the last twenty to thirty years has been so rapid that many of us feel profoundly disoriented. The young-adult challenge to construct meaning and cultivate life-sustaining practices must now take place in a culture that itself is in upheaval. And many young adults are increasingly disconnected from communities of identity and memory as they negotiate this rapidly shifting terrain.

In my primary faith community, one can readily observe a spectrum of responses that young adults are making to the narratives and practices of their Anabaptist-Mennonite faith heritage. Some are choosing to identify with the formative stories of this distinctive faith community and to embrace its core practices. Others are on the margins, drawing identity and meaning from stories and practices that are not Anabaptist-Mennonite, nor even broadly Christian. Many are somewhere in between, sorting through a global menu of options.

With a generous research grant, I was able to form a research team of young adults who interviewed fifty-six of their peers. The following pages share the stories and comments from those interviews. We focus on stories that tell about young-adult experience rather than making broad generalizations or numerical calculations about that experience. For reasons of confidentiality, I have changed the names and some facts for those interviewed; the research assistants' names, however, have not been changed (see the Appendixes for more on research methodology, demographics, and page numbers for individual interviewee stories).

Book's Design

The narratives in this book have come from the field notes and journals of the research assistants. I've done editing work on those materials to bring consistency in voice and narrative flow. The design of the book is meant to preserve a narrative core from each of the interviewee's reflections, allowing us to see comments on a particular topic in the context of one's larger life. A significant excerpt of at least one individual interview was placed at the start of most chapters. Following the individual narratives, most chapters feature clusters of comments on themes that illustrate the topics of a particular interview.

The Group Interview chapters feature the comments of four to six people from various groups and are clustered in response to individual questions. Interspersed throughout are journal comments made by the research team, who offer their observations at the completion of each interview.

Acknowledgments

Special thanks to The Valparaiso Project on the Education and Formation of People in Faith, whose generous grant made this research possible, with particular thanks to Don Richter, associate director of the grants program, whose encouragement made the project seem doable and important. Heartfelt thanks to faculty colleague Lonnie Yoder for his counsel and support throughout the project, and to other colleagues, including Brenda Martin Hurst, Lawrence Yoder, Ervin Stutzman, Nate Yoder, and Gerald Shenk, whose insights enriched the project.

And my profound gratitude goes to the young adults who agreed to serve as research assistants: Deborah Good, Aram DiGennaro, Bethany Spicher, Melody King, Annie Lengacher, Nate Barker, Allan Reesor-McDowell, and Chet Denlinger. The quality of their work is exemplary, as the chapters will demonstrate. With style and grace, empathy and keen listening, they were able to call forth these priceless stories from their peers and record them in a way that becomes accessible to us all. Each of these individuals is enriching their communities with their abundant gifts in one form or another. No doubt they will grow into significant leadership in our communities as their elders dare to entrust them with the future.

Warm thanks to my two young-adult sons—Joseph, whose spark ignited this project, and Timothy, whose good cheer buoyed me along the way; and to my husband, Gerald, and daughter, Greta, whose daily love and encouragement are an elixir of joy.

As a team, we were delighted by the depth, genuineness, wisdom, and beauty evident in the many stories young adults shared with us. The more we listened, the more eager we became to share them with a larger audience, believing that they will give pastors, parents, and other adults entrée into the young-adult world—into their memories, their questions, their dreams for the future. While the stories collected here are from young adults affiliated with Anabaptist-Mennonite faith communities as a common point of reference, our hope is that others will recognize in common the experience of grappling to make meaning amid the cultural crosscurrents.

Part 1

Introduction

Chapter 1
Characteristics of Young Adults

"I love the journey, but I'm not content with homelessness"
How do young adults learn to make meaning in ways that sustain a worthy adult life? And a related question: How do they shape a way of life within a community of belonging?

Sharon Daloz Parks's extensive research and writing on young adults grew out of her concern that young adults may discover a critical perspective that calls into question their inherited, conventional faith. Then, though they are able to enlarge their respect for the faith of others, they may be unable "to recompose a worthy faith of their own." Also of concern to her was the notion that too many young adults are not being encouraged to ask the big questions and are being swept into religious assumptions that remain unexamined.

Faith, she says, refers to "meaning-making in its most comprehensive dimensions." Human beings, whether self-consciously or not, compose a sense of the ultimate character of reality and then stake their lives on that sense of things. In her view, faith is the act of "composing and being composed by meaning."

Human beings, she writes, seem unable to survive, and certainly can't thrive, unless we make some sort of sense out of things—pattern, order, and coherence among the many pieces of our lives. If we experience life as only fragmented and chaotic, we'll become confused, distressed, and end up in despair.

So to become a young adult in faith, Parks says, is to discover in a critically aware manner the limits of inherited assumptions about what is ultimately true and trustworthy, and "to recompose meaning and faith on the other side of that discovery." In that process, she concludes, young adults respond to two yearnings—(1) for differentiation, journeying, and pilgrimage; and (2) for belonging, homesteading, and home.

Deborah Good, one of the young-adult researchers on our team, writes a column, "Beneath the Skyline," for *DreamSeeker* magazine. One of those articles grew out of our reflection together as a research team about the work of young adulthood. It was called "Seeking Journey, Making Home: A Glimpse of Young Adulthood."

I am reading a novel. In it, the author creates a little world of people whose lives weave into and out of each other. The newspaperman plays basketball with the brother of a woman who becomes his lover. This woman's best friend is married to the newspaperman's photographer. And the photographer and the basketball-playing brother meet regularly with the same Jewish organization.

The characters' lives are interconnected as they visit each other, eat together, talk about each other, fight with each other, follow the happenings in each others' daily lives. They may not always get along—they may not even be friends—but in their own odd, unintentional way, these six people are community.

Some days, all I want is my own little world of people. I want to feel at home somewhere—in a geographical place, in a small community of people, in a grounded way of thinking and living. Instead, I feel scattered. I know too many people in too many places who believe too many different things. Too many, too many, too many. And therein lie the bane and the richness of my young-adult existence.

In her book *Big Questions, Worthy Dreams: Mentoring Young Adults in Their Search for Meaning, Purpose, and Faith*, Sharon Daloz Parks develops "journey" and "home" as prevailing metaphors in our lives. "The story of human becoming might best be understood as reflecting two great yearnings," she writes, "one for differentiation, autonomy, and agency, and the other for relation, belonging, and communion"—home.

And what do I mean by "home"? Home is, first of all, a place. It is the familiar braided rug in your parents' living room. It is the stream that runs through the family farm. It is the crack in the sidewalk in front of 1800 Kenyon Street.

But home is more than location. It is a feeling of comfort and stability. Expectations are understood and people are constant. Dad always sits in the biggest chair, Beth's always yelling something at somebody, Mom says the prayer before the meal, and, gosh-darn it, everyone better play Monopoly with Tommy afterward. And although no one asks about the meaning of life, most people in the group would have something similar to say. Home is a geographical place, a group of people, a faith tradition.

I find in my own life, and in the lives of many of my peers, a tension between our desire to explore new territory and our hunger for a sense of home. We read books with ideas that challenge the doctrines of our childhood—and then return to our home church for the annual Christmas hymn sing. We spend a year in an indigenous community in Peru, but we are relieved our parents haven't moved anywhere when we get back. We spend our weekends visiting friends in various parts of the country, but in our search for community closer by, we start supper clubs and have keg parties. Even as we leave much of "home" behind, we seek ways to create it wherever we are.

In a song called "Cathedrals," Jump, Little Children sings about times in life when "you get a feeling that you should just go home—and spend a lifetime finding out just what that is." These words capture what I think is a key challenge for many of us in my generation.

Last July, I sat around a professor's deck with a group of my peers, discussing our stage of life. Sometimes I think young adulthood is like standing in a crowded room of loud people and being told to follow "that voice." We have a gazillion ideas of what our lives could look like and little idea how to get there.

So we meander about, bumping into each other, trying to make smart decisions, trying to pay our school debts and electric bills, still trying to discern what we believe, what we're sure of in life—since somehow we graduated from college without figuring that out—and, mostly, trying to have a good time.

I turned 23 last month. When I reflect on the past few years of my life, I find it no wonder that I have a hard time knowing what to call "home." I am not sure about a lot of things, including what job I will have in three months. In the past five years, I have lived in twelve different housing situations, and I'm about to move again. My college classmates and I are constantly navigating the next decision-making episode, the next transition. Almost every other weekend, I am helping a friend move or attending someone's wedding.

I wonder whether my feeling of homelessness was true of young adults in the past. In part, I think it was—this life stage is inherently full of transition. But technology and travel make my world bigger and more accessible than that of many a few generations ago. Exposure to such a wide variety of people, places, and experiences may have left my generation with less of a sense of home than our parents and grandparents.

This morning, I rolled out of bed and pulled on some clothes. It wasn't until lunchtime that I looked down and realized how much my outfit said about my relationship with the world: I bought my purple "Graceland" sneakers last month while visiting a friend in Germany. My long-sleeve top is from Guatemala where I spent a semester of college. And my necklace of dark brown beads was given to me by a friend who lived in India for several months.

In contrast, my 88-year-old grandmother has rarely left the state of Pennsylvania and recently wrote me a card saying, "You are brave to go so many new places, but I think I would rather stay home." After traveling some in young adulthood, most of her children have returned to live in Lancaster County, a short drive from the farm on which they were raised. I wonder where my cousins and I will end up.

Thirty years ago, my parents graduated from Eastern Mennonite College (now University), my alma mater. Their friends scattered to different parts of the country and world, like mine, and they wrote some letters but gradually lost touch with many of their classmates.

I, on the other hand, live in the age of cell phones and the Internet. I am connected to the world—and to people from my past—in a way my parents never experienced. As a result, my friends from high school and college and I write e-mails and talk on the phone to keep in touch. We visit each other regularly, sometimes driving long distances without thinking it excessive or unnecessary. This may sound like fun, but it also leaves me feeling untethered, scattered, homeless.

Also, I am not grounded in a faith tradition the way my parents were a generation ago. I grew up going to Sunday school and learning Anabaptist values from parents and relatives but am much slower to embrace fully any way of thinking and living.

As a child, the diversity of students in my D.C. public school classrooms taught me to be accepting of many kinds of people and to grant validity to different religious beliefs. As a college student, my friends and I watched *The Matrix*, a movie that asks if what we believe to be real is in fact a deception, and we felt like it said something about our lives.

We are living in an era commonly characterized as "postmodernism," an era that defies definitions of truth and reality, and deconstructs foundational ideologies and moralities. In such a world, it is hard to feel at home or take root in any one faith tradition.

I have loved my life's journeys, but I am not content with homeness. I have chosen to live in a bustling city of over a million people with no one else from my family, and to keep in touch with friends in many different places, but I am trying to create home even in my rather nomadic existence.

Next week, I move into an apartment with two good friends. I look forward to spending time there, filling the living room with furniture, decorating the walls with our things. I look forward to eating our meals around the kitchen table, debriefing together after our days at work, and being community for one another as best we know how.

Recently, I have also started meeting a good friend for breakfast once a week—one more way to build consistency amid scattered relationships. And although I say that I am slow to embrace a faith tradition, I still go to church on Sundays, seeking God and, even more, looking for somewhere to belong.

We are a generation of nomads, jumping from place to place and job to job. But if you look closely, we are also a generation scrambling for stability and community, seeking ways to make home.[2]

The work young adults do to make sense of and live into a way of life is challenging and often lonely work. But when done in the company of others they love and respect, it is the heart and soul of what makes life good.

"*We all need a story to live by*," Parks says, and symbols to anchor our meanings, and songs and dances confirming that we belong with each other. More, "*we need practices disciplining us into ways of life* that make and keep us fully human" [emphasis added]. At their best, Parks writes, faith communities provide these in profound measure. If what a faith community offers resonates with young adults, then their spiritual quest leads to a faith home. And in turn, faith communities that become a home for young adults must themselves be open for ongoing transformation by entering into genuine conversation with the questions and visions of young adults.

In the following chapters the young-adult stories invite us into a potentially transformative dialogue, "loving the journey" together even as we fashion homes worthy of our questions and our dreams.

2. Deborah Good, "Seeking Journey, Making Home: A Glimpse of Young Adulthood," *DreamSeeker Magazine: Voices from the Soul* 4, no. 1 (Winter 2004): 10-13; online: http://www.pandorapressus.com/dsm/winter04/goodde.htm. Reprinted by permission.

Chapter 2
The Search for a Unifying Narrative

"I grew up in a 'big-stories family'"

We define ourselves in stories—personal and communal stories, human and divine stories, mythic and parabolic stories. There are ethnic stories, family stories, faith community stories, national stories, Bible stories, stories of enchantment. A human is essentially a storytelling animal, argues philosopher Alasdair MacIntyre, a teller of stories that "aspire to truth." If you deprive children of stories, "you leave them unscripted, anxious stutterers in their actions as in their words."

Telling stories, narrating our lives, seems to be a universal human activity, one of two basic ways of making sense of life that emerge spontaneously among humans, argues educational philosopher Jerome Bruner. The one way he calls the "narrative mode." This shows up in good stories, gripping drama and is very influenced by its particular context. The other way he calls the "paradigmatic mode." This shows up in good theory, tight analysis, and tries to be context-free and universal. Each in its own way tries to order our experience. And both seek to express truth. If we try to reduce one to the other or ignore one at the expense of the other we fail to capture the rich ways people "know," he says.

Somewhere along the line, we were tricked into thinking "that the greatest truths are contained in abstractions rather than stories," observes Brian McLaren, pastor and interpreter of the church in postmodernity. "Nonetheless, we are regaining perspective these days. So we must start by honoring the stories around us." We are each a story in progress, surrounded by other stories in progress; and in the process we find ourselves part of "God's unfolding story, too, because God's story intersects with ours at every turn, in every breath, pulsing in every heartbeat."

"My story" is a subtext or subplot of time-honored community stories of which I am a part. I may choose to interpret my story in light of the community's meta-narrative, a composite of stories that have provided a unifying continuity over time. For example, it was said of the Anabaptists, ancestors of the Mennonites, that for them, the Scriptures were "world-creating;" they "steeped themselves in Scripture," situating themselves in the biblical "story" from which they derived their self-understanding and empowerment.

Any one of us may also discern that the stories we've received are not adequate to make sense of our lives, provoking us to search for other stories or more honest stories that reliably speak the truth of our reality, or—as for the Anabaptists —a new and more radical interpretation of the stories we've already received.

Each of our lives is in some way a quest for a unifying narrative, for making enough sense of the world so that we can become generative participants in it. But also many of us, and particularly young adults, find ourselves busily recomposing our unifying stories so they more adequately integrate the complexities, contradictions, and surprises of our world.

When Rachel was invited to talk about the different kinds of stories that shaped her imagination and identity during her childhood years, she had many to tell. She also spoke about the stories that have power for her now as a young adult. Through Rachel we see the richness of a "storied life" and the many ways in which stories provide the stuff of which to make sense of life.

Rachel

Rachel said that she grew up in a "big-stories family." There were so many stories and a lot of emphasis on passing down stories.

Rachel's dad grew up in a family of ten kids on a farm, and "the family was weird." While out on the tractor, they often had a book of Frost or Thoreau in their back pocket and would hold the book on the steering wheel and memorize poetry while farming. Education was important. They often recite poetry at family reunions. And the next generation is encouraged to memorize poetry, too. Her mom's side tells "tall tales" based on reality but stretching it, making the stories bigger and bigger each time.

Rachel recounted it this way. One big family story tells of Mom's dad as a farmer. When Mom was two years old, Grandpa took her twelve-year-old brother, nine-year-old sister, and a whole crew of neighbor kids out on a sleigh pulled behind a tractor. He was pulling them around, off-road, on-road. There was a load of high school boys behind them, throwing snowballs at them. Grandpa didn't like it, thought it was getting out of hand, and he wanted to get away from them. At the railroad crossing, Grandpa decided to cross very quickly. A train hit the sleigh and killed all twelve kids except for his two children. It was horrible. All the neighbor kids were killed; one family lost all their children. It made national news. There were stories that Grandpa was drunk; they got mean letters from California. . . . This is a story that everyone knows in that generation. It changed everyone's life. Grandpa was devastated and became very depressed. He also became very gentle, quiet, would "cry at the drop of a hat and would just like to hold us." "We always knew there was something different about Grandpa, but it was never talked about until he died." The neighbors themselves did not blame him. "It was immense forgiveness and immense love." The hardest part for Grandpa, according to the family, was facing the neighbors every day, knowing he'd killed their children and they weren't upset with him.

Rachel's family was also unusual because they were interracial. She related stories about the adoption of her brothers: Her parents talked a lot about how they added her brothers, where they came from, everything they knew about their birth moms (which wasn't much). They all started as foster kids. Rachel's mom asked the agency, "How long am I going to have these kids?" And they said, "Well, you can have them till they're eighteen, basically. No one wants a black boy." And Mom said, "Over my dead body . . . I'm going to adopt." Her brothers faced discrimination, but Rachel thinks it may have been better that they lived in such a small community, where everyone knew who they were.

Rachel doesn't remember Bible stories much because they weren't as "exciting" as the other stories in her childhood, but they did go to vacation Bible school every year, where the adults would set up a village and play different characters. Her dad was sometimes Jesus. Grandma (dad's mom) often quizzed them on Bible stories.

Rachel's parents' faith didn't really fit with that of their church and surrounding community, which were more conservative and read the Bible word-for-word, because they had left the area and come back. Her dad had been in Zaire doing alternative service during the Vietnam War. Dad told his stories with slides and really made them come to life. Her mom told stories from when she worked at Rocky Mountain Mennonite Camp.

Her family had no TV, but they occasionally watched *NOVA* and other nature shows at her Grandma's. As children, Rachel and her siblings always asked for stories before they went to bed. "Mom, tell us a story about when you were young." Her mom also read to them at bedtime. She read Alex Haley's *Roots* aloud to them when they were children. And other books too. Rachel and her siblings were encouraged to read. Her mom said there were three things she wanted her kids to be able to do: (1) read, (2) math, (3) swim. Why swim? "I don't want you to drown!"

When Rachel reflected on what the stories taught her about who she is, she commented that the tragic story about Grandpa and the sleigh was huge. It taught her a sense of community, and the gentleman her grandfather became afterward really impressed her. The actions and attitudes of the neighbors taught Rachel about forgiveness and the power of not retaliating.

Reading *Roots* impacted how Rachel saw the world. She learned the horrible, blood-stained history of African-Americans in this country, which was made more personal because her brothers are black. As she observed the world around her, she saw that racism was not something only in the past and in the South. People are cruel. She came to appreciate her brothers' rich history, with amazing stories of survival, and the terrible truth that their race is only in this country in the first place because of the horrible things white folks did. She became somewhat ashamed to be white. Then she got to high school and college and realized how many people hadn't grown up hearing these stories.

In school, they had a horrible history teacher, and Rachel "always knew there was some story not being told." She remembers asking a lot of questions of this teacher. The narrative that the United States "was great" did not sit well with her. Her dad had Howard Zinn's *People's History of the United States of America*, which she read some in high school and even more in college.

As a kid, her parents took them to diverse churches, including Black churches that gave her a diverse view of God and church. But from childhood stories she had the impression that God was male. The shepherd image for God became very real for Rachel when she helped her dad deliver lambs on the farm, after which she wouldn't leave the sheep.

Now there are a variety of stories that hold power for Rachel. She enjoys it when older people in the local area tell stories about her grandparents at family reunions.

She also hears powerful stories working as an ob-gyn resident at a hospital in a mostly white suburb of Philadelphia. She recounted a recent story of racism in which a patient's husband requested that no African-Americans attend to his wife, or even enter her room. The hospital went way out of the way to accommodate the request.

Rachel has talked intimately with a scrub nurse who faced discrimination as a result. This nurse faces discrimination all the time—most whites would have no idea. Now, the NAACP is suing the hospital. "*Roots* comes back to haunt you," she said.

She lives with the many stories of her patients, stories of extreme joy and pain, and once she delivered a dead baby, for example.

Rachel recently read a newspaper story about a child found in a garbage bag two blocks from her house. The story made the news seem so much more real. It pains her that these things still happen, and she wonders what could have been different in the life of that mother to prevent her from abandoning her baby. What could even just one person have done differently in her life to make it better?

For a while when Rachel lived in Egypt, she was supposed to follow a woman around. This woman was the third wife of a Muslim man. He beat her, and she couldn't really do anything about it. But she refused to make him supper. That was her way of saying no. He then refused to provide her with the food for making supper. Instead of subjecting herself to him, she worked extra hard alone to get food for herself and her kids. This woman's example of nonviolent resistance was very powerful for Rachel. That woman was a "Muslim pacifist."

Rachel keenly feels the contrast of driving from her mostly black, urban community to the wealthy suburbs where she works. She is ashamed to be white. She knows she is privileged and has had numerous opportunities that others didn't. She doesn't want to take that for granted. And she wants to use that privilege to change the world a little for the good, to make it a little better for other people.

Rachel spoke of a variety of media sources she tunes into. She watches TV news and *Jeopardy*. Books she reads include *The Poisonwood Bible,* by Barbara Kingsolver, and fiction and nonfiction, a lot of them stories like *The Red Tent*, by Anita Diamant. Now she reads a lot of material related to her residency. She doesn't read trashy romance novels, preferring the classics; she also reads about adoption since she and her husband are looking forward to adopting. Movies she's enjoyed include *The Power of One,* about South Africa, and *Bend It Like Beckham.* She hates violence and anything scary; she likes movies that have points, movies where good wins out.

Rachel uses the Internet for e-mail and e-Bay. She gets *Time* but hates it; gets the local newspaper, picks up the local Black daily paper, and loves the local paper in her small hometown with all its random story bites. Rachel listens to NPR (National Public Radio) every day on the way to and from work, though the national and international news depresses her.

She enjoys listening to country music because it reminds her of home, which is "embarrassing" because the songs are often racist; she associates it with farming, a sense of community, and knowing all the neighbors. She likes hymns more than "Praise God" songs: "You came from heaven to earth to show the way, from the earth to the cross my debt to pay, from the cross to the grave"—just skips over Jesus's life. Rachel grew up singing from *Life Songs*, and she likes the music to be found in the Mennonites' blue *Hymnal: A Worship Book.*

Rachel says that verbal stories are still the most important to her: stories from her mom on the phone, from patients . . . "Everybody has a story. That's what makes them interesting."

Journal Comments

Unlike some of my interviewees, Rachel had no trouble with the story theme. Her life is full of stories, and she tells them easily. She draws other people's stories out of them by listening and values that practice deeply. Rachel could probably have spent two hours answering the first question alone, telling me her childhood stories. It is interesting, though, how small a role Bible stories play in her memory—probably the least of anyone I interviewed. She remembers the more exciting family stories much better.

Despite the tragedy in some of the stories, there was nothing dark about Rachel. Throughout the interview she was laughing and lighthearted. I was also impressed with Rachel's racial consciousness. I tuned right in since that's a huge part of my own story. Others talked about their identities as Mennonites, Christians, Americans, and women, but no one else really talked about being white as a significant part of their identity formation. Rachel spoke openly about her struggle with the shame of her white skin.

—Deborah Good

Chapter 3
Practices That Become a Way of Life

"I love the singing and the food"

There's a fascination with all things Celtic among a lot of people today, including me. We're not all enamored with the Irish for the same reasons, but when a particular culture excites people's imaginations, there must be something about such a way of life that is compelling, fills a kind of deficit many of us feel, and satisfies a pervasive yearning. I've read some wonderful books about the Celts. But while visiting Iona, a little island off the coast of Scotland, I encountered firsthand the mysterious, beautiful way the "material and spiritual" are closely interwoven in the Celtic way of life.

When Brian McLaren spoke at Eastern Mennonite Seminary several years ago, he remarked that the premodern Celtic era was one of the most vibrant periods in Christian history, lasting some seven hundred years, with far-reaching influence in Europe's awakening from the Dark Ages. He observed that the Celts didn't have a written theology but rather encoded their theology in ritual, dance, song, and a sacramental approach to daily life. Their faith was expressed in their daily rhythms and practices rather than in an elaborate, rational system of beliefs. Many of us are also drawn to practices that reconnect us with the earth and with each other, weaving together the physical and the spiritual in ways that make us whole.

There is something about the Celts that reminds me of my forebears in faith, the Anabaptists, who also did not develop an elaborate abstract theology, but invested themselves—heart, soul, and body—in following Christ in life, internalizing the Jesus story, and recovering Jesus-inspired practices. They revolutionized their communities in practical, bodily ways even as their spirits were ignited with a fervent love.

We use practices to give shape to our everyday lives and to express faith in our communities of worship and service. They involve the movement of our bodies and the investment of our spirits—touching, seeing, tasting, smelling, healing, feeding souls and mouths, singing, loving, reflecting, praying, kneeling, cleaning, washing, opening doors, resting, clothing ourselves, anointing, burying, planting, birthing. . . .

"Christian practices are things Christian people do together over time in response to and in the light of God's active presence for the life of the world," write Craig Dykstra and Dorothy Bass in *Practicing Our Faith* (San Francisco: Jossey-Bass, 1997). These are ordinary activities, "the stuff of everyday life." Yet no matter how mundane, they can be shaped in response to our experience of God's active presence in our homes and communities. When woven together, these practices suggest the patterns of "a faithful Christian way of life for our time."

When done well, practices sustain human communities over time. Ask people to discuss a fond childhood practice, and stories tumble out. Tears and laughter erupt. Connections are made. But there are practices that also made us feel trapped, stifled, and worse. Practices need to be examined to see how life-giving they truly are. When done well, quality practices are gifts that immeasurably enrich our lives.

In our interviews, we asked about narratives and practices. Dave's story is fascinating; he talks about not remembering many stories from his childhood, but what he recalls are all sorts of concrete activities, real-life expressions of family and faith commitments—"loving the singing and the food." Dave's story illustrates well the way in which practices were powerfully formative in shaping a quality way of life.

Dave

Dave doesn't remember many stories from his parents. He does remember that every Sunday during Advent his family would sit around the Christmas tree, with his dad reading from the children's Bible, telling the pre-Christmas and Christmas story. And he remembers the children's books they read, like the Berenstain Bears, Dr. Seuss, others.

When Dave was a kid in the American South, maybe five years old, his dad was pastor at a small church. There were only five kids in his Sunday school class. Dave remembers a teacher who didn't believe in luck but that "God was behind everything in some way. I guess I didn't really think about it too much, but then I told my dad later. . . . I don't even remember what he said except that he asked me, 'What do you think? How do you feel about that?'"

A church camp was Dave's home away from home. He started going there when he was about ten. He loved the singing and the food. He loved campfire time—stories, Scripture, sharing time. He remembers singing "Seek Ye First" and "Sanctuary," and "for some reason that singing clicked with him way more than Sundays at church." The camp taught Dave how to worship, "to just sing some song and be totally wrapped up in it." People talk about things being too emotional, but there is spiritual value in just letting go, not thinking, and being in awe, he said. There were no altar calls; Dave hates altar calls.

Dave calls himself a "news junkie." He used to watch the news two or three times a day, beginning in elementary school. He liked to know what was going on in the world. When San Francisco had a really big earthquake, Dave collected everything he could about it—newspaper clippings, *Newsweek*—and made a scrapbook. His parents never tried to shelter him. They told him about the time they spent in Central America in a cross-cultural study program. Probably, though not overtly, his parents encouraged Dave's exploration of the wider world.

Dave knew he was Mennonite, but no one in his town had a clue what a Mennonite was. He wasn't told Anabaptist stories but did learn from his parents, especially his dad, the theology that made Mennonites distinct, especially pacifism. But he didn't really know about the "ethnic Mennonite world" until he moved to a "Mennonite town" in the Midwest, and all of a sudden he wasn't "weird" anymore. In that town, being Mennonite was the norm.

Faith is and was important to Dave's parents. His dad cares about being a minister and teacher. He "allows a lot of flexibility" in his understandings of faith and is as willing to learn as he is to teach, an attitude that probably helped him in his role as a campus minister for nine years.

Dave had this sense of being Mennonite from the things his parents told him, but he felt different from the others at school. As a result of his belief that you weren't supposed to hit back, he never got in a fight. He was aware of the church-state distinction Mennonites make. He remembers becoming conscious of the Pledge of Allegiance in fourth grade and knowing that he should be pledging allegiance to God, not to his country. He was never directly instructed by his parents not to pledge to the flag, but he remembers having a sense that he shouldn't. He also remembers being at baseball games when everyone stood to sing, and his dad telling him that he stands to be respectful but doesn't sing the national anthem.

Dave was friendly with odd people. He was attracted to them because they were always trampled on and were, like him, not materialistic and not cool. He hated the kids at school who made fun of others. We're all God's children and should be treated as such, he felt. There was one girl that Dave was in band with. Kids would always make fun of her because she had a developmental disability, and Dave was so fed up with them.

Dave remembers his neighbors, who were not as well off. The family had lots of kids, who were always doing "bad" things. One time they even shot BBs at Dave's family from a tree house. But there was always a sense among Dave and his family that they should give their neighbors some grace—be kind and sensitive—because they didn't have as much as his family had. Many had some family issues going on. In other words, there were unfortunate reasons behind their actions, and Dave should be compassionate. Today, as Dave works with low-income families, he constantly reminds himself of that lesson: fight the stereotypes in your head about the poor and homeless. "You don't know their story. You don't know what's going on in their head, or why they're that way today."

Dave remembers that Sunday school stories made God neat and tidy. "Probably by and large those stories don't do a lot of good." His dad wanted Dave and his sister to make a conscious decision to join the church. "He made it clear that 'This is something I've chosen for myself, and I'd really like for you to choose it yourself.'" It was never forced. Dave never *had* to go to church, but he always did.

Dave was quite analytical and scientific (in a "Western" mode). Beginning in middle school, he questioned God's existence some, but he still always went to church. It took a long time for him to decide to be baptized because of being uncertain of God's existence. He took "catechism class" at a Mennonite church. Once a week he met with a fortyish mentor who had walked a similar road to faith. Dave finally decided to be baptized at seventeen. He's not sure why, but he knew that was the direction he wanted to go with his faith, even if he wasn't quite there yet. Being baptized involved going before a committee that asked what it meant to him to become a member of the church. At the baptism, Dave was immersed, which was important to him because of the symbolism of "coming out anew from the water."

Journal Comments

Some young adults journey, others stay or go home. Dave has journeyed some in a geographical sense and in the career sense. He is currently a social-service worker and lives in a major metropolis—two things he has never done before. But it seems that Dave has never journeyed too far in his lifestyle choices (practices) and in his beliefs/values. He has embraced what his parents instilled in him.

Dave was able to continue to embrace the stories and practices of his

Mennonite upbringing even after going to college and the city. Such experiences sometimes push young adults into rejecting their faith and experimenting with lifestyles that fall outside their parents' expectations. I expect that part of the reason he was able to continue in this track is because his parents' presentation of faith was already quite open to interpretation. Their faith "allowed a lot of flexibility." And he grew up in a world that was not homogeneously Mennonite. Even his small Mennonite church was composed of mostly nontraditional Mennonites. This kind of "flexible faith" allowed him room to move.

—*Deborah Good*

Chapter 4
Historical Narrative Springboard

A young adult's trip around the world, a hundred years ago

I've long known about a published travelogue my grandfather A. D. Wenger wrote about his trip around the world a hundred or so years ago. I never met my grandfather, nor did my mother or any of my siblings. He died when my father was seventeen years old, while serving as the second president of what is now Eastern Mennonite University. My dad made sure each of his eight children received a personal copy of his father's book, *Six Months in Bible Lands: Around the World in Fourteen Months*, published in 1902. It is reported to have sold very well in Mennonite circles in the early twentieth century, since A. D. was a well-known evangelist and educator in his day. I didn't have any particular interest in reading it, however, until my young-adult son Joe said that he had begun to read it. He was intrigued with this daring, adventurous great-grandfather.

And so, at age fifty, I finally read the book, but with fear and trepidation, because I didn't think I would like what I found. I read with an intense interest that surprised me. It seemed like a rare opportunity for me to hear a young adult of a hundred years ago tell in great detail his encounter with the religious and cultural plurality of his day, and then to compare it with how today's young adults make sense of their "global village." At thirty-one, A. D. Wenger was still a fairly young man when he ventured around the world. How did he interpret the world of his day, having been nurtured in a particular faith community and immersed in the biblical narrative? How might his story give us depth perception with which we can examine where we've come from and where we're going?

I shared excerpts of A. D.'s travelogue with the young-adult research team during our first session together. What followed was a fascinating "intergenerational dialogue" between their experience with formative stories and practices and his experience. A. D.'s travelogue allowed us to hear from another young adult who is not so far removed that we can't identify with him, and yet clearly represents an earlier time.

A. D. was born near Edom in Rockingham County, Virginia, in 1867. As a twenty-two-year-old, he ventured westward, attending various schools and teaching. He was ordained at twenty-seven and pastored at Bethel Mennonite Church in Missouri, where he held evangelistic meetings. He moved to Pennsylvania and married at twenty-nine, only to lose his wife to disease after one year. Within six months of his wife's death, he left for a trip around the world.

Excerpts from A. D. Wenger's Story

From the First Page of A. D.'s Handwritten Travel Journal

From childhood my mind often reverted to the scenes of the land trodden by the Savior of the world in his earthly career. Six months ago, after only one year of happy life, God took unto Himself the beloved bosom companion he had given me. Since then deep convictions have fastened themselves upon me that I should visit some of the foreign lands. First, that I may be relieved somewhat of that intense loneliness and keen sorrow which I realize while [at] home and which those only know who have experienced the loss of a chosen life companion. Second, to visit the land of our forefathers who several generations ago fled from a martyr's death to a land of religious freedom. Third, to visit the scenes of Bible action and become better acquainted with the Word of God. Fourth, to learn more of the work of those who have gone forth into heathen lands as missionaries in obedience to the commands of the Lord Jesus. . . . Left Millersville, Pa., Jan. 16, 1899. . . . Sailed on the ship *Servia* of the Cunard Line for Liverpool.

From A. D.'s Published Manuscript

In Liverpool: "I felt strangely insignificant as I left the great ocean and stood for the first time upon the shore of the Old World, in which are the Mother country, the 'Fatherland,' the Holy Land, the cradle of humanity, and over twelve hundred millions of people" (8).

When visiting Oxford: "We are glad for the educated men of the past who have given us the Scriptures by translating out of the original Hebrew and Greek. Here John and Charles Wesley were educated, and founded the Methodist Society in 1729, which body now numbers more than five millions in the United States alone. Here the founders of State and builders of Empires have studied and gone forth to move the world" (14).

Near London: "Some of these aristocratic gentry squeeze their numerous tenants to a bare living, while they themselves live in great luxury in their magnificent mansions and stroll up and down their lovely parks, in which are spotted deer, rabbits and other animal" (15).

In Paris: "The minds of the French people have been largely influenced by Voltaire and other infidel writers. They have ignored God and the Bible and enthroned carnal reason as their guide. In conversation with a few Parisians that could speak English I found them without even an intellectual faith in Christ and His Word" (24).

In Switzerland: "The Swiss are an humble people, happy and sociable, not as haughty and reserved as the English and French and I feel quite at home among them. . . . One appreciates the society of humble lovers of the Lord when far from home and friends" (27-29).

Later, in Germany: "They spared no pains to make me feel at home in a strange land. Before retiring for the night they never failed to sing some spiritual hymns, read from the Book of truth, and kneel around the family altar in prayer to the Father of mercies" (41).

Reflecting on the "barbarian" ancestry of Germany and thus of many Mennonites: "We are not the descendants of the Jews, but of these Gentile barbarians. The early missionaries bore the gospel of salvation westward and northward from the Holy Land until it reached our forefathers several centuries ago. . . . Truly we are glad that the story of salvation by Christ came to us in our great darkness and idolatry" (31).

In Germany: "The laboring classes are hard workers, especially the women. You can see them doing all kinds of slavish work, even hauling on the road with ox teams. Nothing appears too hard for the weaker sex. . . . When will Germany awake to give woman the position she deserves?" (48).

When reflecting on what he's observed of European Mennonites: "The one hundred and twenty thousand Mennonites in Europe and America would today wield a wonderful influence for the betterment of the human race, had they all remained true to the principles maintained by their brethren a few centuries ago. Why have those of Europe become guilty of gross deviations, and division into factions? They have been poorly organized" (81).

In Rome: "In such a mansion lives the Pope who pretends to be infallible and able to forgive sins, while the One who actually is infallible and abundantly able to forgive every sin had not where to lay His head" (112).

En route to Turkey: "There is perhaps no better place in the world than on a ship in the Orient to compare the citizens of the different nations. There is no getting away from your ship companions while on the wide sea; you are penned right up with them for days in the same floating house. You cannot compare religions so well for they seldom wish to talk religion. But just touch them up on politics and they are full of the subject and each ready to claim that his country has the best government. A comparison of their dress, complexion, facial features and physical structures [is] quite interesting. On board our vessel were natives of Germany, Austria, France, Russia, Greece, Armenia, Turkey, Palestine, Spain, Poland, Denmark, Italy, Egypt, Bulgaria, England and America" (133).

En route to Syria: "Mr. A. Adiassewick, a Russian and a member of the Greek church, was a passenger on board the ship on his way to the mountains of Syria to prospect in mines. Shortly before our voyage ended he took me to his cabin where he strapped to his body a long sword that hung nearly to the floor, and got two well loaded revolvers out of his trunk; then he said, 'This is the way I'll travel when I get out there. They tell me those people are savage and if they come at me I will shoot. What will you carry?' I replied that I would also carry a sword, a Bible, which is 'the sword of the Spirit.' With that a man is better armed than if he had a deadly weapon in every pocket" (149).

In Syria: "Wherever it was my privilege to call upon missionaries and learn of their work and say a word of encouragement to them I was glad to do so. It seems to me there is nothing more self-sacrificing, yet beautiful and grand in the service of God, than to break away from home and friends and go to some far-away secluded place, where Christ is not known and there is no society and few comforts, and there spend and be spent as an humble missionary for Him who said, 'Go ye into all the world and preach the gospel to every creature'" (155).

In northern Palestine: "Three men, ministers of the English Church, after wandering over the wild country on both sides of the Jordan for four weeks, came to our hotel on the evening of May 6, tanned and toughened with their journey. When asked if they were not afraid of the Bedouins, they replied, 'No, we are all armed.' That doesn't seem right, does it, for ministers of the gospel of the Prince of peace to carry carnal weapons? And it is not right, for Scripture saith, 'The weapons of our warfare are not carnal'" (162).

In northern Palestine: "Of all the places in the Holy Land I desired most to see the Sea of Galilee next only to Jerusalem. Here so very many events in the life of our Lord took place, and when you walk upon the very shores, climb the very mountains and sail upon the very waters so often hallowed by the presence of Jesus Christ strong emotions well up in the soul and vainly seek to be clothed in language" (176).

At Jacob's Well, central Palestine: "Our Moslem attendant asked the priest for a drink of water from his jar. Upon being refused he grabbed up the vessel and drank anyway. This insulted the priest and they were just beginning a fight when two men caught the Moslem and forced him without the gate. It seems strangely singular that a Christian priest should refuse a drink of water on the very spot where once a despised Samaritan woman was so willing to give a drink to the world's Redeemer who offered in turn to her . . . *living waters*" (206).

In Jerusalem at the "Jews' Wailing Place" (the Western Wall): "It is indeed a touching sight to see them standing and kneeling here reading their prayers and mourning over their departed glories and the destruction of their temple and kingdom, just as their fathers wept long ago by the waters of Babylon. Here they come again and again, and have been doing it for centuries, and we cannot doubt their sincerity. Old men with long gray beards, . . . old mothers of Israel wrinkled and deformed by many hard years, . . . young men and women and even boys are among the number with tear-stained cheeks and bitter lamentations. . . . It is a strange gathering, different from any other. I never before in my life felt so much sympathy for the Jews as when I stood there and watched them in their solemn service of wailing. At that service you will recall much of their suffering and persecution through the ages that are past and be compelled to 'weep with them that weep'" (247-49).

In Jerusalem at the Church of the Holy Sepulchre: "A civil guard of Mohammedans is always at hand to keep peace between the various sects who profess to follow the Prince of peace. . . . About all these Mohammedans know about Christianity is what they see of it here at Jerusalem. Can we wonder that they are hard to convert to the Christian religion when they must stand on guard to keep these so-called Christians from killing each other? More than one riot has taken place within the walls, and the church floor has been covered with blood and heaps of dead bodies. . . . What a shame to the Christianity of the day and what a pity these Mohammedans have not bright Christian lights around them! Is it any wonder they call us Christian dogs?" (251, 322).

In Jerusalem: "May the time speedily come when the women throughout the land will be educated equally with the men and thereby be lifted from her degraded position to be man's equal. . . . The church right where it began needs reformation and extension. Education would lift the natives higher, especially the women, but it will take a thorough conversion to Christ to raise them to true manhood and womanhood" (347).

In Egypt: "I can see very plainly that our new country is following right after the old countries in many things, especially in the oppression of the poor by the wealthier classes. The few who are extremely wealthy control almost every enterprise by their various combines and monopolies and thus grow richer and enslave the masses, who are poor, more and more" (404).

Reflecting on ship while en route from Egypt to India: "The world is very wicked and cold toward God, but it has always been so, and we should not be discouraged in our Christian work. Our own land is the best one and yet it is full of drunkenness, profanity, immorality, pride, skepticism and hypocrisy" (452).

In India: "What work could be more pleasing in the sight of God than that of lifting these widowed women from a life of slavery and heathen blindness to a glorious life of liberty and joy in Jesus Christ? . . . There is no higher calling than that of living for the temporal and eternal good of others" (463).

En route from India to Ceylon: "On the morning of December 20 we saw the evergreen shore of Ceylon in the distance. Just as we entered the harbor a war vessel loaded with soldiers left the harbor for Manila. A United States flag floating over it told us from whence it had come and we well knew its mission. On board the ship I had just been talking with a highly educated Buddhist who claimed that Buddhists are better than Christians. He said, 'Christians are false and cruel. They do not live according to the teachings of Jesus Christ whom they profess to follow. He has taught that His followers shall be merciful and that they shall love their enemies. The leading Christian nations, England and the United States, are now both waging cruel war.' What could I say? Yonder only a few miles away was a warship from our own country sailing for the scene of bloody war" (499).

Leaving Japan for home: "At last, after one full year of travel from England to Japan the time had come to sail for home. It was a season of joy and heart yearning that no one knows who has not been far away for a long time. In this life we constantly look beyond and wonder how it will be at other times and other places. In my long journey I often wondered how it would look beyond—beyond a mountain, beyond the sea, beyond in some other country. And now there was a looking beyond the great ocean to the dear land so far away. . . . O how glad one is to get home once more from a long journey and enjoy the society of friends and the communion of saints. To a merciful and loving Father be all honor and praise for keeping His servant through dangers seen and unseen and bringing him safely home after many wanderings in strange lands" (542, 546).

Limitations of A. D.'s Worldview

In hindsight, we quickly detect limitations in A. D.'s worldview from a historical period in which many assumed America was a superior nation, with responsibility to Christianize and civilize the world. That worldview reflected confidence in progress and the bright optimism of the age before World War I.

We can see racism and ethnocentrism in A. D.'s appraisal of his world. For example, he seems to assume at points that Germany, England, and America are peopled by a superior race. He seems to have an inflated regard for the "light of our own country." He talks about some people as "low and degraded" and describes some people as civilized and others in a disparaging tone as "half-civilized." Some of what he says is offensive to those of us shaped by sensitivities raised after World War I and II, the Holocaust, the devastation caused by colonization, the civil rights movement, postmodern philosophy, and much more. In retrospect, the clear limitations of some of A. D.'s perspectives provide us with sober reflection on how we also are shaped by the prevailing narratives of our times, as well as by the biblical narratives.

"Intergenerational Dialogue" with A. D., About Narratives

After reading these excerpts and many more, the research team engaged with a variety of observations about A. D. and about themselves. Here are some of their observations:

A. D. had a distinct sense of how Christians "should behave" that is impressive. He had "a powerful meta-narrative that he took with him everywhere he went." He derived all of his interpretations of the world "through that paradigm."

A. D. "took his truth with him," which he used to evaluate the world. He was "certain about his truth claims," and his "presuppositions were confirmed" in what he saw and experienced. In contrast, now there seems to be no "measuring stick" against which to measure the truth claims of others. We are taught "to listen to different stories" and acknowledge the truth that's in each of them.

A. D. showed "no hint of cynicism." He was "very sincere." He "gave credence to people's stories," but he was very clear in saying "what was right and what was wrong."

A. D. finds that his "narrative holds up," but he can also take "other stories seriously."

For A. D. there was something of a "seamless existence": everything fit together.

He shows "a lot of bias," yes, when he's trying to make a point. And there are "definite themes he pushes out" for his own purposes. And he shows a lot of "optimism about education" and the possibility of "progress." This is a contrast to current young adults. The vast number of "today's young adults are overwhelmed. A. D. isn't."

A. D. clearly regarded Christianity as a way to better the world. He severely critiques the "hypocrisy of Christians" he observed in Palestine, often being harder on those hypocritical Christians than on the "heathens of India."

He was a man who clearly valued consistency of word and deed, suggesting that "by their fruits you shall know them." He clearly connected Christianity with "a way to better the world."

"Intergenerational Dialogue," About Practices and Values

A. D. Wenger was passionately committed to the renewal of faith practices and a robust spirituality in his day, primarily among Mennonite youth and young adults. After reading excerpts of his travelogue, the research team identified these characteristic practices and values:

- Values adventure, with significant initiative in exploration and risk-taking
- Attends "divine services" preferring to go to where he can "hear the word of God" rather than to the "theater"
- Takes the side of the lower classes, with great sympathy for the poor and ignorant; very critical of the wealthy
- Upholds pacifism, conscientious objection, comparing carnal warfare with spiritual warfare, the "sword of the Spirit" with the gun
- Appreciates the hospitality of "lovers of the Lord"
- Esteems humility and a humble spirit
- Lauds a "missionary spirit"
- Highly values education and frequently commends it as the way to solve multiple problems
- Frequently calls for consistency in word and deed, for integrity of faith and practice
- Appreciates the Word preached in purity and simplicity
- Values authenticity of songs and prayers
- Commends spiritual renewal when he sees it
- Frequently refers to reading the Scriptures
- Talks of engaging in silent meditation, imaginatively reconstructing biblical stories in geographical context
- Values equal education for women
- Shows reverence for nature, demonstrating a poetic regard for nature
- Calls for baptism of believers
- Refers to nonswearing of oaths as expected practice
- Practices abstinence from alcohol
- Thinks it's all right to dance to the glory of God, but other dancing is not appropriate
- Admires self-sacrifice and self-denial
- Practices foot washing, the kiss of charity, the Lord's Supper
- Appreciates simplicity and modesty of dress (valuing natural beauty, comfort, and nonconformity to what is considered fashionable; includes "head covering" for women)
- Honors the Sabbath (rest)
- Commends sexual fidelity and purity

- Commends play and recreation as important aspects of child development
- Again and again lauds the "humble teaching of Jesus"
- Appreciates the *Martyrs Mirror*
- Critiques bigotry, fanaticism, intolerance in each faith—Muslim, Jewish, and Christian
- Values the quality of Jewish home life
- Values the study of other cultures (their language, environment, ancient arts)
- Calls for conversion to Christ and growth in newness of life
- Calls for a balance of evangelism and social development
- Loves the church with ardent devotion and loyalty

A. D.—One of Many Young-Adult Activists in His Generation

Brenda Martin Hurst, a colleague from Eastern Mennonite Seminary, joined us for our conversation about A. D. She talked about several young-adult Mennonite leaders of the late-nineteenth and early-twentieth centuries who significantly impacted the character and future direction of the Mennonite church of their day: George R. Brunk I, A. D. Wenger, Menno Steiner, Daniel Kauffman, and others. She described how significant change happened in the Mennonite church at that time, much of it initiated by these enterprising young men—and women, who were less prominent. She said that it was young adults who reshaped the church in the 1890s and 1900s.

The end of the nineteenth century was a time of significant change in the United States—change from a largely rural, agrarian society to an industrial, urban society, with a new emphasis on education. Brenda commented that A. D. and his young-adult peers were bent on "redefining what it means to be Mennonite in the world and what the Mennonite relationship ought to be to the world." The common thread she found among George Brunk, Daniel Kauffman, A. D. Wenger, and others who later became significant reshapers of the Mennonite church of their day was that they all had been exposed to other denominations. They all seriously questioned whether to join the Mennonite church or join with others who were more engaged in the wider world.

"Why did these young men decide to embrace the Mennonite church after seriously flirting with leaving the church to become politicians or educators?" Brenda asked. She asserted that it had a lot to do with John S. Coffman, who was about ten years older than the pioneers named above. In the evangelistic meetings that Coffman organized, he tried to encourage educated young men and women to throw their energies into building the church. Brenda argued that Coffman and these other young adults increasingly redefined what it meant to be Mennonite. One could be Mennonite and be educated, Mennonite and evangelistic, Mennonite and bold—not backward and ashamed of one's faith. He redefined being Mennonite in a way that was attractive to these young men, and many bought it. "A. D. gave his energies to the church in a big way. The whole thrust of his work was to get young people to join the church, to make the church and the gospel message meaningful and attractive to young people," she said.

One of the research team asked Brenda, "When was the last time a group of twenty-somethings significantly reshaped the church?" Brenda responded, "I don't think it's happened in the same way since this core of young men transformed the church at the beginning of the twentieth century." The dynamic at work then was that as they made a strong move to become more a part of the world and to impact it, they also gave more intentional energy to self-definition, to who Mennonites are as a group. It was a time to unite resources and talk about what we hold in common so that we could share our story and those resources more effectively with the rest of the world. And, she observed, they were able to exercise incredible power to shape that new common life, enacting a kind of uniformity that hadn't been present in the church before. This had mixed repercussions for the life of the church that followed, with much that was good but some that was harmful.

One of the team members marveled at how those young adults started publishing together and that they drew up a common confession of faith. They were "confident that there is a better way." In contrast, we also "inherited the idea that we're to make the world better," but we've seen so many failures, we wonder "how." "I think," he said, "that today's young adults have high interest but low involvement. We are not trusted with church leadership."

Another marveled at how "those young adults claimed their voice, put themselves out there, and that John Coffman validates them." Now, he said, the "generation gap is incredible." There is a lack of "those bridging people."

Conclusion

Despite the disturbing aspects of A. D.'s worldview, I was pleased and surprised while reading the travelogue at the integrity of his core motivating vision, which runs throughout his journals. I would describe that vision as his confidence that a few faithful Mennonites could "wield a wonderful influence for the betterment of the human race" if they remain true to "the humble teachings of Jesus, and thus be a great power for good to the world." He was sure that there is no higher calling than to live for "the temporal and eternal good of others."

And even more, I am stunned at how A. D.'s core vision shows up throughout the stories of the young adults that follow in these pages. This same vision is expressed over and over again, though often in different language and reflecting somewhat different assumptions about the nature of the Christian calling. This suggests a strong, continuous core of vitality that links the generations even amid shifting worldviews and global dynamics.

Part 2
Narratives

Chapter 5
Formative Childhood Narratives

"They *are* my stories and they *aren't*"

All of us are deeply formed by early childhood experiences and by the stories that have shaped our early imagination, our images of self, others, God and the world. We spend our adult years trying to mine the goodness of that narrative legacy and to uncover the source of pain and struggle that may also be part of that bequest.

Each of the interviewed young adults was invited to reflect on the different kinds of stories that shaped their imagination and sense of identity during their childhood years, and also on what stories have power for them now but weren't a part of their childhood. A few of these are collected below. The rest appear in the lead-off narrative to many of the following chapters.

Below, Kate reflects at some length on the power of story in her childhood and young-adult years.

Kate

Kate was born to a family steeped in the Russian Mennonite stories and tradition from her father's side. Only later in life did she come to know and appreciate the Appalachian Scotch-Irish heritage on her mother's side.

Kate's paternal grandparents in Russia underwent hardship and hunger "because they were Mennonite." As a child, the idea of being persecuted for faith was significant for Kate. In contrast, she says, her mother's parents "weren't Mennonite. They made money. They were in the world. Of course," she adds later, "the Russian Mennonites were also persecuted because they were rich landowners."

Kate did some weeping as she retold story after story: How her *Oma*'s (grand-ma's) uncle tried to convince the community to flee Russia. They refused, and the Bolsheviks massacred the entire village. How her *Opa* (grandpa) proposed to her Oma while they were hiding in a basement during an air raid. How every year since they were young, her Opa has gathered into books for his grandchildren stories about the people he knew and countries where he worked and traveled.

The stories didn't end with Kate's grandparents. For years her parents were in Asia with Mennonite Central Committee (MCC), so there were the MCC stories. And then there were the martyr stories: "The guy who went across the ice, the woman who got a screw in her tongue. Other kids I knew didn't have to deal with this stuff!" she says.

These stories taught Kate that she was part of a community, that she was different from the world, and that she was safe.

"As a child," she says, "I was obsessed with security, always worried about my family. But I knew I would always be taken care of, because Mennonites take care of each other."

Her ideas about God conflicted.

"All these stories taught me that God takes care of you, even in ways you don't understand, even through pain. But at the same time, he pushes you into dangerous situations that aren't safe! Like I said before, I just wanted to be sure my family would be okay, but you have these martyrs that give their sons pears before they go to the stake!"

When Kate was in high school, her father had health complications, and during one severe illness, his heart stopped. Kate remembers praying desperately in her room down the hall, "Please, God, don't let him die!" Her father survived but was depressed for months afterward. Kate also struggled with depression during high school.

"I felt very betrayed by God for a long time," she says. "My father was just a shell. And while I still had these stories, it was like, 'These stories are lovely, but they aren't for me.'"

During this period, Kate traveled with her Opa to Germany, Switzerland, and the Netherlands for three weeks to meet the people and see the places in his stories.

"It was incredible seeing how all these giant people were just human, how their strength couldn't have come just from themselves. I met these people, and I realized how frail they were! It changed the stories for me."

The experience also seemed to make Kate more open to faith again.

Several books and authors were also influential during high school: Madeleine L'Engle's *Walking on Water*, George MacDonald's *The Princess and the Goblin*, Kurt Vonnegut, and C. S. Lewis.

In college, Kate started to learn the stories on her mother's side as well. She worked for a summer at a data-entry job and listened all day to NPR's *Prairie Home Companion* and *This American Life*.

"I was realizing that Americans have stories, realizing the worth of those stories, and trying to understand what it means for me to be an American, because I *am* an American, strange as it is. The stories I have from my grandparents, parents, and the *Martyrs Mirror*—they *are* my stories and they *aren't*. What stories am I going to live in my life? And how am I going to recognize them if I'm just looking for these epics? My grandparents' stories are epic! I mean, they're fleeing with hundreds of thousands of Mennonite refugees, being smuggled out from Soviet-occupied Berlin under the cover of night! They're encountering famine on massive scales! They're surrounded by this hurt and pain; and amazingly, with the help of the church in North America and elsewhere, they survive and are able to begin a whole new life.

"And here I am, living my life in middle-class America. I'm white. I'm privileged. I don't know if I knew it at the time, but I was trying to find an American equivalent to my grandfather's stories, to get used to other stories and recognize God in other stories as well."

Now Kate in a way is following in her grandfather's footsteps, telling stories at Mennonite College coffeehouses, But these are stories about her third cousin Johnny from Appalachia—on her mother's side!

At the same time, Kate emphasizes that her family was different from other Americans, and that as a child she was keenly aware of that difference. As she puts it, "Americans watched cable TV, ate white bread, and celebrated Christmas with Santa Claus."

While it's difficult for Kate to say she's a Christian, she considers herself very solidly a Mennonite: "I'm Mennonite. I'm Mennonite. I'm part of this body of believers. I go very easily from 'Mennonites' to 'people of faith.' It's easy for me to say I'm Mennonite, because that's my main community, that's what I really believe, those are the lives that have impacted me the most, that's who I am right to my core. To say that I'm Christian—that just means that I believe in Christ as my Lord and Savior, right? That just lumps me in with a lot of people who have done a lot of things in the name of Christ, the Lord and Savior. I don't feel that it lumps me in with people who have a similar relationship with the God I understand. 'People of faith'—that sounds similar."

Journal Comments

When I asked the first question about stories, Kate didn't hesitate—she dove right into about fifteen minutes of retelling the stories of her Opa and Oma. Obviously, her identity is rooted in these stories, and they're tangled up with her ideas about God and the Bible, with what it means to be Mennonite and Christian. As she herself said, these are epic stories that seemed to set for Kate—early in her childhood—a beloved but impossibly high bar for faithfulness.

In real life, Kate keeps running into her own frailty, the frailty of her father during his illness, even eventually the frailty of people in her grandfather's stories. She knows she can't live up to these stories, knows she needs something more, and for her, that seems to be community. Even as Kate is interpreting her *own* stories—those of being American, Mennonite, a biology major, a law student—even though that process seems in some ways to liberate her from the pressure of her grandparents' stories, she definitely doesn't see herself as autonomous. She's deeply communal—even her own stories are rooted in bigger communities, in larger stories—from the Mennonite community to the natural world.

—Bethany Spicher

Below are the reflections of other young adults who remember the formative power of their childhood narratives. To draw these out, we had asked several interview questions: Tell me about the different kinds of stories that shaped your imagination and sense of identity during your childhood years. What did you learn from these stories about who you are and about who God is? How do you feel now about the importance these stories were given in your childhood? Do you wish other stories had been given more attention? Which ones?

Matt: Matt observes that all types of stories have shaped him. His mom bought children's books at Christmastime and every Christmas read a new one; these stories had a purpose for all ages; he learned distinct lessons in morals from them. He remembers a specific story about a shoemaker who helped anyone who came to him; one day Jesus came and visited him, and he was able to extend the same help to Jesus.

Matt is interested in family history, the Mennonite game, and ties to the family farm; he enjoys hearing about his dad's experience of growing up on a farm. Often his grandparents would tell stories about childhood and show him pictures. He still spends hours looking at old pictures whenever he visits them.

The Bible stories of significance were introduced to him through the "now-you-can-read Bible stories." Joseph and his brothers, Noah and the flood, Rebecca and Isaac—these were important stories in his childhood. As a young adult, he now relates more to the New Testament and the prophets.

Matt reflected on the function of stories as he was growing up. They gave him a sense of identity, a sense of where he wants to go, what he wants to be, and where he has come from. They gave him confidence and encouragement for the next steps in his life. The stories showed him how his parents' experiences have shaped them, a formation that then has rubbed off on him. They also show God as faithful, compassionate, and full of grace. Matt feels that the stories created a strong base in him as he grew up and fostered his social, spiritual, and educational development. He would like to reread some of the Old Testament stories to refresh his childhood years.

Recent stories come from Matt's Mennonite history class and his cross-cultural experience. There are stories of how people have been sustained through times of hardship, massacre, war, and economic difficulties. Matt is amazed at the faith and joy displayed through the hard times. He enjoys stories of grace like *Les Misérables*, Tony Campolo's stories at a youth conference, and South African stories. Stories have also shown God's grace to Matt. They are important to him because they have modeled generosity and hospitality, influencing him to be more welcoming in spirit, taking time for people, having a greater interest in people's needs.

Amy: Amy's mom would read her Bible stories at night. Her family read lots of stories together. She remembers one storybook in particular called *Nobody Listens to Andrew*, with which Amy identified because it was the story of a youngest child whose family was inattentive until the end, when he is vindicated. Amy is a youngest child.

Amy's grandfather would also tell stories from his childhood, about her aunts and uncles, or from happenings on their farm. Amy and her siblings much appreciated those stories. It gave her a sense of fitting into the family, a sense of inclusion and of history.

Amy's grandmother died when she was seven, and Amy always enjoyed hearing stories from her life. This woman "obviously made a big impact on her family and community" and has become a model and encouragement for Amy as she considers the kind of person she wants to become.

Amy has been exposed to and intrigued by "stories of God working overseas" in mission settings. This, along with some personal experience, has given her a desire to be involved in mission efforts.

Craig: From his childhood Craig remembers the story of Daniel in the lions' den as a powerful one. Craig identified with Daniel because he was a rebel, against the system, and he sticks to his principles even when things look bleak. The story underscores the power of this position, and "that's a real powerful" inspiration for Craig.

He also remembers the children's storybooks about Curious George. Craig could really identify with George's playfulness and inventiveness. An aunt used to work with Craig to write stories along the lines of Curious George, with Craig as the implied character.

He was also taken with the *Knights of the Round Table*. Craig's dad used to read him these as bedtime stories, and Craig found himself just drawn into the literary quality of this work.

Craig values the influence of these stories. He would definitely like to pass them along to his own children. He thinks that, in general, literature should be a part of children's lives. He doesn't feel that these stories have too much immediate influence on him. "Stories aren't the sort of thing I consciously latch onto," he says. But he is sure they affect him somewhat, and is glad of this.

Renee: Renee is from a Mennonite Brethren family, and her mom told many stories about her childhood and family. Renee's grandfather died of illness when her mom was sixteen, and there were many stories about how the death affected the family. Grandma got a job, and Renee's mom, the oldest child, ended up taking on many of the maternal roles in the family. There were also funny stories of bee stings and all the crazy remedies Grandma had for them, and stories about fights between Renee's mom and her brothers because they would sit around while she did all the household chores.

Renee's mom's family lived in a village with several other Mennonite families. The community was centered around a business, for which her Grandpa did the accounting. But the community fell apart somewhat about the time he passed away.

Renee loved when her grandmother would talk about all the children she grew up with and about eating culturally German foods. Renee found this communal spirit fascinating.

There were stories of Mennonite heritage in which Renee took an interest as she grew older. She would ask her grandmother lots of questions. But TV and movies were not an important or shaping part of Renee's childhood.

Renee loved the fact that her family was Mennonite. This was very shaping and so much a part of her identity. The stories from her mom's side reflected that family was a value stressed for generations. Renee's dad worked for the oil business and had opportunities to move around a lot. The opportunities could have advanced his career, but he and Renee's mom decided it was important that they stay in one place so Renee and her sister would have the continuity of family and place.

Christian faith was considered very important in the family. Renee grew up understanding God to be very loving, since everyone around her—family and church—loved her. Stories taught her that God isn't biased but cares for everyone, and that we have a responsibility to do likewise. Renee had a very positive experience with church and had no negative feelings toward God.

At summer camp, though, Renee rededicated her life to Christ over and over, because she knew she would feel guilty if she didn't go forward when the invitation was made. This feeling of guilt was tied to the things Renee was told while growing up about what it meant to be a Christian. This image of perfection left her feeling like she didn't quite measure up.

Laura: The stories Laura experienced in childhood also told about a loving God. In Bible school, she was also told about the "justice of God." If she didn't give her life to God or if she did something bad, she believed she would go to hell. As a kid, she wanted to make sure she was going to heaven, so she recommitted her life over and over.

In seventh grade, she rededicated her life to the Lord at a concert. She realized then that there was more to faith than being a good person. It was about being in relationship with the Lord in her daily life. It was about sharing it with others, reading the Bible, praying, building a relationship with Jesus—things she didn't necessarily see in the people at church and youth group, or even in her parents.

She recalls an experience she had at a concert. "I remember very vividly. I was there with two girlfriends from middle school. They were playing 'Not Ashamed' ('I'm not ashamed to preach the name of Jesus Christ') and saying that if anyone wanted to rededicate their life, to raise their hand. And I raised my hand, but when they asked us to come forward, I didn't quite have the guts. And so this one girl obviously had her eye on me and asked if I wanted to go up front. So I went, and I was so glad that I did. It was just really refreshing. . . . I was just bawling. . . . This is so much more than what I was thinking."

Tom: Tom relates stories from his childhood in Germany as the ones that have formed him. He recalls the story of how the German Mennonite church got started in the area where his parents were working. Everyday his parents met for coffee with the neighbors. One day the neighbors asked for prayer for their sick child. The child experienced healing, and the neighbors came to know the Lord. Another story involved the dramatic transformation of a man who had been doing hateful things toward the missionaries; and yet another involved Tom's own physical healing.

Tom related other stories that give evidence of supernatural intervention and says that they form him "whether he likes it or not." They remind him that God is faithful and that the battle belongs to the Lord. "I have a bad memory, and stories help to remind me of God's faithfulness." Stories of struggles in past life also help him keep perspective in the present.

What I Hear

Formative stories have many sources: family lore, the Bible, church, community, folk and classic tales, cross-cultural narratives. Some are heroic, epic stories, and others tell of human frailty; some stories set the bar impossibly high, and others teach us about grace. Some stories are rooted in bigger communities, and others seem uniquely personal. Some stories show how "my people" have experienced God, and some tell of discovering God in other people's stories as well.

These stories will continue to unfold in the chapters that follow. They often illustrate the joy and the pain that each of us experience in uniquely personal ways, but also as "my story" set in the context of a much larger community and even a cosmic story. In some paradoxical way, as Kate says, the stories we receive from others "are my stories and they aren't." Questions remain: "What stories am I going to live in my life? How am I going to recognize them if I'm just looking for these epics?"

Chapter 6
Formative Church Narratives

"You don't even know who you are"

The community dimension of formative stories pervaded story after story. The community is more specifically described as the church, in most cases the Mennonite church. We didn't ask for "church stories" per se in the one-on-one interviews. Instead, we asked about "different kinds of stories" (Bible stories, family, denominational, ethnic stories, books, literary classics, movies, music, TV). What showed up in many of the stories, however, was powerful evidence of the church community's formative impact on individuals. That impact was often appreciated, sometimes not.

Experience with the church story is often indistinguishable from one's family and community story. In the three stories that follow, "the church" shows up as a prominent player from childhood into young adulthood.

Peter

Peter grew up in Virginia, except for four years he spent in Ethiopia with his missionary parents. One of Peter's earliest memories is listening to his parents talk at the kitchen table about how they felt God calling them to Ethiopia.

"There was really a sense that we were going to help people who aren't as fortunate, and I learned that that was important." There also was always a sense for Peter that he was different from other kids—because in Ethiopia he was white, and back in Virginia he didn't watch TV.

Peter was influenced by a story that his family read every Christmas, the story of a poor family burglarized on Christmas morning. The youngest daughter of the family approached the robbers and offered them her Christmas money. They didn't take it, and the whole crowd ended up eating Christmas dinner together. Peter gathered that this was the kind of "brave, compassionate action" that was required of him.

As a child, Peter believed that "God demanded a lot of me. My idea of God was definitely a sheep-and-goats kind of image. I thought that God would stack up all the good things you did and bad things, and whichever stack was higher, that would determine your eternal fate." In a fourth-grade Sunday school class, Peter's teacher told him that "deeds" didn't matter, and that it was a personal relationship with Jesus that counted.

"It sort of shook my world up," Peter says, "because I'd been trying to be good. Now I hear that Jesus died and I was forgiven, but I still thought there's got to be a catch somewhere. That kind of stressed me out a lot."

Peter remembers responding time after time to altar calls all through junior high, "but it was never quite enough." He was baptized in the ninth grade after his youth pastor approached him at the roller-skating rink and asked if he'd ever thought about baptism. Peter remembers thinking, "I think I should get baptized. I think that's the answer he wants."

"There was this mushy sentimentality to the religion I learned at church. You had to have this emotional experience, and I never really had that, and it bothered me." At the conference youth retreat in Peter's junior year, the speaker encouraged the youth to "go to another country and do missions." Peter felt called to do STAT [Summer Training Action Teams], evangelistic training in which the outreach is practical service, but he had mixed feelings about his summer with STAT.

"I learned about taking spirituality seriously, but the theology was, 'We have answers and we have to bring them to everyone else.' That's something I've questioned since then." At the STAT training in Baltimore, one of the speakers had just come from the "Toronto Blessing."

"And what do you know, it descended in Baltimore. Nothing happened to me. They kept saying nothing has to happen, but when you're seventeen years old and everyone around you is laughing or dancing or falling into comatose states, you think something's wrong with you. But I didn't want to fake it. On the second night, though, I thought, 'The heck with it. I'm going to dance around on my own.' All the while knowing I could stop at any moment and just stand there. I came back from STAT feeling very spiritual—this responsibility to be on fire for Christ—and feeling like I should be critical of my church for not being on fire. But after awhile I said, 'Aw, this is too much work. They're fine.'"

Peter paused to characterize his home congregation: "One time they invited a speaker who said that Islam is a lie that Satan made up to trick people."

At his Mennonite high school, Peter and some friends who'd also been to STAT started a weekly prayer group and Bible study. "We were the spiritual pillars of the school."

For Peter, his Mennonite college was "refreshing," especially the peace club, PAX. "We talked all about simple living and peace." Regarding activism, Peter was influenced by his parents: "I had this sort of idealized view of the 60s. In high school I had long hair, wore bell-bottoms." However, he didn't connect peace activism to faith until PAX club late-night talks: "We had lots of discussions—are we a Christian group or a secular group? Eventually, some people who were further to the left split off. They didn't want to do our peaceful vigils; they bought gas masks and went to the IMF [International Monetary Fund] protests in D.C." Though Peter was one of the "peaceful vigilers" who appreciated the links between pacifism and faith, "evangelism went by the wayside, and I found something to replace it—peace activism, and this seemed like something I could relate to."

Journal Comments

Peter is highly self-critical, as he himself said, and I wonder if that's a result of having such a demanding God! From his experience in youth of responding to multiple altar calls to his current feeling that war tax resistance isn't enough, Peter seems to understand, as he put it, the Jesus of challenge more than the Jesus of comfort. Another theme is his continuing struggle with not having the "right" emotional responses to faith.

He seems to have a quite practical, works-based faith, even as a child when he believed that God kept a tally of good and bad deeds. Peter strives to be authentic, not to use religious language unless he's sure of what it means. He makes decisions because they make sense and fit with the action-based compassion he learned as a child, not necessarily because they're what God has called him to—though he's fine with explaining things that way if he encounters someone who seems to want that language. Peter is very conciliatory, even though he said at one point that he often finds himself defying whatever prevailing theological-political framework he's around at the time. Yet his defiance is never open; relationships seem to matter more to him than ideologies.

—Bethany Spicher

Jason: Jason's dad, who was Amish as a boy, left the church at sixteen and became Mennonite, along with his siblings. Jason's mom grew up in a conservative Mennonite home—strongly influenced by fundamentalism. Jason grew up in a quite Amish area, but not many Amish are left there today. He reflects that Mennonites from an Amish background are different: they're moving away from the rigid rules of the Amish lifestyle without a strong sense of Mennonite philosophy-theology and without strong Mennonite leadership, leaving the community very vulnerable to outside influences like Christian fundamentalism. Jason didn't learn about a lot of Mennonite teachings until he attended a Mennonite college.

Jason's parents read Old Testament stories from a children's Bible before bed—Ruth, Moses, Adam and Eve. They also read him Sesame Street and other children's books. There wasn't much TV, just a few cartoons. He wasn't allowed to watch a whole list of sitcoms. The Jesus stories were told over and over: the standard Christmas story, Jesus as a thirteen-year-old in the temple, Jesus's three years of discipling, and the resurrection.

The stories did not include much hellfire and brimstone. His parents were turned off by tent revivals when they were younger. Jason remembers, though, being very scared about Jesus coming back, about not being able to grow old. He used to have dreams about it. He vividly remembers one dream in which Jesus would walk down the driveway to his house to get him, and he wasn't ready for it and didn't want to go.

"I could never understand how everybody else was so excited about this even happening when life would be *over*." A part of the fear was also his worrying about not being taken, and a fear of losing his family through it. He remembers worrying about reaching the "age of accountability." He wasn't exactly a "good" kid and was taught that there was this age, maybe around thirteen or so, when if you didn't accept the teachings and do what you should do, well, that's it. Before that age, you would go to heaven regardless.

Jason's dad had a band with some of his brothers—sort of a contemporary Christian type, kind of country-rock-folk group. They would tour around on Sunday nights. Jason would often go along. One day, Jason went out to his dad's shop, where he was writing a song called "Sweet Memories": "Sweet memories we'll have to hold until that day when we'll all sing again in perfect harmony." It was about Jesus coming back. Jason was really affected by it and broke down. His dad prayed the "Christian prayer" for him—what you pray when you become a Christian. He was probably eight or nine.

Politics intrigued Jason. He was quite into the Dukakis run for election when he was eight years old. His family and a few friends were the only Democrats in town. In sixth grade, he had a bet with his teacher over who would win, Bush or Clinton. He won a big bag of candy. He followed politics and current events mostly through watching TV and through conversations with peers. He would have political debates at school even though he didn't know much. He'd go home, ask his parents about something, and then go back with that "ammunition" for the next day.

He learned to be comfortable with, and even to like, being a dissident. He learned that a strict line separated Mennonites from the rest of Christianity. His grandfather would talk quite negatively about Catholicism. Jason got the idea that unless you were Mennonite or Amish, you were wrong.

As Jason talked, he identified a significant difference between the God he learned about at home and the God he learned about in school, a difference he had never thought so clearly about before. At home he learned of a God of compassion, understanding, and grace. As Jason grew older and his parents' perspective changed, the Sermon on the Mount and teachings of Jesus were stressed more. At school, God was somewhat a tyrant, an enforcer of rules. God didn't encourage freedom. God was intrusive, inescapable, angry if you did something wrong, and not compassionate. Jason thinks this view had a much greater impact on him.

Jason was scared of God, thinking: "I have to live a certain way, or bad things are going to happen to me." God was distant, looking down with a lightning bolt. God was *not* in everything, and *not* a personal buddy. There was some emphasis on a personal relationship with God—"they sang touchy-feely praise songs at school"—but this was stuff he never understood. It was like a different language.

Jason wishes he was told more about historical Anabaptism and fewer stories about the mythological Old Testament—Noah's ark, and so on, stories without much meaning. He wishes there would have been more emphasis on the New Testament, which he finds more relevant. He wishes he could have explored more of what was prohibited—things considered "of the world" and taboo: TV shows, conversations about sex (he remembers being shocked in sex ed class), and pop culture. He feels that being so removed from the world created insecurities around other kids who were allowed and exposed to those things.

Jason doesn't remember any stories of Anabaptist history from his family. "My parents don't know anything about Anabaptist history," Jason said. He learned more about that in college. He definitely considered "Mennonite" part of his identity in grade school, even though his knowledge of what that meant in contrast to mainstream Christianity was limited. Jason describes his sense that his parents and pastor had more understanding of Mennonite uniqueness than the community at large, which though Mennonite in name, was more influenced by mainstream fundamentalism.

After his freshman year of college, Jason no longer considered himself a Christian. He saw Christianity, especially the Christianity with which he grew up, as being too legalistic and rigid and limiting of freedom. But at the same time he was also learning what being a Mennonite was: the peace stance, simple living, nonconformity, service. And so, these were "things I picked up while discarding everything else." He remains quite respectful of what it means to be a Mennonite and glad of his upbringing, but calls himself a "secular Mennonite."

Jason remembers with appreciation stories from his dad's construction business. Jason was impacted by his dad's respectful treatment of his employees. Jason relates to others with a faith in individuals, believing that people are generally good; he believes in human potential.

He has a theory that there are moments you stumble upon when you reach transcendence temporarily, moments when everything makes sense. Jason reflects that maybe he is trying to live in a way that stimulates those moments.

Jason doesn't belong to a congregation. His level of commitment to the church is nonexistent, and he would expect not to have any involvement in the future. He could see himself belonging to an interreligious group of people who would look at different religious and secular texts, bouncing around ideas. He may be interested in trying a secular community that shares belongings. Any community he's a part of should be welcoming of everyone, he said.

Journal Comments

It was interesting to me that the choices Jason makes about how he spends his time appear to have little to do with the ideas and values he argues about in his head. He talks about valuing the peace stance, nonconformity, and simple living as core values of his Mennonite heritage. Jason talks about picking these up in college while discarding the more dogmatic Christianity he had grown up with (and a belief in God), and yet his practices don't strongly reflect these values.

He's really into the *stories* of revolution and utopian thought, but his own life doesn't strike me as particularly revolutionary, utopian, or challenging of the status quo. Similarly, he had an easier time thinking of stories and ideas he'd like to pass on to his children, but a very hard time with the question about practices he would expect to regularly incorporate into his home life (shown elsewhere). In other words, I found him quite thoughtful about ideas but far less thoughtful about how those ideas affect how he lives and will live in the future.

—Deborah Good

Miguel: Miguel was born near the Mexican border, the youngest of five brothers and one sister. His siblings are all married, and he has lots of nieces and nephews; his extended family is large on both sides. Miguel's father was born in Mexico and emigrated when he was four years old, coming to Texas during World War II. Miguel's mother was born in Texas.

"Her family dates back to when this side of the border was still Mexico," says Miguel. "They're true Tejanos."

Miguel's father was converted from Catholicism while he and his wife were employed by Mennonite farmers as migrant workers in Ohio. Miguel's mother had grown up conservative Methodist. Every night she prayed for her husband, who before his conversion drank, smoked, and danced. Miguel is amazed now at "that perseverance and love."

"So here's my dad in Ohio, struck with arthritis at the age of twenty-seven, with three kids, and these cold Ohio mornings. It takes him two hours just to get ready for work. And he begins to realize that 'I can't keep doing what I'm doing.' He would take mom to church. One night he's outside in the car, it's cold, and Dad says, 'What the heck, it's too cold. I'm going inside.' He slides into one of the back pews and begins to hear the preacher. This preacher makes a connection with him, and he goes up for an altar call and accepts Jesus Christ as his Lord and Savior. He comes back a changed man."

Miguel adds that his father said after that, "I want to go back to my people."

"Mom didn't believe him for five years, but he proved himself by being a minister with the migrant people there. He really felt that he was anointed by God, that God had a place for him and a message for him, and he went back home to work in his barrio. That story is huge in our family."

Miguel's father came back to Texas and started a Mennonite church out of his brother's garage, along with his brother and father, who were still Catholic but supportive. Miguel grew up in Texas, as he says, "on tortillas, baloney, and TV." On the hot days in the "barrio," where there was no air-conditioning, he and his siblings would watch hours of TV, and tape-record the sound to listen to before they went to sleep. "I was raised by women." His playmates were his sisters and female cousins, who lived in the same neighborhood. Miguel remembers that his parents were always busy with church.

"We were living the story, the church story. Church was your life. You lived to go to church, to be with the family."

As a child, Miguel was afraid of God. "Hell was a huge hole. You would go down and keep falling forever and ever. It used to worry me. Fear of God, fear of the devil, fear of going to hell—it was very much a part of my story at our church. Dad wasn't yelling that from the pulpit, but somehow I knew that God was something to be feared, so you'd better stay on the right path, dress appropriately, and go to church."

Miguel remembers his dad reprimanding him and his friends from the pulpit: "Miguel, stop playing. This is church!" Miguel was a self-described "rebellious kid, always fascinated with cigarettes and beer."

Growing up, he says, "I had this idea that we were good people, that I was a part of something good. My friends at school were Catholic, and I felt separate from them. My sisters didn't have quinceañera, and we couldn't go to other quinceañera. There's probably going to be beer and a dance.

"We said, 'We're Mennonite.'

"'Well, what's a Mennonite?'

"I got along great with friends at school. In some ways I felt like a normal Chicano kid."

The church youth group, however, was where Miguel felt most at home.

"To us, we were the coolest at the church. We were the ones being deviant. As we got older, we started bringing a six-pack of beer and drinking it behind the church."

Miguel's dad preached pacifism from the pulpit.

"I always knew that I wasn't going to the army. A lot of my friends went into the Marines, and then they came back. There was none of this 'I'm out of here' that you see in a lot of small towns."

The expectation seemed to be that you'd return to "the [Rio Grande] Valley" and start a business.

"So I said, 'I guess I'll stay here, too.'"

Miguel worked as a paint salesman at Sears and says, "I connected with what I missed growing up—drinking and partying." He also attended the University of Texas for two years.

At this point, Miguel says, "I wasn't connected with what it means to be Mexican-American, a Chicano. I didn't hear stories of César Chávez. I knew who was white. I knew who had it better, and I always felt that it was our fault, that we just weren't as smart as them. We would travel up north to go to church conferences in these ugly cars, and these Mennonites would have a really nice little Camry. We kids were always excited. We were going to sleep in a really nice house! They have carpet, air-conditioning—sweet!"

After two years at the University of Texas, Miguel participated in an MCC antiracism drama troupe with three African-American women and Anna, who would later become his wife. Miguel calls it "a spiritual and cultural revolution."

"I saw four women who loved God, had a commitment to church and education, loving who they were as people, as part of a cultural group."

Of Anna, Miguel says, "She got after me a lot of times. She'd say, 'You don't even know who you are!'"

Anna, who was born in Mexico and grew up in a migrant farmworker family in California, amazed Miguel with her "love for Mexican culture and love for God. Cultural rituals and church were so natural to her, and I said, 'Here it is! This is how it is!' It was the experience that I look at in my faith journey that really turned me around."

After the summer with the drama troupe, Miguel says, "I committed myself to connect with God again, to figure out who I was as a Mexican-American." He brought his learnings back to his family. "My family right now is going through a cultural renaissance, even my mother and father. Their theology has changed! My dad's stories of growing up Catholic in the barrio—that's now something that was good, not something he needs to look down on. My family wants to learn Spanish. They're saying, 'Let's throw a quinceañera.' It's been an incredible journey. I'm still trying to figure out what it means to be Chicano and Mennonite."

Journal Comments

Miguel's an animated storyteller. I could tell when he became excited because he started speaking in Spanish. He's also very self-aware, naming the stages he's gone through: from being unaware of his cultural background to integrating his Chicano heritage into his faith and life, from feeling that inequality between races was his fault to becoming an antiracism activist. And he wants to share his learnings with his people.

Perhaps one blessing of being so family-oriented is that one person's education becomes the entire community's. And "one's own story" doesn't fit with Miguel's understanding anyhow. He very much sees himself in the church, in a family, in a "people."

—Bethany Spicher

What I Hear

Faith, family, and church are inseparably intertwined in these stories, sometimes building on each other, deepening and enriching each other, and sometimes introducing discordant themes—exaggerated emotionalism, fundamentalism, and racism—that detract and confuse. In one way or another, all three stories express fear of a demanding God and apprehension about how one's actions would impact one's eternal destiny. Each storyteller talks about mixed messages they heard regarding who God is and what God expected of them. And there are mixed cultural messages—being different from other kids, carrying responsibility to help other less-fortunate people, being separate from another taboo culture, which for Jason seemed to lead to some insecurities, and for Miguel to an attraction toward what he "missed growing up."

But there also are the strengths that endure. Peter finds a new kind of integrity in an integration of faith and peace activism. Jason learns an enduring respect for his Mennonite heritage even as he declares himself a "secular Mennonite." Miguel hears the call—"You don't even know who you are"—that awakened him to a new, vibrant connection with God as he discovered the richness of his own Mexican cultural heritage, reclaiming its colorful gifts for his family and church.

Chapter 7
My Experience with the Bible Narrative—I

"Scripture is very rich, deep, and refreshing"

To say the Anabaptists were "crazy" about Scripture isn't far from the truth. They so immersed themselves in the stories, images, songs, symbols, practices, and poetry of the Old and New Testaments that they came to be formed in body, mind, imagination, and spirit primarily by the Scriptures. And that immersion was driven by a passion to live faithful lives as Jesus's disciples.

In the research team's discussion of A. D. Wenger, they noted with surprise how powerful the meta-narrative he took with him proved to be for making sense of everything he saw and experienced. He "read" his world almost entirely through the "eyes" of the biblical stories.

Since the time of our Anabaptist forebears in faith, and since A. D.'s time, biblical scholars have given us tools for critical evaluation of the Bible's narratives. These tools have enriched our understanding of the many different contexts and eras out of which those stories arose. Yet even as we celebrate new subtleties of insight and fresh appreciation for how revolutionary the stories of liberation and salvation are, we also have gathered ample evidence of how those stories have been misused in oppressive and violent ways. Critical analyses have sometimes made it seem that the biblical stories are not reliable, and that only the experts are equipped to truly understand them.

For reasons beyond what we can discuss here, many of us no longer have the passion of our forebears in faith to immerse ourselves in Scripture. We tend to be more circumspect and uncertain about the relationship of Scripture to our lives. And yet, as is evidenced throughout these young-adult stories, there is a pervasive longing to know the Scriptures better.

Below are the stories and comments from a variety of young adults who seem to have a relatively positive relationship with the Scriptures. For example, Jessica exults in the way Scripture has enriched her life.

Jessica

During Jessica's childhood years, the dominant stories she imbibed were Bible stories. The family frequently gathered in the evening, and Jessica's dad would read from Bible storybooks. But rather than just reading the stories, he would personalize them, adding humor, adding the names of the children or acquaintances. "So the shepherd was counting the sheep and he said, 'Yes, Jessica is here, and Anna is here, but where is Billy?'" These stories were very formative for Jessica, and she remembers this from earliest childhood. The stories became *her* story, even though that identification was as yet unconscious, and her voluntary commitment to the narrative was not yet possible.

Watching the *Jesus* film in sixth grade was the most prominent example of this identity emerging into consciousness. Until that point, Jessica did not know that she was a Christian, although in retrospect she seems certain that she was. Nonetheless, she is grateful to have had the opportunity then to make her commitment conscious.

Jessica is grateful for being soaked in these formative narratives during her childhood. When taking Bible classes during her first years at a Mennonite college, she felt they were "ridiculously easy" because "all that stuff was already inside her." She is grateful to have been formed in this way. If she could change anything, it would be to add other narratives—denominational ones, for instance. She assumed nonviolence as a part of her faith, because it was part of the New Testament in passages such as the Sermon on the Mount. But she did not perceive that this or any other Mennonite teaching was different from other Christians around her. However, during her time in Youth With a Mission (YWAM), she began to recognize and appreciate what she shared with others in a Mennonite community: martyrs and potlucks and turning the other cheek. Classes at Mennonite colleges served to further define and reinforce this identity.

Another narrative thread Jessica would like to have had in her childhood is some basic awareness of pop culture. She has often felt like she is playing catch-up in this area. She feels left out of conversations about what it means to be an eighties kid or what is happening on television. When Jessica has a family, she would like to keep the biblical narrative primary, but also expose her children to a broader range of narratives. They should have enough knowledge of popular culture and classical literature that they do not feel so isolated and different.

Now in college, other threads of narrative are being added to Jessica's consciousness as well. The narratives of neo-hippie counterculture appeal to her. She has friends who are into it, listens to its music, and appreciates its emphasis on peace, justice, ecology, and political criticism. She also has begun reading novels of science and speculative fiction, especially those that wonder about the future and try to comment on what it would be like if certain current themes on earth were taken to logical conclusions. She identifies easily with characters who are intelligent, perceptive, and who both wonder about and shape the future.

Denominational stories have also been reinforced in college, and Jessica has come to appreciate church history and the history of her own denomination.

As Jessica moves into young adulthood in her last years at college, the Bible is still a rich source of guidance and inspiration. She loves discovering things in the biblical narrative that surprise and challenge her—violent stories in the Old Testament, the beauty of the Psalms, the idealism of the church in Acts, the guidance for her life and choices today. Scripture, as familiar as it is to her, is still quite rich, deep, and refreshing.

Jessica feels she has known the Jesus story "forever." But when she talks about it, her eyes begin to glow a little. She wishes she could hear it for the first time and be shocked by it because it has lost the impact that it should have. She knows that this story is actually as she saw it in the *Jesus* film in sixth grade—an amazing and gripping drama.

Bible classes at the Mennonite colleges she's attended have often seemed to undermine or attack what she believes about Jesus and the Gospels. Jessica often feels confused after hearing the variety of views that are out there, hearing Scripture attacked in so many ways. It would be tempting to stop believing, but Jessica finds that at the core, her early knowledge and experiences go deeper than these attacks can. Even if all the "evidence" points in the other direction, she has concluded that her faith is so deep that she "can't not believe." The depth of this faith, and the realization of its depth, is a tremendous comfort, even in places where Scripture is not valued very much.

As a writer, Jessica senses that her life story should have an overarching plot, the conclusion to which will be hearing, "Well done, good and faithful servant." She tries to focus her life, in all its many details, into accordance with this theme.

Journal Comments

Jessica had strong roots in a quite evangelical, traditional Mennonite sense. She is experiencing and experimenting with a lot of new ideas at college, but her vision for the future and her future family is in line with her upbringing. I wish I would have asked her why this was, but I was impressed by the strength of the early narratives and practices.

—*Aram DiGennaro*

Interview Questions

Tell me about your experience of reading the Old and New Testament Scriptures? How often do you read in the Bible? How do you feel about the reading that you do? How important is it for who you are and who you want to become?

Miguel: As a child, Miguel developed a love of writing and reading from his father and remembers reading through the encyclopedia set in his house. Currently, he's interested in books that "reconnect me with my cultural heritage and with my faith journey," and he's been reading the Bible in that light, as well.

"It feels like I'm reclaiming my Old Testament, my background, my history, reclaiming something that's been taken away from me. I understand the Gospels better. There were people in the Gospels whose identities were almost nonexistent: the disciples who didn't know who they were either, the woman who touched Jesus from behind, the multitudes that were being abused. Jesus says, 'Reclaim your power to change systems that are oppressing you!' When we understand who we are as humans, we can better understand what God has in store for our lives and for our communities. It's not an individual story; it's a community story. When I go back to my church and talk to them, I tell them, 'You shaped me.' It was *los hermanos y las hermanas* [the brothers and sisters] at church—not just my mom and dad—who helped me stay on God's path or prayed for me or encouraged or reprimanded me."

Regarding the Bible: "It helps us to understand who God is and who God was at the time. I'm open to God changing. It's amazing because these people were so radical. We didn't grow up with a critical theology of how radical they were. The crazy disciples [were] always wanting to put fire down on somebody."

Miguel adds that by studying the Bible and "big books on postmodern, postcolonial theology" (he cites Marcus Borg as influential), he's come to understand how the Bible calls for social justice. He and Anna lead Bible studies in the Valley churches, and "it's amazing to see what happens to other people too—women who have lived a certain life with their husbands and families, people suddenly reunderstanding our roles as men and women in church."

Renee: Renee has spent two years working at a rape crisis center in a major U.S. city. These years have been tremendously shocking, shaking, and then shaping.

She grew up thinking quite traditionally about gender roles, in the church and elsewhere. Women were never encouraged to take leadership roles. Her college did not challenge this way of thinking. In the city, Renee found herself surrounded by people with a very different theology and way of thinking about women. At first this was difficult because it was a challenge to what she previously understood the Bible to say. How could people interpret the Bible so differently?

The idea that God was not male was scary at first, but now, after hearing stories at the rape crisis center, Renee understands how it would be really difficult to see God as male when men have treated you so terribly. It's been good for Renee to understand her gender as represented in who God is—that many of God's attributes are female in nature. Renee also took a seminary Internet class that was quite formative and helpful as she redefined her theology and understanding of what the Bible says regarding gender roles.

Ajay: Regarding the Bible, Ajay said, "I still see it as something that shapes my daily life and walk. That doesn't mean I read it every day." Ajay also cites as influential C. S. Lewis's *Chronicles of Narnia*, the autobiography of Martin Luther King Jr., Orson Scott Card's Enders Series, and Walter Wink's *The Powers That Be*. The latter, Ajay says, "helped me put together the social, nonviolent themes of the Gospels." Ajay adds that he'd like to learn more about "drawing from the Bible for how I live my life."

Matt: Matt reads in the Bible three to four times a week. He doesn't feel that it is shaping his faith too much right now. He's not sure how it is impacting who he is becoming. Currently he has more interest in the academic side of Scripture, studying theology. He finds it helpful to have an outline or structure for reading Scripture, reading through the Bible book by book. Matt likes to read *The Hymnal* as an alternative to the Bible sometimes.

Christina: Christina reads the Bible every day, or every other day. She finds her perspective shaped by academics now, especially since she's taking an Old Testament class in seminary. She is receiving a new lens for reading Scripture. Christina thinks that biblical reading is very important. While she had to do it as a child because it was enforced, the wisdom she found in her reading shapes who she is becoming, especially in understanding God's character. She thinks of the Bible as the most important book in her life.

Mary: When asked about the Bible, Mary said, "It's fantastic—such good stories! If it's real, all the better!"

We learn through stories, mixing up all ideas of life lessons. In her Mennonite

Youth Fellowship (MYF) experience, she remembered, they didn't read the Bible a lot. "We were *told* what was in it. It was offensive." The Bible was presented emotionally first without attaching any sort of analytical, critical thoughts.

Mary says she doesn't read the Bible very often. She prefers a scholarly version that is open to interpretation.

Will: Will feels that he knows Scripture quite well. If he is deficient in any area, it is not in reading and knowing, but in applying. Since "we are accountable for what we know," Will is concerned that he works to apply Scriptural teachings. He says: "We should read Scripture with the wonder and simplicity of a child." "Wonder and simplicity" should be central, even as we use study and knowledge to enhance that perspective.

While "none of us are entirely conformed to Scripture," Will feels that Christians "should be governed by Scripture," "be submissive" to it, "wear it," and generally seek to let it impact us. He believes Scripture has a perspective-giving function. "The more you read Scripture, the more you see that earthly things unrelated to the kingdom of God are of infinitesimal value."

Sherri: Sherri often reads Psalms and Proverbs. She reads the Bible when she is having a bad day or needs help. She thinks that her reading is very important for who she wants to become. She chooses to read the New Testament because it's easier and more applicable and the Psalms and Proverbs give her encouragement.

Tom: Tom reports that he was exposed to a lot of Bible as a PK (preacher's kid) and an MK (missionary kid). He says he must constantly look at Scripture for "fresh insight." He sees the Bible as stories of "God's faithfulness to the church throughout history. I'm a child of God, and the people in the past were as well." The Bible also gives him direction on how to follow Christ.

Tom believes that "God works through the Bible." Tom shows God that he "cares enough to read and believe it." Then God uses the words to "change us."

Right now he is inconsistent in his reading even though he craves space for it each day. He tries to read a mix of the Old Testament and the New Testament. He chooses what to read on the basis of what he feels he needs that day. For wisdom, he goes to Psalms or Proverbs. For insight on better living, he goes to the Gospels and the New Testament letters. When he needs a "cool" story, he goes to the Old Testament. He also has been keeping a chart of the books of the Bible he has read for about the past three years.

Laura: About two years ago Laura decided she was going to read through the

Bible "to make sure that I had read every word." She said, "Sometimes when I read the Bible, I feel like I'm just reading because I should, and then sometimes I'm like, this is so fresh, . . . and a Bible verse will just hit me, just telling me what to do. I'm like 'Whoa! Where'd that come from?'"

Laura, who is attending a community college, said that right now she has a class on preschool that she doesn't enjoy at all because she doesn't plan to teach preschool. But then she was reading Proverbs and came across something about being a "happy learner" (she laughs) and decided she needed to change her attitude.

She finds the Old Testament harder to read, but she's learned to appreciate it a lot more. It happened so many years ago, but she realizes "that really happened to them; they're not just stories; this is real life." The main ideas are important: "to have faith, to believe, to obey." The Israelites were so disobedient, and yet God loved them so much that he kept waiting for them to come back to him, she commented.

Laura is amazed by the miracles Jesus performed and that the same power is in us. She also finds Acts important. She is struck by how passionate the church was. "That's how I want the church to be [now]," she said. The Bible is "essential because it's the truth, and it's the Word. I was just thinking that if I lived in Bible times and didn't have that to follow, I would be lost because it has the answers."

Laura puts Bible verses in notes to people to encourage and comfort them. "You can turn to it for all reasons," she said.

Amy: Amy is reading through the Bible in a systematic way and tries to read some every day. At first her goal was to make it through in a year, but she is finding it is often more fruitful to stay with a shorter passage each day.

Brian: Brian often reads the Bible. He believes the term "Christian" needs to be revived, to have a meaning closer to the New Testament model of being a follower of Christ. He finds reading the New Testament refreshing. He enjoys reading Proverbs because it opens his eyes to what wisdom is and provides guidance for his life. He would like to grow into a wisdom that can handle any situation and believes that through reading Proverbs he gains wisdom.

The story of Job is important for Brian. The book shows that you need to trust that God hears and answers even when circumstances are difficult. Brian finds it helps him understand God working on his own time, in his own way. It shows Brian that God provides blessing in the midst of hard times, and that God's "got your back." Brian appreciates when the Bible is put into song. The lyrics impact him and help him form ideas.

Alisa: As a child, Alisa participated in her family's nightly devotions and prayer. "As I got older, I realized the importance of doing my own devotions. Usually I would have a devotional book, and there would be a passage to read. I remember my dad's Bible. It always sat by the recliner in the living room. If we came down early, we'd find Dad sitting in his chair, reading the Bible. To this day, I'm amazed at his discipline. To this day, when I'm looking for a particular Scripture, I can always ask my dad, and he knows where it is. I hope that I can do that someday, but I have a long way to go." Alisa struggles with how to get the most out of the Bible. She finds her weekly small-group Bible study to be a valuable help.

What I Hear

Most of these young adults appreciate the Bible-reading skills they've been taught. Those skills allow them to better understand Scripture. They also appreciate that Scripture, in addition to including many great stories, is open to interpretation. We are therefore invited into active deliberation about its many-layered meanings. This is liberating and energizing for many young adults, who acknowledge that they turn to Scripture as a "rich, deep, and refreshing" resource for personal nurture, encouragement, and guidance.

Chapter 8
My Experience with the Bible Narrative—II

"I would like to be able to navigate my way around"

While some young adults in our interviews spoke in glowing terms about how the Bible feeds their spirits and imaginations, many clearly feel that they don't relate well to the Bible and express regret about that. The comments in this chapter reveal a more conflicted relationship with the biblical narratives.

The legacy of our forebears in faith, for whom the Scriptures were "world-creating," can't help but leave some residue of guilt when our own experience with the Bible seems so minimal and unsatisfying. In certain ways some of us have experienced the Bible as primarily a rule book. The Bible stories are obviously a mixed bag, often full of vengefulness, pettiness, and war, and these stories don't sit well with what Jesus taught about loving our enemies. And then there is a literalist approach that seems to take the music, the poetry, the archetypal grandness out of the Bible.

Bruce Feiler wrote a bestseller called *Walking the Bible: A Journey by Land Through the Five Books of Moses* (New York: Morrow, 2001). The book describes his "epic odyssey"—by foot, Jeep, rowboat, and camel—through "the greatest stories ever told." Sometime in midlife, Feiler says, he felt like the stories of the Hebrew Scriptures that had been formative for him in his childhood were no longer "a part of me in any way. And yet I wanted them to be. . . . Suddenly, almost overnight as I recall, I wanted these words to have meaning again. I wanted to understand them." Despite several attempts to get into the Bible, however, after several years he was "no closer to reconnecting to the Bible than I had been at the start." Then, he says, "I went to Jerusalem."

He recounts a fascinating saga of discovery. "It had never occurred to me that that story—so timeless, so abstract—might have happened in a place that was identifiable, no less one I could visit. It had never occurred to me that the story was so concrete, so connected to the ground. To here. To now."

The Bible, observes Feiler, is "the culmination of a profoundly near-Eastern sense of how to build a people through storytelling." At its heart, he says, the Bible is a great adventure story, whose principal story line is the relationship between humans and the Divine.

So what are the suggestions and longings of these young-adult commentators on the biblical narrative?

Jeff: Biblical stories are the important narratives that first come to mind for Jeff. He grew up with his father reading to him and his siblings at breakfast time from a large blue book of children's Bible stories. Through these narratives he became familiar with the Bible and the fascinating and exciting stories it contained. After he was in a Mennonite college and taking Bible courses, he remembered hearing these narratives as a small child and appreciated having a base from which to work.

Jeff laughs as he describes how he didn't learn about the Bible from the church he attended while growing up—an urban house church—but from the Bible school at his uncle's church. His own church was made up of individuals from conservative backgrounds that had formed a church which, in Jeff's view, was at the other end of the conservative-liberal spectrum. More focus was given to socioeconomic issues than to biblical narratives. In retrospect, he wishes more attention would have been given to Bible stories and to Mennonite history.

Along with biblical narratives, Jeff's family also placed an emphasis on oral tradition. His paternal grandfather often provided vivid word pictures of the days on the farm where Jeff's father grew up with seven other siblings. Jeff's father carries on this oral tradition. There are numerous stories, and it's hard to think of just one to focus on. Nevertheless, the stories illustrate themes and values of humor, generosity, and grace, and they infused Jeff with a vision of a gracious, generous God. Jeff recalled that living on a farm, the children would often get into mischief or simply have accidents in which equipment would be broken. Their father chose to find humor in these situations and handled them with an abundance of grace.

As a mature college student somewhat older than his classmates, Jeff desires a greater knowledge of the Bible. Besides reading for classes, Jeff only reads the

Scripture given on Sundays for the church service. But he speaks of a strong desire to have a better grasp of what the Scriptures offer. He believes that it is a substantial book, with the potential for great meaning and direction, but he needs "an external prompt" to take him into the text. He states, "I would like to be able to navigate my way around" in significant Mennonite texts and the Bible "for my own discernment process."

Presently, he finds himself surrounded by people's biased opinions of what the Bible and other important faith-based texts have to offer. What he desires, however, is a way of deriving meaning for himself from the stories, of gaining an objective look at the words themselves. He was disappointed with his Old Testament class. It had the potential to be that external prompt but came as a general education requirement at the college he is attending. Hence, he found himself in a large class of people who did not want to be there, and in an environment that did not encourage discussion of personal faith issues.

Journal Comments

In a post-interview conversation, Jeff and I talked briefly about the minimal praying and Bible reading he does. I asked him more about his feelings on this because I sensed an awkwardness and nervous laughter when he talked about it during the interview. Jeff acknowledged feelings of guilt and shame. Yet he feels that the examples of these practices he's observed are either insufficient or do not bring meaning to him. He fully believes, however, that prayer and Bible reading potentially bring an added dimension of "overall well-being" into his life.

I wonder where he (and I) will find what he called "the external prompt" to understand and navigate through the Bible and the ambiguous practice of prayer.

—Melody King

Interview Questions

Tell me about your experience of reading the Old and New Testament Scriptures. How often do you read the Bible? How do you feel about the reading that you do? How important is it for who you are and who you want to become?

Mark: Mark finds reading Scripture a chore. He never really has given the Bible a chance, he says. He doesn't read the Bible that often. It wasn't pushed for him as a child. Then, he only read it in Sunday school or in church settings.

Now he's reading John, but he doesn't feel the reading is really impacting him. He thinks it would affect who he wants to become if he understood it better. He sees the importance of reading the Bible through other people and trusts their judgment of Scripture and its relevance.

Mark wishes he knew more about Scripture reading to make it relevant to his life. He wishes he were more comfortable with prayer, but praying aloud is hard for him.

Hannah: Hannah doesn't have a good concept of what the biblical stories mean. She grew up reading the Bible and singing the songs in Sunday school, but later she realized that the stories didn't really sink in. She feels sad about her lack of Bible knowledge, which she says is slim to none. She can't quote Scripture, though she does know key verses that are argued about.

Hannah went through a Ministry Inquiry Program during college. She lived with a family and found it to be a healing experience. During that time she decided to read the Bible in two weeks. It was so good to see how it all fits together, she said, in contrast to Sunday school teachings or sermons that take one story from here and another from there. But she doesn't really remember that much about it. "I have to experience something in order to remember it," she said.

Hannah's parents tried to provide an incentive by offering to help out with college expenses if she read the Bible. But though there are certain things about which she is very disciplined, reading the Bible has never been one of them, and she finds this reality frustrating.

Hannah's favorite book is *Traveling Mercies*, by Anne Lamott. It's easy for her to click with something like that, but she can't connect with the Bible.

"I can't sit there and plow through some of this stuff unless it's going to connect to me," she said. Lamott—it's her story, raw and real, not flowery. She didn't care who was offended.

Hannah said she didn't grow up with devotionals, conservative radio, or books around the house. Her parents didn't do daily devotionals but read faith-related books. She goes to church for the music and the people, not the sermons. "I hate the sermons," she said. But she has found two pastors, including her current one, that connect with her. They present theology with grace, without shoving it down her throat, she said.

Hannah said that while attending Mennonite high school and college, the Bible wasn't taught in a way with which she connected, but instead in lecture format. When asked how the Bible may be important for who she wants to become, Hannah said she didn't know that she will ever read the Bible regularly unless she has a leadership role in the church. She doesn't disrespect the Bible's richness, but claims there must be a discipline in place if she is to read it. She says she most likely won't ever have that discipline because she knows herself too well. The Bible feels dry and disconnected unless someone connects it for her.

The most life-giving scriptural experience she had was creating a sermon on

Ruth for use during the Ministry Inquiry Program. At that time the pastor's advice to her was to read the Scripture out loud several times and listen for what jumps out. That's God moving.

Mike: Mike says he wishes he knew more about prayer and reading the Bible. He finds fulfillment in neither, except when things aren't going well. "I wish I could pray and read the Bible and enjoy it. That'd be great," he says. He believes that both practices could make life more fulfilling. He just doesn't feel he has time for them right now.

Mike acknowledges that he often doesn't feel connected to God when reading the Bible. He hopes he's not at this "stage my whole life." He does believe that Scripture is important, but there are so many questions and different interpretations.

He reads the Bible about two to three times a week for about ten minutes in the morning before going to school. When life is tough and things become uncomfortable, the Bible is what he goes back to as a result of his mom's practice. When things are going well, he doesn't read as much, and he acknowledges some guilt feelings about that. He would love to sustain the practice of reading Scripture, but it's not real for him right now. He says he has to do what he feels is real, and relationships are more real for him right now than the Scriptures.

Working on his relationship with God is important to him, but right now Scripture is not a huge element of that process. Journaling and other types of reading are more fresh ways to work on the relationship.

Ben: Scripture stories are still valuable, but they are not as vivid as they were in Ben's childhood. When one is young, stories capture one's imagination in a way that they cannot do later. Now Ben's tendency is to analyze and abstract, to look for various meanings or the reasons the author had for writing a passage. He asks more questions. In a way this is frustrating because it doesn't have the freshness and imaginativeness of his childhood experiences with Scripture. But it is also rewarding in that Ben is able to see more content in passages. Scripture provides an alternative way for Ben to look at his life and gives him another way of explaining or reflecting on things that happen to him.

Dave: Dave says he doesn't read the Bible "often enough." By whose rules? "By my own," he admits. He reads maybe once a week. He has every intention of reading lots of Scripture. He thinks it's important because it's where we learn about faith and where we should be going and what we should be doing.

He says that not everything in the Bible is of equal importance. The Gospels are most important. He mostly reads the Gospels. He doesn't read the Old

Testament much because he finds it hard to understand and contradictory in relation to the New Testament. But he has gained an appreciation for it. College helped give him more perspective on what was really going on in the Old Testament.

He also remembers an Old Testament scholar at Mennonite World Conference who gave a seminar on violence in the Old Testament, explaining that he feels it is not about violence but about peace. Deuteronomy tells us to choose life, not death. The violence of the Old Testament, then, is really about the Israelites taking things into their own hands.

In one class Dave also especially learned to appreciate the Psalms. They express anger and all kinds of negative feelings. The church doesn't give room for those feelings, he says. He wants to read the Bible more to know more.

Greg: Greg commented: "If it wasn't for the Old Testament, I wouldn't be a Christian." The story of Job is a specific narrative that has been quite important for him in understanding himself and his personal narrative. He wishes somebody would have introduced him to the book of Job much earlier in life. Greg discovered it in college. "The first time I knew I had gotten somewhere was when I understood the book of Job," he said. He was humbled by its teaching and realized that the answers of God to Job are not answers: "It's not for you to know" and "How can you understand what I do?"

"That's how God answered me every time I pleaded and begged for an answer or just lashed out against God." It's not about an argument with God. It's impossible to know God's will. "I was so confused and so easily swayed everywhere and was so engrossed with trying to figure out answers."

"I came to know who I was and became a lot more stable person when I started realizing how little I was actually going to be able to figure out and how little I needed to know."

Greg says he reads the Bible once a week and wishes it were more frequently. The Bible is important, but so many times it has been misinterpreted. He has a strong desire to know the truth. He remembers that in church as a child, he observed that the Bible "was theirs." They held it tight under their arms, but there was nothing in there that they needed to know for living.

"I have so many bad associations with the Bible." We seem to make it too inaccessible or complex. The academic community tears it apart till it doesn't quite mean anything anymore. Yet so many people literalize so many things that it causes the spirit of it to be lost. It is so easy to disrupt a balance.

Greg wishes he were more consistent with fasting and prayer. He didn't have excuses for not reading the Bible. He just always picks up another book first.

John: John's interest in the Bible began with an Introduction to the Bible course. He also began going to a conservative evangelical church, which stressed Scripture quite a bit.

Regarding relating to Scripture now, he says, "Frankly, it's quite a struggle." It reminds John of "old antagonisms" that were strong in his family, feelings that the church and the Christian faith needed to be called to task for past evils, from the crusades to slavery to the oppression of women. He recognizes that there was something of an antireligious undercurrent in his family, and a view of God as judgmental and whimsical, sending people to hell. John struggles with this picture of God even though he doesn't believe that's how God is.

Rachel: Rachel doesn't read the Bible much, except to look at a passage as it is read in church. While growing up, she had a poor experience with the Bible. After her sister was baptized, she tried to convert Rachel by making her read the Bible and do devotions. Then in high school, Rachel joined the church's Bible quiz team, which was "horrible." All the emphasis was on memorizing and on beating the other team. Not memorizing well meant losing and more rigorous study and practices. It was like getting punished. These experiences really turned her off.

Rachel prefers reading the Bible in French because she associates it with a very positive time for her in France and West Africa. Singing certain hymns does the same.

She works with a lot of Jewish people and sometimes finds it interesting when the Bible comes up in their conversations. They know more about the Old Testament, while Rachel knows more about the New Testament. It's neat to have the Bible in common with so many people.

Rachel regards the Bible as a guide, but she doesn't take it word for word. "Just like I treat recipes—I don't follow the recipes ever. It's just more fun to experiment. More fun to do what tastes good. There is some of the Bible that is not relevant today. My mother-in-law would die if she heard me saying that."

Peter: Regarding the Bible, Peter said: "I find a lot of stuff to be a little bit boring. I don't get into Psalms—they sort of harp on the same thing all the time. All the prophets basically say that society is judged by how it treats its poorest people. As a pacifist, it is hard to know how to deal with the whole Old Testament battle stories. Certainly that was the perspective of the writers, but that doesn't mean God told them to slaughter all the women and the children. Most of the problems in the church today come from Paul—not that it's his fault—but not allowing women in leadership, not allowing gays and lesbians in the church. What Jesus has to say—that's where it's at for me in the Bible. Jesus is great—the way the

Pharisees try to trap him, and he always has an answer that threatens their power. I'm not a biblical literalist—I see it as a book that humans have written, but I still would say that it's the most useful book for me."

In childhood, Peter sang "The B-I-B-L-E, yes that's the book for me." All through high school, he didn't really question the Bible.

"The Sunday school teacher would ask a question, and it was clear that there was a right answer. It took me a long time to have an honest relationship with the Bible," he said.

Kate: "It's minimal," Kate said when asked about her relationship with the Bible. She memorized Scriptures in Sunday school.

"My grandfather gave me books about women in the Bible. They were badly written. I've always been a discerning reader, and there are very few well-written books in Christian literature. I was also very sensitive. I had this feeling that if I opened the Bible and started reading, my faith was going to crumble, because I knew that there was stuff in the Bible that I didn't agree with, and I didn't want to encounter that by myself.

"To this day, I have not read the whole Bible. I know that if I would open the Bible and start reading, it would make me sick to the stomach. There are so many stories of pettiness and vengefulness, so many wars, so many things about women and gay people. I've taken Bible classes. I've read the writings of women who are reclaiming the Bible. I've decided that Paul didn't really hate women, but still I skirt around the Bible, knowing that if I just come to it like I am, I won't be able to accept it, and I'm scared about that.

"How I understand God is by touching trees and talking with people. Not with anything that involves the Bible." But, she adds, she *wants* to have a relationship with the Bible someday, especially in the context of a church community.

"I would like to be acquainted with the Bible better. I would like to be like my grandparents' generation, which has all this Goethe, hymns, and Bible memorized. Of course, they were memorizing it so they had something to hold on to when they were in the concentration camps. I'm just waiting. I think I'll know it when it comes."

Jason: Jason doesn't believe in God and doesn't believe it's important to know whether God exists, though he sees religion as playing a vital role in society. Sometimes he discusses God with believers and acts as though he also believes, because he thinks it is still important to relate to believers despite his change of faith. If Jason did believe in God, he says, that God would be the kind that is okay with everything. He/she would be full of grace, all-loving, and following him/her would not be hard. There would be no hell and no suffering. Jason thinks this kind of God contradicts the Bible.

If it turns out that God is judgmental, Jason will stand before God on judgment day and tell him to piss off and send him to hell. He doesn't want to spend eternity with a God like that. Jason believes things about the universe are "ultimately unknowable." He generally believes in the golden rule as a guide for right and wrong, but believes nothing is universally right or wrong. Everything depends on the context.

Jason never reads the Bible and hasn't since going to college, except for class. He holds it on the same level as other religious texts and classic literature. There's wisdom in it. The prodigal son story is his favorite Bible story, and he likes other stories of grace. Through studying narratives in college, Jason took interest in the notion of archetypes. He sees the Christian story as an archetype. It has lost its importance for him as the paramount of things one could believe in.

What I Hear

I'm impressed with the longing, the ambivalence, the struggle, and the baggage associated with reading the Bible in many of these comments. Person after person seems to be aware that there is a rich resource here available to them, but that too often it seems to be obscure and distant from their reality, taken too literally, misused, misinterpreted, or not interpreted at all.

Yet beyond the conflicted feelings of being drawn to the Bible and also put off by the Bible, time and again the respondents in one form or another mention a desire for an "external prompt," as Jeff described it. And Kate with transparent frankness acknowledged her fear that if she reads the Bible, her faith might crumble, and she didn't want to encounter that by herself. She, like Jeff and many others, wants to be able to "navigate my way around" in the company of discerning others.

Chapter 9
My Experience with the Bible Narrative—III
(Group Interview)

"Group interaction is the best way to encounter the Bible"

During Bruce Feiler's "odyssey" in the lands of the Bible, he spoke about how early in his adventure he was "consumed with the factual foundations of the stories." The longer he journeyed, the more he moved toward trying to understand the power of the stories, the motivation of the characters, and their evolving relationship with God. And then even more, he tried to grasp the raw human emotions underlying the stories of people forging a new identity during a difficult wilderness journey.

Feiler talked of needing to break away from modes of thought "I'd used since being a teenager—reason, skepticism, logic, learning"—and to move "toward modes of relating to the world—emotion, intuition, trust—that I probably hadn't relied on so much since I was a child." Rather than proving or documenting the story, he was drawn more and more toward the spiritual power of the story. And it was drawing him into his own encounter with God.

"The one thing I knew for sure," Feiler wrote, "was that I had less and less interest in voices that had all the answers, in people who were sure, who never questioned, or rediscovered. I was drawn instead to a manner of speaking, a tone, a sense of exploration. I was attracted most to people who wanted to engage the text in a dialogue, in an ongoing conversation."

As we've observed from the one-on-one interviews, many young adults are able to enter the Scriptures with imagination and an intuitive ability to make meaningful connections with the ancient stories. They are surprised and delighted at how the poetry, wisdom, and prophetic words animate their lives. For others, however, there is more longing than fulfillment, more frustration than animation, more conflict than comfort, and more calls for reading it together in conversation, than contentment with reading it alone.

With multiple stories that indicated a somewhat conflicted relationship with the Bible, we wanted to hear more from young adults in group interviews. Segments from those interviews are below, separated by a symbol.

Group Interview Questions

The Bible and its many stories have played a significant role in Mennonite and other Christian faith communities. After listening to what several other young adults said about their relationship to the Bible, talk about how you relate to the Bible, or what relationship you would like to have with the Bible? What would help to make the Bible more meaningful and accessible to you? In what context do you or would you feel most motivated to explore and become better acquainted with the Bible?

Phil: "One way I relate to the Bible is as one of several avenues to truth. That's how I find that middle ground between being completely critical and being completely literal. Bible has truth; it's the story of Christ and God's redemption in the world, which is applicable to my life. But I struggle to see it as absolute truth, and there are so many people that seem to just worship the Bible. I also want to emphasize community, the Holy Spirit, and a personal relationship with Christ as sources of truth."

Rose: "I don't feel like I'm afraid of the Bible, I don't feel like I need to get defensive about it, or be afraid to read it. I sort of see myself as a container. So when people are debating the fine points, I can collect it all. But when the dust settles and I sort through what has been said, I am able to make the decisions on a personal basis. Hearing a bunch of different opinions doesn't overwhelm me."

Derek: "The Bible sometimes scares me—even the word 'Bible.' The word doesn't sound the way I want it to sound. Because of the way people have abused it as a big, huge rule book. Jesus didn't write down a word of it. The Bible we have now is a narrative that reminds us of a God who has acted from Abraham on down, and now becomes my story as I try to enact what Jesus told his disciples to do—follow him. And that's it; that's what I want to do. That's a story that I'm a part of, that I want to be a part of. I don't believe in the Bible; I believe in God."

Anita: "The Bible is a kind of a base when I'm feeling down. It helps me learn about God's unfailing love and graciousness, forgiveness, and even our need to repent. But I don't think that just following the rules is really the answer. The world is a lot different than it was back then."

Rose: "The Bible isn't something that gets in the way of faith. What I meant by saying I make decisions on a personal basis is that I weigh things between God and me as a kind of conversation."

Phil: "The Bible is taking abstract concepts about God, love, and forgiveness and putting them in a context we can understand: people, stories, concrete acts of God. Take all that away, and what understanding would I have of God's love? What understanding of forgiveness would I have without the specific examples? All that would be left is a set of rules."

Derek: "Yes. For example, the rich young ruler and Zacchaeus—Jesus didn't tell them to do the same thing. He expected different things of different people. Zacchaeus responded, for example, by giving things away as restitution. In the case of the rich young ruler, Jesus tells him to give it all up. That's what the stories allow us to see."

～ ～ ～

Ken: "I'm reading *Saving the Bible from Fundamentalism*. For me, it's a test whether or not I want to go to seminary. I think the Bible, much like this sense of Mennonitism that we've been talking about, has stayed with us, many of us, and we can't shake it. For me, the only thing I can try to do is salvage it. While the Bible is pivotal, there's a lot in it that I don't connect with or that has been misused as proof texts for things I don't agree with. What would help? A trust that someone's there with you, interpreting it with you."

Jennifer: "I have a lot of fear about the Bible. I don't yet read it on my own. I'm finding that during these years when I haven't been reading it, I have forgotten a lot. It's kind of exciting that I don't remember the order of the books of the Bible so I have to use the index to look up books. It's something a bit fresh.

"I consider my relationship to the Bible to be sort of like during the medieval period: I'm trusting others to interpret it for me. I need it to be filtered through people I trust, who speak in a language I can relate to. I know some people who can glean things I'm unable to find. When I open it, I see a lot of things to be angry about, but through other people I have found a connection to it. I see myself gaining confidence, but I'll stick with my medieval ways for now.

"What bothers me about Bible radio stations? I need to know and trust the person who is interpreting Christian faith for me in order for them to offer me anything spiritually. I do have a few people in my life like that: an older friend in her midforties I met ten years ago while doing volunteer service in Boston. I trust her life; I trust who she is. I'm finding it a little bit at church. My pastor finds nuggets in Scripture that impact me and to some degree my parents, and some friends, but mostly people a little older."

Karla: "My relationship with the Bible seems quite different from what I've heard so far. I've had a lot of people fail me in my life. And I've had an opportunity to crumble many times. The one thing that has been consistent has been my relationship with God. The teachings and the Word of God become your breath— your very existence. I have to trust that God continues to speak through other people and through his word. The Bible gives me guidance on how to live, and I'm learning how to filter it for that guidance."

Ellen: "For me, the Bible has a lot of truth. I'm leery of saying I don't believe certain things because I can't relate to them. I like to be open and admit that I don't understand it when I read it. I'm dating a Catholic. Before, I could always take it for granted how to read it and what it means. So for me, I feel like there's truth in it. But how you interpret that truth is what can turn it into meaning something it's not meant to. People are always going to read it differently with different lenses. 'Is it the body of Christ, or is it *really* the body of Christ?' [laughter] You do have to trust that the Bible holds truth to make it meaningful."

Lisa: "I stopped reading the Bible in high school. I liked [studying] biblical literature in college. I learned a lot about these stories I had heard again and again and was really fascinated by the cultural underpinnings of all these stories. Every night before bed when I was little, we had a Bible story and a 'secular' story. I want to share Bible stories with my children, too, and hope to provide more context than I was given. I agree on the importance of knowing the context."

〜〜〜

Josh: "I don't often read the Bible, especially when things are going well for me and I am not having any problems. But when I have tough times, [that's when I find that] I read the Bible the most. Sometimes I feel guilty for not reading."

Greta: "Where do you think the guilt comes from?"

Josh: "I don't know. I read for twenty-four years until I came to America, and my parents were there to remind me every day to read the Bible. Since I've been here, there is no one to tell me to read it, and I just kind of stopped doing it regularly."

Don: "I have had a similar experience because of Bible memory camp. I feel a sense of guilt because of that experience. They would ask us questions like, 'If your house was on fire, what one object would you take with you?' I said the family pictures, but that was the 'wrong' answer. I was supposed to save the Bible. My argument was that there are so many Bibles in the world—my grandma has a dozen! But it was pushed on me. I think that's why now I feel a sense of guilt associated with the Bible."

Josh: "My freshman year I took a New Testament class. I remember I used to read the Bible every day. It was a new concept to study it in an academic way. When I took the class, I was so interested because I was studying the context behind it and all kinds of details I had never heard anyone preach on before. That was great."

Margo: "I am experiencing that now as well. Learning the context and background is great. It sparks an interest in me so that I can relate more to the Bible in new ways."

Don: "Yes. There is something about that. I hate to agree with everything. But dissecting it makes things come alive."

Margo: "I don't think that a class is necessary to take something from the Bible, but at this point in my life it is beneficial to me. And it can be beneficial to others."

Al: "At different times I have been frustrated by reading stuff without any background knowledge. I feel as though I am either taking everything literally, or not taking anything away at all. Because of this, I decided to go to Bible college. One of the things was taking a Romans class, . . . reading the book straight through several times and getting the big picture. Another part of my ideal for relating to the Bible is that it be done in a community setting: walking with a group of people, with a commitment to receiving what God is trying to say, and then being accountable to living that out."

Greta: "I would agree with that."

Curt: "The Word is so good. It is insanely good. I think that most Mennos grow up hearing the Bible in such a way that it is a heavy load. It is not life-giving. But we are called to digest the Word. It is our lifeblood. At times the way we talk about it can sound like Bible camp. But it should be something that we see as good. We should want to eat it up like a good feast, not like a hundred pills. It is a dialogue with us and God. You have your group of friends, and you share with each other. Teaching the Word is important, and that is how we can be fed."

Don: "For me as a child, the Bible was so intimidating. You're reading kids' books, 'Dick and Sally did this and that.' Then your mom brings this twenty-pound load out and opens it up. It's scary. I also had an idea about how it had to be read. I remember watching public TV, and they were discussing it in a book-club setting. I didn't think it was okay to talk about the Bible in that setting. I asked my dad if you could do that. He said it was okay to have discussions about the Bible in that way."

~~ ~~ ~~

Tara: "The downfall of growing up in the church is the attitude of 'Well, I don't need to read it, there's nothing new in it.' I've learned more from friends who didn't grow up reading the Bible. When I was younger, I just accepted it for what it was. Now I need to rethink all that I took for granted. A book called the *Purpose-Driven Life* has helped me approach the Bible in a new way. I have found that group interaction is the best way to encounter the Bible. On my own, I don't let it challenge my life, but in a group, there are a variety of perspectives."

Tony: "I never owned a Bible until I went to a Mennonite college. The Catholic Church just reads it to you. When I got to college, I said, 'Wow, you guys actually read the Bible!' I find it to be a really confusing book if you don't have others to talk with about it. I would like to have a better relationship with the Bible. I believe it is God's Word, but it takes deciphering, talking it out. I want a community that has a group study, where it is okay to be different, okay not to understand it all. It would help me a lot to have a group of four to eight [people] to hash it out."

Linda: "I wish I wouldn't have owned a Bible until I was twenty years old. I know how stories end now, and I would like to experience the Bible as if it were a novel where I didn't know the ending. I would like to see new things, be refreshed, inspired. I 'fasted' from the Bible for a year . . . and was very bitter against it. When I began reading it again, it had a fresher perspective. I was not so bitter, so the time off was really good."

Ray: "As a seminary student, I work with the Bible a lot. It's a little like a lawyer working with a constitution. The Scripture doesn't nurture me spiritually. I see others nurtured through it though, and I would like to experience that someday."

ᔆ ᔆ ᔆ

Beth: "Sometimes the Bible seems like a history book that's missing pages. When you take a New Testament class, they fill you in on the history. I find it hard to read the Bible because I feel lost. I don't read it that often. I feel like I read it more when I'm involved in a class. In reality, I am interested, but when I read on my own, I don't feel like I get much out of it."

Tim: "I relate to the Bible on an academic level. I went to a Bible school, so I've had to know it, even the Hebrew words. Besides sometimes appreciating the stories, I've never wanted to have devotions and never had a desire to open it for my own pleasure. I struggle with reading the Bible on my own. It's so big, and I don't understand a lot of parts. I run into walls and think 'this is too much.' I'd rather talk about it with four or five other people. I want to be with more people if I'm going to study it."

Beth: "I definitely agree that the group is important. It would be exciting to be part of a small-group Bible study. What Tim said, I agree with that. The Bible is interesting. I just want to know more about the history in order to understand it."

Michelle: "I read the Bible in rough times. It's not a part of my daily life. I connect more with it through prayer or music. But I would like to have it be part of daily life."

James: "I don't relate well to the Bible. I would like to, but any interaction with it is pretty nonexistent currently. But I would like to know more about the Bible. Perhaps it would help if I lived in a monastery."

Michelle: "I don't think accessibility is the problem. It is right there beside my bed. If only I had a better understanding of the history, especially in the Old

Testament. As it is, I read about these people, and I don't know how they fit together. It would help to have someone read it with me, or like now, it currently helps to have my Sunday school class read it together. Individually, we read through the week and then come together on Sunday morning to discuss what we've read."

What I Hear

These comments, in combination with the repeated calls in the previous chapters for "tangling with" the Bible in the company of others, make it sound like it is high time to recover fresh and diverse expressions of a time-honored Anabaptist ideal. The Bible can and should be encountered in a gathered circle of people trying to discern what in the world God has been up to all these millennia and how others' experience of God in the past might help us make sense of the challenges we face now. Tara put it succinctly: "Group interaction is the best way to encounter the Bible."

Chapter 10
My Experience with Jesus Narrative—I

"I learned about the crucified Jesus, the dying Jesus"

While accompanying my husband on a sabbatical journey to Israel/Palestine recently, we visited many sights associated with Jesus's life. There truly is nothing like being there for getting close to the "Jesus narrative." And in my experience, there was nothing very romantic or sentimental about it—in part because of the grinding conflict between the Israelis and the Palestinians. But even more so because the most horrific violence, occasioned in large part by competing narratives, has played out with a bloody grimness over and over throughout many centuries in the very place where Jesus wept and cried out: "If you, even you, had only recognized on this day the things that make for peace" (Luke 19:42).

But there is also an awe-filled realism that infused my experience of the biblical stories after visiting the dry, barren Judean wilderness, walking through olive groves, eating fresh figs, and praying by the Sea of Galilee. And that realness profoundly stirred my imagination and spirit.

We visited a place called Banias, which is one of the springs that feeds the headwaters of the Jordan River. This place is associated with Caesarea Philippi, where Jesus is said to have asked his disciples, "Who do you say that I am?" (Mark 8:29). To this day, one can see vestiges of ruined temples, altars, and statues. There used to be temples to Augustus, Zeus, and Pan, the god of the forest and the shepherds, from which came the spring's name: Banias. Archaeological excavations conducted here indicate the performance of sacrificial rites and the bringing of offerings to Pan, as well as to other Greek gods such as Zeus, Athena, Hera, Aphrodite, Artemis, Dionysus, and Aris.

In this quasi-marketplace of gods, considering Jesus's question "Who do you say that I am?" adds intrigue to the story for me.

We all have different experiences with the Jesus narrative. We receive different pieces of the story, often told out of context. Or favorite parts of the story are emphasized at the expense of the whole story. Our experience of the story always comes through lenses tinged by someone else's interpretation, someone else's experience layered on to our own.

"What was your childhood experience of the Jesus story?" we asked these young adults. "And what is your experience of it now?" Here first is Renee's account, and then others—and more in the next two chapters.

Renee: Renee wishes there were fewer stories with an evangelical emphasis in her childhood. Her church, her mom, and definitely her Mennonite grandmother spoke often of being concerned about the status of other people's souls. She remembers worrying about her dad's mother, worrying that she wasn't "saved" and wouldn't go to heaven. She remembers traveling with her cousin to visit this grandmother, and discussing with her cousin how they might bring her to Christ, maybe by giving her a Bible. Renee feels that even though these conversations always happened with the best of intentions, they were often destructive to relationships, and efforts to evangelize often were not helpful and turned people off.

She wishes there had been more than just saving souls, more stories about peace and social justice, and our responsibility to the world. She wishes Mennonite Central Committee workers had visited her church instead of only Wycliffe Bible translators. Renee wishes her family had talked about these things, too. She wishes she had had more exposure to different cultures, different ways of doing things. Instead, Renee feels there was a lot of fear of differences.

At church, "typical" Old Testament Bible stories (Abraham, Jonah, Noah) were often told. Jesus was talked about, but the Old Testament stories are more vivid in Renee's memory.

"I think the Jesus that I learned about a lot was the Jesus of Golgotha, the crucified Jesus, the dying Jesus, the one who loves you so much that he's dying for your sins. And I feel like that was especially played upon in high school, because it had an emotional element to it that they—whoever—felt they could use to . . . to get us."

Over and over again, during high school, at church and at camp, Renee was shown Michael W. Smith's music video *Secret Ambitions*. The verses would tell about Jesus's life, but the chorus would cut to scenes of Jesus's walk to Golgotha, the crucifixion, the burial. The words, "No one knew his secret ambition. No one knew his claim to fame," implied that the principal reason Jesus came to earth was to die.

On the Smith video, "you see the whole passion story, of them actually nailing his hands and his feet, of them raising the cross, of them putting the thorns on his brow, of them beating him—I mean it's vivid of them beating him—of the blood dripping, of them shedding him of his clothes. And at the very end—Smith has already sung his last passionate chorus—you see this sort of ghostly figure of Jesus." Renee is struck with the violent images in the video.

Now Renee is working at a Rape Crisis Center in a major city. She hears stories on the hotline and especially in her individual counseling sessions with survivors of sexual violence; stories about the pain others have experienced when someone had power over them, assaulting them sexually or forcing them to do things they didn't want to do.

Renee is living at a Mennonite Central Committee house where, over meals, she has had the chance to talk with all kinds of people. Many are MCCers passing through. They tell stories about what is going on in other communities, in this country, and around the world. Renee feels very good about being part of an organization like MCC, which does not go to other places with the purpose of converting others to Christianity. She was proud to see MCC recently featured in *Time* magazine, contrasting their work with the work of Christian evangelistic organizations. Renee finds it arrogant when people go places believing they have "the answer."

She has also come to see God as peaceful in nature. God has a goal of seeing peace in the world and reconciliation among people with each other and with God. She likes this better than what she grew up with, the idea that God's goal was the conversion of all people.

Renee believes her life should reflect what she thinks God cares about. Often she spoke about the interconnectedness of her faith, her life, and her work. Faith doesn't have to be talked about, she says, but should be lived out through work.

What does this mean for her? "Ultimately, I want my life to work toward appropriate treatment and care for all people," says Renee, "and especially for women."

The stories of the past two years have also affected Renee's relationships with others. She values relationships highly and gives them much nurture, time, and care. She tries to treat all people with God's love—not just people of faith but *everyone*.

Renee reads the Bible about twice a week. Why? Mostly because she's been told that she's supposed to do so. Most often she reads the Psalms and the New Testament. The Old Testament can be rich, and she wants to enjoy it, but sometimes she gets lost in it. She likes the New Testament, particularly the Sermon on the Mount. The New Testament is most important because "this is who we follow." Jesus teaches us to love people, care for the underserved, notice the outcasts, and be countercultural without being embarrassed or afraid about it. Jesus was empowering all people.

Journal Comments

For Renee, dramatic change happened with her move to the city. I was especially interested in the role feminist/womanist thinking and women's stories played in her transformation. God was no longer just male. Traditional male/female roles were no longer acceptable. And the painful stories told by sexually abused women at the center meant that Jesus could no longer simply be a vehicle to heaven but had to be a radical healing presence here on earth.

At the same time that she was being exposed to a new perspective on women, Renee was also encountering people from different cultures and backgrounds whose experiences had formed them into people very different from her. She learned to listen, to love across lines of difference. She discovered, in a setting much more pluralistic than the one in which she grew up, that it would be arrogant to believe she had "the answer."

—Deborah Good

Interview Questions

When you reflect on the stories from your childhood and those that have come to have power for you now, where does the Jesus story fit in? What is its importance in your life now, and how important is it to who you want to become?

Mike: Mike said that Jesus was the way God showed how he loved us. He doesn't know how to neatly fit the Jesus story in to the other stories of his life.

He suggests that there seem to be "cosmic rules" surrounding the idea of Jesus, a line that is followed along his life story to help us reach salvation. He believes his life was meaningful, but he doesn't believe as strongly or get as excited as some do about Jesus's death and resurrection. "Perhaps my perspective is too cynical," he remarked. Instead, he likes to focus on the paradoxical example that Jesus was: counter-cultural, throwing power systems on their heads, the enigma of weakness equaling strength.

Greg: "As a grown man, I so appreciate Jesus now. He's so abrasive and *rude*!"

As a child, Greg thought that Jesus always seemed either to be the smiling, clean, bearded man, or to be only about dying on the cross. Since then, he's discovering so many different parts of Jesus's life that the Bible tells to give depth to his character. The Jesus story seems so amazing, so new, and there's so much left to explore about it. Whenever he talks or reads about the Jesus story, he just has a feeling that he knows this is right.

Jason: Jason says that Jesus is a good model for how to live a life based on compassion, love for others. There are a lot of similarities between the Jesus story and the stories and teachings of Buddhism, for example. The crucifixion and resurrection are not the relevant parts of the Jesus story, he says.

Peter: Regarding the Jesus story: "At this point in my life, I'd say that God forgives us through grace, but I don't think grace is contingent on Jesus's death. I think that Jesus's death was about the message he brought and a humanity that was unable to accept that message." Peter cites Walter Wink as influential in his thoughts about salvation.

"Now I alternate between the Jesus of comfort and the Jesus of challenge. But I'm not necessarily living out the Jesus of challenge. I do war-tax resistance, but to me, it doesn't feel like it's enough. There's a lot more—like racial reconciliation—my friends are so white and middle-class. I struggle with the fact that I don't have the energy to do what I'm called to do, and then I drift into apathy.

"I often feel awkward and inadequate, and I know other people don't see me that way, but I'm very self-critical. I feel different from my society. Most of my friends are also different from society, so I don't see it that often, but particularly after 9/11, I had a distinct sense that I am not part of this, this resurgence of patriotism."

Peter also seems to question his motivation for following Jesus: "It's not just that I do these things because Jesus wants me to; I do them because they just make sense. It makes sense that this person needs something, I have it, I should give it to them. I'm influenced a lot by logic. To do something because God says so doesn't cut it for me—a lot of people hear God saying a lot of things. When I'm talking to people who don't understand it otherwise, I can refer to the fact that it's what God says." In decision making, Peter says that he wants to rely more on emotions rather than on pure ethics.

Rachel: And about Jesus? Jesus was a normal guy. We are to focus on his life and model ours after it. The focus for me, Rachel said, is on how he promoted peace and how we should resolve conflict without violence. She doesn't focus much on his blood, and so on.

Rachel says that more important than Scripture is attempting to live her life based on her understanding of Jesus's life—"the whole justice thing," for example. Seeing people wear WWJD [What would Jesus do?] makes her gag, Rachel says. What is their interpretation of what Jesus stood for? She knows someone who wears WWJD around her neck and also a pin that says "Support our troops."

"Just seeing those together makes me cringe," she said. "That's not who I understand Jesus to be at all."

When Rachel talks about her understanding of Jesus, she says, "I don't know. I don't understand Jesus." She questions a lot. Jesus was for the underdogs in the world. He could have been anyone: male, female, gay, straight, black, white, whatever. His sense of justice was immense. He was so creative in working out peaceful solutions. You can find Jesus in many people every day.

In many respects, she said, this is the Jesus she grew up with. Her dad would say: "Rules are like fences. There are always gates in them." You get taught a certain way about who Jesus is, and then he grows into something different: more gentle, more complex.

Mary: Mary says we'd all be better off if we could meet Jesus. We'd be better able to understand his humanity. Pieces of his life are being left out—he got hungry, smelled funny, laughed at awkward moments. He was abrasive, sharp, and Mary thinks she wouldn't have gotten along with him. Christian means "little Christ," but God doesn't necessarily want little Christ puppets.

Matt: The Jesus story is the most significant part of Matt's life, even more now than in the past. It affects how he lives perhaps more than a personal relationship now. Matt is working toward a more holistic view of faith as he tries to live in grace and finds that the horizontal connection with others is part of experiencing the presence of God, not just a vertical relationship. Following Jesus's modeling and teaching is central to Matt's life.

Mark: The Jesus story is more important now to Mark than it was in his childhood. Before now, it was just like any other story in his childhood. Now he notices a pull toward Jesus, an overall pull in his life. He feels Jesus nudging him. It's never really sunk in until the present, but now it is the most important part of who he wants to become. Mark wants a deeper connection with Jesus.

Christina: Christina has understood Jesus as the Savior of the world. Now this view has expanded to see the relationships of Jesus with other people, and Christina finds it important to see the divinity of Christ through his humanity.

Amy: Amy sees the Jesus story as "an example to follow." She recognizes that it would be impossible for us to be sinless as Jesus was, but still thinks he should be the pattern for our lives. She identified the elements of love, peacemaking, and a close relationship with God as central to the Christian faith as she understands it.

Will: Will recognizes that his response to the Jesus story has varied throughout his life, yet he now has a desire that the Jesus story be a pattern for his life. "There was a chunk of my life where I didn't want it to shape me. There was a chunk when I only wanted it to shape me in certain areas. Even now I certainly could stand to have it shape me more."

Another shift has taken place in the way Will prioritizes different parts of Scripture. During a time in a fundamentalist setting, he felt that the writings of Paul "were unduly elevated. Yet Paul said, 'Let the words of *Christ* dwell in you richly [Col. 3:16].'" Will does not believe that we should slavishly or simplistically imitate the *acts* of Jesus—like fasting for forty days after baptism—but that "we should esteem the red letters above all else." Jesus's teachings should be the last word, and nothing should detract from emphasizing obedience to that pattern.

Will does not want to know more, but rather believes he needs to practice more faithfully what he does know. As for practices he would like to do more often, Will replies, "All of them, from holy kissing to reading Scripture."

Jeff: From childhood stories Jeff learned a view of a God full of grace and generosity. That view is also represented in the Jesus story, he believes. But the story has become more important in recent years as Jeff has moved from an urban, secular environment, to a more rural environment, surrounded by more Mennonites. Growing up in a major city, Jeff had many Jewish friends and recalls feeling his own set of values differing from theirs. They did not share the values of service, peace, and so on, taken from the Jesus narratives. His Jewish friends more readily sought revenge, held grudges, and argued openly.

Being in tune with socioeconomic issues is another aspect of Jesus's example that Jeff wishes to emulate. He grew up in a high-class neighborhood and had a high-paying job before deciding to come back to school at a Mennonite college. He frequently thinks about the comfortable lifestyle he leads, the privileges he has, and what that means for him and the people around him.

Alisa: Regarding the importance of "the Jesus story" in her life, Alisa says, "I don't ask 'What would Jesus do?' I ask 'What would Jesus have me do?' I make daily trips to the 7-Eleven, and often there's someone there asking me for money. I still haven't figured out what I should do."

Alisa also wonders how to best care for the kids at the Neighborhood Learning Center when they misbehave. "How do I express to these kids that 'This isn't something you should do, but I still love you and God loves you'? I really have felt God convicting me sometimes and saying, 'No, there's a better way.'"

Ben: Ben sees the Jesus story as clearly being a model for the way we should be living our lives. Jesus gave us the commandment, "Follow me." While he does not discount the great commandments of love for God and neighbor, Ben feels that following Jesus is the most important thing for Christians to work toward. And since Jesus was so full of love for God and neighbor, emulating him does fulfill the greatest commandments.

Lately Ben's interpretation of this has moved more toward social and justice issues, but he does not see this as surprising, since he is attending college at a Mennonite school that is much into these things.

For Ben, the Jesus story is not only a good example, but also normative. Ben personally wants the Jesus story to be the overarching pattern for his life. Even though Ben feels he falls short in many ways, this is his ideal for a way of living.

What I Hear

Many of these young adults express ambivalence about the meaning of Jesus's death and resurrection. In comments here and elsewhere, they suggest that the Jesus story was reduced to its most bloody chapter and used in ways that seemed contrived to have a particular kind of effect. These ways were not true to the original story and took advantage of their childlike trust and desire to belong. Not that the adults intended any harm; they were simply playing out a script that had "worked" for them. Many of them talk about how now as young adults they have a heightened admiration for Jesus as a "grown man." They admire his radical, sometimes abrasive and smelly humanity, and they value Jesus's down-to-earthiness more than some spiritualized meaning associated with Jesus's death. In some ways, they seem to be experiencing a deeper, centering connection with Jesus.

Renee's expanded understanding of Jesus is strikingly in contrast to the overwrought image of her childhood. She speaks for many of her peers when she compares the "Jesus of Golgotha, the crucified Jesus, the dying Jesus" of her childhood with the Jesus she has learned to know as a young adult. This Jesus "teaches us to love people, care for the underserved, notice the outcasts, and be countercultural without being embarrassed or afraid about it."

Chapter 11
My Experience with Jesus Narrative—II

"Jesus is the only way, and everyone else is going to hell"

Many young adults wrestle with the questions Jesus posed at Caesarea Philippi: "Who do people say that the Son of Man is?" And the more personal, "Who do you say that I am?" (Matt. 16:13, 15).

In one way or another, many of the young adults who related their experience of the Jesus narrative also distinguished the personal question from the more general question—who is Jesus for me vs. who is Jesus for others. There seemed to be little angst about how "I" regard Jesus other than the repeated acknowledgment that though I hope to model my life on Jesus, I have not achieved perfection. But the angst shows up in having a satisfactory answer to who Jesus is or should be for others, particularly people of other faiths, and a related question, "What is my responsibility toward them?"

Craig wrestles with this question, as do several others in this chapter. Then there are others for whom the question did not arise.

Craig: On a daily basis Craig spends time on a bus and a subway. He works in human rights for an international church agency in Washington (DC), and spends his day meeting with people and talking on the phone. In the evenings he catches up on things, drinks a beer, reads, plays guitar, does schoolwork, and goes ballroom dancing—his current hobby.

He sees this routine as indicating that he actively values people and likes to interact with people from a variety of backgrounds. What his practices obscure is that human rights work is emotionally draining; there often seems to be little hope in many of the cases on which Craig works. He values connecting with people on a philosophical level, discussing things of importance to life, the world, and faith. In his present context, that is not as much of a possibility as when he was studying on a campus.

Craig reads his Bible some every week, though not as much as he would like. He talked about how his work is an expression of his faith. He believes that Christians' faith should be deeply connected to their work and vocation. Being faithful to God should make a difference in what we do for a living. He is deeply involved in a personal discernment process regarding direction for his life. This is an ongoing process that involves prayer and listening on an almost constant basis.

Craig had much to say about his experience of reading Scriptures and went into some depth. He said that the kind of experience he has depends on what part he's reading. Right now he connects most with the Gospels and the Psalms. Even for these parts of the Bible, it is often "hard to read with fresh eyes" since he has been reading and hearing them for many years.

Craig realizes that there is much he does not understand in the Scriptures, especially the application and the meaning for today. He can see perhaps what *happened* or what is said, but it is not immediately apparent how this is to affect his life now.

When looking at Scripture as a whole, Craig feels a tension between the Old Testament and the New Testament, between a God who endorses violence and a loving and healing God.

How can these be reconciled? "If you don't read the Bible from the point of view of the Israelites," then what happened in Joshua or other Old Testament accounts of war is rather awful and unfair.

Craig wonders if the Old Testament can be read as historical only, descriptive rather than prescriptive or held up as an example. Alternately, the theme of Scripture could be identified as "God reaching out for relationship to humans; then when humans screw it up, God tries again."

Craig finds the Jesus story "thought-provoking and insightful." He perhaps would boil Jesus's message down to love for God and neighbor, and healthy relationships with both. Jesus said "some really simple, straightforward things," but it is much more complicated and difficult to discern what it means for us to follow these.

The Jesus story was "not more than nice stories" for Craig until some time in high school. Since then, Craig has been "fired up and challenged" and finds Jesus's message provocative.

When looking at the Jesus story, a major problem Craig has is the "lack of harmony between what I see in the text and what I see happening [in the church]." Throughout history, Christians have been the best and the worst elements of society and influence on it. The church often seems to not "get it." In the past it was easy for Craig to see the church's response as error or even conspiracy. Now he would guess that 95 percent in the church are walking honestly, sincerely trying to live faithfully according to the teachings of Jesus as they see them.

Along with this shift in the way others interpret and live the Jesus story, Craig is less certain about his own interpretations. He definitely "has his own opinions" but is not as positive that he is exclusively correct.

What is Craig's personal journey with the Jesus story? He has no problem with the values that Jesus teaches but finds it hard to arrive at the exclusivity that many Christians seem to profess, claiming: "Jesus is the only way, and everyone else is going to hell." In some ways, Craig would like to accept these and other classic teachings of Christian doctrine, but he always has many questions. Thus far, Craig has held off being baptized until he can settle some of them and be able to repeat a creed in good faith.

Journal Comments

Craig is exceptionally intelligent, articulate, and further from the evangelical end of the Mennonite spectrum. I was impressed most by his exceptional intellectual honesty and sincere grappling with both his own questions and those raised by the interview. It was a pleasure to work with him, and I hope to be able to maintain communication with him.

—*Aram DiGennaro*

Interview Questions

When you reflect on the stories from your childhood and those that have come to have power for you now, where does the Jesus story fit in? Tell me about its importance in your life now. And how important is it to who you want to become?

Kate: When asked how the Jesus story has figured in her life, Kate answered: "Minimally. I definitely feel this force in the universe of goodness and light and darkness and life and God connecting us and binding us—I have felt that throughout my life. Okay. We'll call that God, call it the Holy Spirit. But then, intellectually, I'm supposed to look back on this one very live dude and be like, 'Now I just thank you, Jesus, Lord, Father. I just want to thank you, because before Jesus, God was whuppin' everybody's ass, but now through Jesus we are saved.

"When I was baptized, I was so grateful to feel God again. I was so grateful to *feel* again after being depressed, and I was so grateful for this community that was the Mennonite church. I knew that I had to say something about accepting Jesus as my Lord and Savior. I knew I had to say that to get in, and so I did. I did that because I've learned so much from the stories and parables of Jesus, and I knew I would keep learning from them, that my understanding of them was still limited, that it could grow. I felt that I had a lot to learn from this Jesus guy. I felt that we were all partly human and partly divine—or wholly human and wholly divine, that we're all sons and daughters of God, that there is a lot to learn from Jesus just as there is a lot to learn from Buddha, and so on and on.

"I also didn't tell anybody this.

"I did have a moment where all of a sudden it fell into place and it was like, 'I do believe in Jesus!' One morning in college it was just like, 'There we go! Whee! This feels great! I finally feel like I'm part of the gang! I believe Jesus is my Savior!' That kind of faded, along with this whole idea of Jesus as a gateway and all these people that I know and love not passing through that gateway. But still, I just wanted to believe so badly.

"Then it didn't stay with me. It wasn't like I woke up one morning and said, 'Jesus Meesus, I'm gonna go pick my nose!' It just got harder for me to believe it again, or to understand what these people were praying about when they were praying in church. And it went on the back burner. It was like, 'I bet the answer's in that there Bible. I'm just gonna put that on hold. I'm gonna wait till I find a community that I love and that loves me, and then I'm really gonna try to figure this out.' But in the meantime, I don't feel a big loss. Don't tell any Mennonites."

Journal Comments

Of all the interviews, Kate's was the most delightful. Not only is she very funny; she's also incredibly vulnerable, self-aware, and good at making connections. She recognizes inconsistencies in herself (such as wanting a diverse church community, but also requiring a particular brand of theology—mentioned elsewhere), but she gives herself grace, seeing herself as on a journey, recognizing that she has much left to learn. Eventually, Kate wants to find a community that can help her through the more difficult pieces of faith—what it means to follow Jesus apart from traditional definitions of salvation, and how the Bible fits together. She also seeks out community for accountability in her vocation. Ultimately, her "mission" is to help others connect to their own communities.

—*Bethany Spicher*

Dave: Dave claimed that his time in Guatemala and the Middle East "reinforced the importance of what I feel the New Testament—and the Bible—is all about, what I feel Christ's message is all about: care for each other, brothers and sisters. It's not a message for rich people; I mean, it is a message for rich people in the sense that 'you guys are the ones that got all this changing to do, and poor folks got it much more right than you do.'"

Dave feels that living out faith looks like this: "Be less materialistic—don't build up treasures on earth, stop building expensive churches." A lot of it has to do with money. Dave has a hard time with people driving BMW's to church. He has a really hard time with the prosperity gospel he heard in Guatemala, that money is a blessing from God: "Be a Christian and you'll get rich." It does not make sense to him—he called it "a load of hogwash"—and is not found in the Bible. "I think the Christian church just can't ever forget where it came from, who God's people are, . . . who the church needs to be serving."

Dave says he was taught that Jesus was God's Son on earth, that the crucifixion reconciles us to God. But he's argued with himself a lot about that. He has no problem saying, "Christ is my way." But he's not sure if he wants to say that he is *the way* for all people. And yet he does believe that there is a unique and special way that Jesus did things.

"And so again," he said, "I come to one of those points where I have to realize that I don't have the answer."

"Jesus came because we keep screwing up," he said. Jesus shows a different way "that is really, really hard to follow if you want to do it all the way." Trust in God, be willing not to know what's coming, be willing to give up everything, to leave your comfort zone, to buy a house in a bad neighborhood. "I'm not there."

John: In John's family of origin, Jesus's existence was assumed, or at least not contradicted. Now it is a struggle to know where Jesus fits in. It is easy to accept him as a role model, yet John realizes that the church claims him not only as role model but also as a "figure of faith," someone to be believed in. John can't really pin down where he stands.

Laura: Laura commented that for her, Jesus is the reason for living. He is what Laura's faith is based on. Jesus, she said, makes Christianity different from other religions that also believe in God. This difference is important because Jesus is God in human form. He came to earth to die and rise again. He did amazing things on earth, too, but the most amazing thing was saving us; through his death, he took away all our sin.

Brian: The Jesus story is important to Brian in the way Jesus lived as a "normal" person. As a child he needed to learn as other children. It helps Brian to connect with the humanity of Christ. Yet the Christ who died on the cross also became real for him three years ago. "The Jesus story is powerful," he said, "because it is about grace. Jesus is grace."

Eric: Eric asserts that Jesus Christ is his purpose, his cause, and that everything is an expression of Christ's example and gives him new life. This past year, Eric read Lee Strobel's *The Case for Christ*, a rational, intellectual approach toward making truth claims. Eric also read Newbigin's *Foolishness to the Greeks: The Gospel and Western Culture* and Philip Roth's *The Human Stain*. These books and some time in West Africa have helped him understand the Western resistance to the gospel.

Hannah: For Hannah, Jesus is the God who was presented to us by our parents versus the God of her high school friends or the Old Testament God. Hannah thinks the church does a bad job of connecting the Old Testament God with the Jesus story. Her dad told some extreme tent revival stories, about peoples' reactions, and he spoke of wanting a more loving and caring God and finding this in Jesus.

Jesus dining with the prostitute is a powerful image. It demands the question, "Who am I relating to? Who do I have in my home?" Hannah is taken back to the desire to be in the world but not of it. "How far do we push ourselves," she asked. "How much space do we keep sacred for ourselves? Where is that balance?" She observed that Jesus, while he often surrounded himself with the outcast, also surrounded himself with his disciples. Maybe that example tells us that our congregation is our group of disciples, and we need comfort in relating and giving to the broader community around us, outside our somewhat homogenous congregation.

What I Hear

Clearly, it is a challenge to take the image of God and the violence perpetrated by the people of Israel described in the Old Testament, and to reconcile that with the Jesus for whom these young adults all express admiration. Perhaps Dave's comments in chapter 8 help to point the way: The violence of the Old Testament is really about the Israelites taking things into their own hands, and Deuteronomy tells us to choose life, not death. Certain interpretive handles may help to show the way toward a reappraisal of what was really going on. And flawed portrayals of what God is like are corrected over time as the Israelites gradually figure out with what kind of God they are in covenant.

Such an evolving or developing image of God also seems to be the experience of these young adults. An increasing awareness of the world's complexity requires them to reassess what they believe about God and Jesus. Living with the questions is unsettling but not immobilizing. Rather, the questions provoke stirrings that reach for new and more adequate answers than have often been given. Somehow for Craig and for the others mentioned above, the standard answer—"Jesus is the only way, and everyone else is going to hell"—doesn't do justice to what Craig has come to understand about the values Jesus teaches, values that have Craig "fired up and challenged."

Chapter 12
My Experience with Jesus Narrative—III
(Group Interview)

"Jesus is the crux of things"

Reading Scripture and modeling our lives on Jesus relates both to our narrative and our practice themes. Scripture is in narrative form, and the "Jesus story" is in narrative form. How we access these narratives relates to practice. How we model our lives on Jesus relates to the embodiment of the story of his life individually and in our communities.

Philosopher Alasdair MacIntyre has a definition for "tradition" that I like a lot. Tradition, as he describes it, doesn't imply rigidity and maintaining the status quo. Rather, he calls it "a historically extended, socially embodied argument" about how best to interpret and apply the formative text(s) of a particular community. Tradition, then, isn't only a deposit of narratives and related practices that are passed on, but also a living experiment or argument about how a community's formative stories will find their most life-giving interpretation and embodiment here and now.

The group interviews for this project were not debates, but they involved a group conversation about how best to interpret and apply the church narrative, the Bible narrative, and the Jesus narrative. They modeled the kind of conversation necessary for a tradition to become a living and vital force. Here we can listen in on what the groups said about their experience with the Jesus narrative.

Group Interview Questions

Who and what is Jesus to you? After listening to several quotes from your peers about their experience with the Jesus story, describe who and what Jesus is to you and how Jesus and the Jesus story are relevant to your life.

Derek: "Jesus is Lord. If I claim to follow him, then he is Lord of my life, and he is the Savior of all people. I am wrestling with the question of whether Jesus has saved all people, whether people have to respond first by making a pronouncement about Jesus as Lord, or whether there is universal salvation. But Jesus has done such a wonderful thing that I can't imagine not talking about him. He has done such wonderful things and has given such wonderful things."

Anita: "Essentially, I agree with the statement that Jesus is Lord, but I still wonder what will happen with Jews, for example, who believe in God but don't recognize Jesus."

Rose: "I feel that Jesus is so profoundly human, though I expect myself to swing back and forth on the emphasis of human or divine. I have experienced things and thought, 'Jesus went through this.' Something happens and you feel betrayed, and then this story of Judas, it just clicks. I definitely feel that Jesus is the crux of things. In the last couple of months, I have read some interesting books about Jesus being sent to die: What does that say about God as a Father—or parent, and what does that do to our internalized ideas about God? But I still want to keep Jesus at the center."

Phil: "Jesus is the fundamental part of my faith. But he's a bridge to God, and I'm hesitant to say that Jesus is an end in himself because he leads me to God. I am a follower of Jesus, but ultimately I want to get to God. I also have wrestled with the question of Muslims, for example, who are fervently following the same God, but they don't do it through Jesus."

෨ ෨ ෨

Greta: "The first thing that comes to my mind is that Jesus is how God showed his deep love for us. He is God's Son, someone we can strive to live after. Jesus is salvation for us. He is how we get to God. If Jesus did not come and live his sinless life, how would I know how to try to live? God is God, omnipotent, unfathomable. How would I know how to live if it weren't for Jesus? Jesus is our connection point with God."

Don: "I really identify with the idea that Jesus is the model of how to live. I would love to pattern my life after him. . . . but he set the bar rather high. I see Christ as a way to live, but I also agree with Greta that it is the relationship point of my religion."

Curt: "Right now, the most provocative and important Scripture for me is where it speaks of 'this mystery, which is Christ in you, the hope of glory' [Col. 1:27]. Without that I could follow any dude and do pretty well with that, . . . and do some good stuff. Christ isn't just my friend or buddy; he is within me, a part of me. It is a mystery, but it is also our hope. The bar is set high, and Jesus said, 'Be perfect' [Matt. 5:48]. Sometimes I'm like, 'Are you kidding me?' 'For mortals, it is impossible, but for God all things are possible' [Matt. 19:26]."

Don: "I am interested in other world religions. But Jesus is the thing that ultimately keeps me within Christianity. That is the best part—Jesus."

Josh: "For me, Jesus is the way to God. I agree with Greta."

Greta: Jesus is the way "because you can connect with Jesus. He has been through things you are going through."

Margo: "And you can turn to him for help. One image of Jesus is as the 'Comforter' [John 14:16, KJV], and the love and grace that come along with that. People will let you down, but Jesus will never let you down. In his eyes, you are perfect the way you are."

Curt: "Jesus's death alone doesn't save us. You need the resurrection, too! It is so painful to read the account of his death. It's just an emotional roller-coaster! But when he pops up again, it's like 'Yes!' Imagine the response of the disciples. They must have been totally pumped."

Don: "Yeah, the resurrection has to be quite important."

Greta: "Everyone dies, but nobody since then has come back from the dead. That's definitely something special."

Josh: "I had a friend who provoked a thought. Jesus died, and if you believe in him, you will be saved. Why didn't he automatically save everyone when he died, the way everyone was condemned when Adam sinned? I've never really been able to answer that argument, but I have concluded that maybe I can't, and I just have to leave some of those questions to God. For me, what is important is that I do believe in Jesus myself."

Al: "One question that I have been thinking about is this: What risk was there in God handing over his Son, knowing that he was going to be resurrected? I'm not sure where I have come out, but I know that God loves me for it and is passionate about me because of what Jesus did. He saw fit that Jesus should die and rise again."

⌐⌐⌐

Linda: "Jesus is my friend. I see Jesus as a buddy figure in a phenomenal way. I am amazed at his persona, the way people gravitated toward him, the way he mixed and mingled with groups and brought healing to people. I don't understand the God part of Jesus. Jesus being human, I can grasp, but Jesus being God is tough to grasp. And the whole 'Jesus died for our sins' stuff is hard. But I want to be like him, this dude that I admire."

Tara: "My thinking about Jesus has shifted a bit. Coming from a traditional church, I saw Jesus as a strict father. I read Philip Yancey's *What's So Amazing About Grace*, and that changed things for me. I saw who Jesus was hanging out with. Now Jesus is more graceful and accepting. I can't put Jesus in a box as just one thing."

Ray: "For me, relating to Jesus is not a really personal thing. Jesus is how I know things about God. I don't really like the idea of a 'Jesus story.' I don't connect with that type of thing. It seems like the 'Abraham Lincoln story' or a 'Winnie-the-Pooh story.' But I'm all about Jesus. He's cool. And Jesus's life and example is how I'm coming to see what is right. I used to call myself a Christian and not really care too much about how Jesus lived."

Tony: "I'm still figuring this out. Like Ray, I used to call myself a Christian and not really care too much about how Jesus lived. But then I started seeking Jesus, and he became a friend, but in a different way. There are different levels to friendship with Jesus. I don't want to be a Christian just because that's what I'm told to be, and I don't want to have the attitude that 'I don't [care] about my faith,' which is the way I see some of my friends act."

⌐⌐⌐

Beth: "Those people you quoted from other interviews had interesting things to say. I can identify with the part about Jesus being 'my way' but not the only way. I struggle with that, too. The Jesus stories have value because they model the way we should strive to live, though not as a rule book, nor word for word. The resurrection and crucifixion are amazing. I don't know how I could identify with what Christ went through. But saying Jesus is the way for everyone is a strict interpretation. I can't swallow that right now. He is the way for me, though."

Tim: "It's hard for me to put into words an answer to that question. It's very deep. I feel like I should write a paper on it. I would like to use the word 'model.' His teachings and his legacy are for us to abide by. I have certain beliefs, too, but some of them don't coincide with what the Bible says. I'm not a literalist. But Jesus is relevant to me. He's my model, but I wouldn't say you have to follow everything strictly."

Michelle: "Jesus is my example of how I should live and treat others. He is my Savior, my way to heaven."

James: "Jesus is my buddy. He teaches me how I *should* interact with people."

ↄↄↄ

Andy: "Jesus is huge. The goal in my life is for Jesus to be more. I'm not very good at it. God sent him to save us from ourselves. I feel like we're always seeing parallels to that in the movies, like *E.T.* People are searching for something, a savior, someone to give them hope and meaning. Jesus is the best."

Conrad: "Jesus is the Son of God. I believe in the salvation of the cross. He is the final authority. There is always a lot of ambiguity, but it always comes back to what Jesus said and did."

Aaron: "I grew up on Jesus. My life was formed around Jesus's teachings. That was my parents' choice, and I really value that and give credit to them for that. I think Jesus was an amazing man and had incredible things to say. . . . But for my life, I don't really feel like I'm searching for meaning right now, not searching for a map or direction. I stopped that after college. I just want to figure out what I want to do with my time—how I can be the most productive and happy, how to interact with the people around me. Thoughts about Jesus also remind me of time spent in Indonesia during cross-cultural experience during college. While there, I heard from people from all different religious backgrounds. I learned from listening to them that there is a common base among all faiths, basics like 'Love your neighbor as yourself.' That was comforting to find."

What I Hear

Responses from these groups expand on some of the same themes that showed up in the earlier one-on-one interviews. Jesus is often referred to as a model, the one on whom we pattern our lives. In nearly equal proportions in these interviews, however, Jesus is also referred to as "salvation for us," as one whose death and resurrection are vitally important and the one whom "God sent to save us from ourselves." More than a model and source of salvation, Jesus is experienced as a personal friend and mysterious presence "within me."

While people see Jesus as central to their faith, and even as their Lord, many still wonder what will happen to the Jews and the Muslims. And what about universal salvation for all? It seems truly remarkable, however, that even with the questions and the different words and ways used to describe him in these last three chapters, Jesus is admired by all, sometimes for different reasons. Yet he's clearly "this dude that I admire," "the best part," and "the crux of things."

Chapter 13
Relating to People of Other Faith Stories—I

"So many missionary stories"

The one-on-one interviews didn't include direct questions about relating to people who aren't followers of Christ, people of other faith stories and practices. But this theme came up again and again as these young adults told their stories.

Because there were so many comments about encounters with people of other religions and cultures in their formative stories, it seems appropriate to group such comments with an ear toward listening for common themes. The encounters described here are sometimes transformative, other times disconcerting, and most often enormously enriching, enlarging their appreciation for the rich complexity of the world.

First we listen to Ajay discuss his formative stories about multiple encounters with persons of other faiths and cultures.

Ajay: Ajay was born in India and lived there until he was thirteen, when his family moved to the American Midwest so his father could study theology.

When Ajay was young, his mother would read stories from a children's Bible every Sunday night. He remembers that when he asked about the miracles, his mother responded, "God did them."

"So that was a really strong grounding," Ajay says. His mother would often relate current life experiences to the Bible. When his bike was stolen, she told him the story of Job. (The bike showed up later!)

Ajay was born into a family of missionaries. His maternal grandparents were missionaries in a Thailand leprosy colony, his paternal grandparents ran a home for underprivileged boys, and his great-grandfather was "a big-name preacher." Two of his father's three brothers were with Indian Evangelistic Missions, and one of them knew eight or nine tribal languages.

His family, he says, has been Christian for seven or eight generations. Before converting, the family was known as medicine people, or healers. Western missionaries who came to South India had set up a church, a hospital and a school, Ajay says. One day a missionary was conducting a service in a church, "and old grandfather was grazing his cow and making too much noise." The missionary came out and asked him to quiet down, and he said, "I'm going to bring your church down with my magic." As Ajay tells it, "He ended up ramming his head against the church wall because he was so mad, and he got hurt." The missionary took him to the hospital, and when he became conscious, he was so touched by the missionary's compassion that he became a Christian.

Another family story that's important to Ajay's faith is his father's, whose first wife died in childbirth. "It pushed him away from God for a long time," says Ajay. Eventually, church leaders and family members planned a prayer service for him. Still angry at God, Ajay's father decided to go to the service, tear the Bible in half, and express his alienation. According to Ajay, "These are quite conservative, fundamental Christians."

During a nap before the service, Ajay's father says that God came to him and said, "'Don't kick against a rock, because you'll only hurt yourself.' So he went to the church service and was comforted by the people there." That story is influential for Ajay: "God is always there. He's not going to leave me."

With so many missionary stories, Ajay felt called to missions at an early age.

"When I was a little kid, I used to think of living in a tent in a jungle somewhere, and I used to get scared that snakes would crawl into my tent.

"I've always felt that God has placed a call in my life to be a peacemaker— I've always broken up fights."

Interestingly, Ajay waffled for a while as a child between wanting to be a missionary and wanting to join the Indian military! It wasn't until his father studied at a Mennonite college that the family encountered Mennonites and the idea of pacifism.

In the United States, Ajay encountered racism firsthand in his family's experience with the Native Americans his father pastored.

"In that town, the racial lines were rather visible between the Native American and white community. I always identified myself with the Native Americans. I would tell my friends, 'Man, I'm the real Indian.'

"I witnessed a lot of one-on-one racism but also systemic racism. One of my friends trespassed on someone's property, and the cops took him to the county jail and beat him up completely. Later, on Halloween night, we were hanging out, and arguments broke out between Native American kids and white kids. The night ended with one of the white kids pulling a 12-gauge gun on us. The police came and picked him up, took him into the local chamber of commerce room, had a talk with him, and let him go."

Another story Ajay told was about the local Mennonite church where his dad pastored. A gym was open in the evenings for neighbor kids to play basketball. Even though Ajay's father was up-to-date with electricity payments, the local electric company cut off power, claiming he hadn't paid. Ajay's father called several times, but it took the white conference minister from the next state to call before power was restored.

"Many of us asked, 'Why does it take a white man to call?' At that time, I became very antigovernment, antiauthority. I was very angry. So when I read about nonviolent resistance in college, that really spoke to me. In college, my social mind changed. At home, we weren't poor, but we were always scraping for cash. When I finished high school, my goal was to make money. That's why I did computers for my first year of college. I still love computers, but that was the reason. Things changed. Before I went to college, I wasn't a complete pacifist. I still thought that war could not be helped. But in college, I learned about what the gospel has to say about peace."

Journal Comments

It's fascinating to me that Ajay (like Miguel, chapter 6) started out their "stories" section with stories about their relatives' conversions, often going back generations to describe the faithfulness of ancestors. In Ajay's case, he knows the story from seven or eight generations back, and that history seemed fresh and real to him, as did the story of his father's narrow escape from turning his back on the church by tearing the Bible in half. This sense of being a "converted" people intrigues me. I wish I would have asked Ajay more about what it was like to be Christian in India, what it's like to be here in a "Christian" nation, where he's no longer a minority.

Ajay's stories certainly show how he has a keen sense of peoplehood that gives him purpose. From feeling called to serve "in the jungle" as a child, to responding to the racism he witnessed in his Midwest state as a youth, Ajay seems to see himself as following in the footsteps of his fathers and mothers. He's committed to eventually returning to India to work there. Still, some of Ajay's theology and practices are uniquely his. He's the first in his family to grow up with Anabaptist understandings of faith, and his pacifist convictions have led him to work at issues related to conscience and war—to be a witness for nonviolence to his friends.

—*Bethany Spicher*

Interview Questions

Are there stories that have power for you now that weren't a part of your childhood? What are they? Where have you heard or seen them?

Dave: College trips made Dave think more internationally. He spent a semester in Guatemala. "The world is a much bigger place than the United States of America," he discovered. Ninety percent of the world doesn't have half of what he has. In Guatemala, seeing the poorest of the poor at the city dump gave him a reality check about what is really important.

While studying there, he attended Mennonite World Conference meetings in Guatemala City as a delegate for his conference. Seeing Mennonites from all over the world expanded his understanding of Mennonites. Only a few "ethnic" Mennonites of European origin were there. He commented, "We have a lot of shutting up to do and a lot of listening to do." Many Latin American leaders have "more validity in their peace teachings, and we Mennonites have a lot to learn from local churches that pray their hearts out."

Dave's experience in various countries leads him to observe that God is relational. Witnessing people's relationship with God has been powerful and humbling. It is "awe-inspiring" to see how people get through awful things like miserable poverty by being really religious, going to church all the time, and trusting in God. This kind of faith draws Dave. He wishes he could get a piece of it.

Dave never had a hellfire-and-damnation notion that God was fearsome. God is one of love and comfort, he said. Dave also reported that he sees his belief in God as an individual reality, not a universal truth. He doesn't want to tell anyone else they are wrong. This attitude comes from not wanting to exclude people.

"That's oversimplifying things, though, because I also believe that community is incredibly important," he said. "You come to God through the church. It's not just a me-and-God thing."

He referred to his wish not to exclude people as "cultural baggage." Excluding people "is not part of the American way."

"There are so many different people in the world, so many different belief systems. And in a way, being a Christian and hoping everyone else in the world becomes a Christian is . . . exclusive."

Has he reconciled this? "I think I've made peace with myself that I just don't know. Probably my viewpoints will change at some point, and that's okay. I've just got to keep trying to fight the fight and keep learning along the way. I have to be willing not to know all the answers."

Hannah: Hannah tells of influential biblical stories like the good Samaritan, which she remembers acting out at church with her two brothers and mom. "It stuck," she says.

Hannah grew up in a mixed urban community. As a kid she related to people of all different colors equally. Her parents taught through word and example that we were to treat everyone the same, she said. She felt the story revealing to her the "blindness of God to faults, differences, and weaknesses." She has always wanted to be in a racially diverse setting. This desire related to her childhood environment and to the prominence of the good Samaritan story.

Hannah was very taken with the Nelson Mandela story and the struggle against apartheid.

"I was going to stop apartheid," she said. "Then someone got to it before I could."

She spoke of an incident at her Mennonite high school. Members of the Zimbabwe Brethren in Christ Church came and presented a play depicting missionaries coming in and demanding change. She described the play as "raw and stark!"

During college Hannah did a cross-cultural study in Kenya. She learned about the history of colonialism, how faith was linked, and about missionary tales. She heard people saying, "Yeah, I became a Christian because they had money and I knew I could get money. Yes, I still have my African religion and my multiple wives, but I'm a Mennonite." This experience was so important for her in examining the church's role around the world. She tried to understand what it means to be a Mennonite in Kenya and wondered if she could fit in and find a place there. But she made a discovery.

"They have their church established, and it's growing way more quickly than anything here. They don't need me anymore. Why is it growing so quickly? Gee! They finally have their own people leading the church. Oh, there's a thought!"

Hannah came to realize that she can't ever be Kenyan. She has the privilege of choice whenever she goes traveling. She observed that she'll always have an out if it's too difficult.

"If I did choose to live there, I'd have to have a couple things to keep sane because I can't throw away where I came from. I'd have to live in a small community, be married to avoid constant sexual harassment and proposals, know the language, and have my own home, where I could escape."

Hannah is also sensitive to conservative thoughts and lifestyles because of summertime spent on an Amish farm as a small child. She remarked that comments against conservatism and groups more conservative than Mennonites can rile her just as much as racist remarks.

Hannah finds her current work as an elementary teacher in a city school life-giving.

"I always feel much more stagnant in my faith when I'm in the Mennonite community than when I'm outside of it," she said. "I don't know that I could work in the church. I need that public outside-the-church experience as my daily reality. My co-workers are my family, my support community. I try to balance who I am in that setting, not to be embarrassed of who I am—my Mennonite identity."

Hannah is a firm believer in Mennonite World Conference. She attended MWC Zimbabwe the summer of 2003. This was a rich church experience and reopened all the questions of her place in the broader world.

She remembers feeling frustrated by a lack of respect from peers looking down on those who chose to work at a normal job in the United States. Many of her peers idealize MCC and international work. While Hannah firmly believes in MCC's work, she feels respect is also due to those who serve in the United States.

"As a church, we need to learn to relate to the people here," she said. "What church here is opening itself to African-American and Latino people? We need to step back and examine ourselves, in addition to giving respect to international leaders."

So Hannah is juggling respect for conservative churches, international churches, and churches right here.

Journal Comments

In this interview I was struck by Hannah's articulation and confidence about her faith. She is sure about many things that she believes in and practices. Her job, her living situation, her lifestyle choices are all quite intentional, and she is not afraid to express her convictions. This is refreshing to me after interviewing so many questioning people who don't know where to look for answers. Hannah, like the others, is searching, but not necessarily for answers to questions about personal belief and who God is.

Hannah has challenging questions for the greater Mennonite church. What are we doing with international mission? Are we really trying to be welcoming and inclusive of all races and orientations? Is it necessary for a congregation to be racially diverse, or can we be okay with the idea that all kinds may not meld together? Hospitality received a strong emphasis throughout this interview, alongside the desire for fellowship.

—*Melody King*

Rachel: Rachel observed that she didn't really notice much distinction related to being Mennonite until she moved away from her childhood home. Her husband, on the other hand, talks about growing up with a real sense of being different from others in his schools and community. Rachel's family had the *Martyrs Mirror*, and she remembers looking at the pictures, which she found scary.

For Rachel, being Mennonite was closely tied to the peace stance. That changed in college when she went to France and met Mennonites for whom that wasn't as important. Her experiences in France redefined "Mennonite" more broadly.

Through Rachel's travels, her understanding of God became indefinable and all-inclusive.

"You grow up thinking, 'Oh, God is this.' And he is a he, and he is white, and he has a beard, and he is God of your church and does what you want him to do. But God just became much bigger."

Rachel's experiences with Muslims led her to believe that they worship the same God she does.

She says she doesn't understand God. She doesn't understand why terrible things happen. She doesn't understand why one child is born in a hospital room to a joyful family while another dies in a garbage bag two blocks from her house. It is so unfair. She questions God. She gets pissed at God. And yet she still believes.

Rachel is much more of a *doer* than a thinker and believer. Her faith has mostly to do with living out her values. To be Mennonite used to mostly mean living your life as Jesus lived his. Now it means more than that. It means believing that everyone deserves to have a say in their future and live a peaceful life, without suffering harm.

She lives out of a sense of justice, of valuing equality—what Jesus wanted for the world. This understanding was there for Rachel in high school, but it has grown more prominent as she has seen more of the world.

Journal Comments

Rachel is definitely a doer and identified herself as such. She has much more clarity about how she wants to live her life than about what she believes. She prefers to act out of a commitment to justice and a love of other people than to discuss the theology behind those actions. I think she would identify herself as Christian, but I don't think she actually used that word once in the whole interview (except maybe when she was talking about a fellow resident who is always proselytizing and drives her nuts).

—Deborah Good

Laura: Laura says that Youth Evangelism Service (YES) training after high school graduation changed her life and was the kind of thing she'd been desiring all through high school. She soaked up teachings about how God works, the love of Christ, that God desires the best for us, that "he's everywhere," and the importance of continuing a relationship with God.

Laura heard stories of missionaries in Africa and Asia reemphasizing that God is working in the lives of people everywhere. While living in an Asian country as a part of a YES team, she also heard stories. Yet a somewhat romanticized vision of missionary work was moderated for her when a missionary family she knew went home to the States and ended up getting divorced. Laura was quite critical of this couple's divorce, but through their story she also recognized that missionary work is hard.

These stories helped Laura gain an international perspective. "When you're in one setting," she says, "you sort of think, well, that's how God works, or that's how it is, or that's how church should be. But then you go to another place, and you see other people who are so devoted to the Lord, and they do things really differently, and that's okay because you can't put God in a box. He works in different ways in different areas, . . . and that was good to see."

Living for some months in another country broadened Laura's idea of God, and she observed that there are certain truths. But a lot can be different from one culture to the next, specifically when it comes to how church is set up. She learned how much people have in common and commented that the more you share with people, the more you realize others are going through similar things. It's important that we help each other through, she says.

Journal Comments

Laura's black-and-white understanding of Christian ethics was challenged by the complexity she faced when she started encountering cross-cultural differences. God works differently in different cultures, she says. But when I suggested, "So, God is different to different people?" she responded with a hesitant yes. Then she quickly went on to clarify that we are all to believe certain truths. But some things—about how church is done—can vary from culture to culture. This paradox—believing in an absolute and universal truth while trying to be open to the idea that people different from us might have some things right, too—is one I think many in my generation wrestle with, some more explicitly than others. And we come out at different places.

—*Deborah Good*

Peter: After high school, Peter said he wanted to do something that was "less evangelical" than Summer Training Action Team (STAT), so he went to Uganda with Serving and Learning Together Team (SALT). There he still encountered the sense—from the people he worked with, and from himself—that he was a missionary.

"I met a friend in a nearby village," Peter said, "and we hung out a few times.

Then I found out that he was Muslim, and I avoided him like the plague because I knew if I was with him, I'd have to try to convert him. I got over that eventually, though."

In Uganda, Peter often compared himself to a family that was, as he says, "culturally inept. They stayed inside and read and never learned the local language." But then he "struggled with feeling prideful."

Peter also experienced conflicting feelings in his appreciation of the Ugandans' faith. He wanted to see himself as not just Mennonite, but as part of a global church, At the same time, he missed the congregation back at home (especially hymn-singing).

"I still appreciate the songs we sang there and the steady faith of the people, who have few resources. The economic inequality bothered me back in the States, and it made me ready to get away from it."

Peter remembers someone from his home church telling him, "Welcome back to the real world" when he returned from Uganda. He was disappointed to encounter that degree of ignorance.

Jason: Jason has been powerfully impacted by his own travel and the people he has met. Two people in particular influenced him. One is Jen, a young woman from Australia with whom he spent a lot of time. In talking with her, he learned that "my own history [as a Mennonite] is interesting to someone else." The other important person is Kevin, a fashion designer from New York. In Jason's upbringing, fashion was considered worldly and excessive, and the fashion world felt artificial. But Kevin taught Jason the importance of being "really true to yourself."

Most of all for Jason, Kevin and Jen shattered an idea with which he grew up: that you have to be Christian—and maybe even Mennonite—to love others and to have a conscience. It was a surprising discovery that there are good people out there who aren't Mennonite or religious at all. This was reinforced in Indonesia, where he lived with a Muslim host family. These Muslims were some of the best people Jason has known, in the importance they gave family relationships, sitting around talking all night. Jason realized that he could shed the Christian narrative and still live a "good" life by helping others, living outside himself, and thinking globally. He also learned about other religions in college, which made the Jesus story seem less unique.

While in college, Jason wrote his senior thesis on Mennonite missionaries in Somalia. The missionaries he studied first took a fundamentalist and evangelical approach. But when that didn't seem to work, they adapted and developed instead "a mission of presence."

"I thought that was rather remarkable," he stated, "especially for the early

Sixties, amid all the turmoil going on in the church. It stood out as an exceptional case compared to the other mission organizations there." Other mission groups left when they were required to start teaching Islam in their schools, but the Mennonites stayed.

"It was a good story for me to be exposed to, I think, because it said a lot of really good things about Mennonites, how the core beliefs Mennonites take into the world can adapt, and how they can be respectful of other cultures."

What I Hear

I'm impressed most by the crosscurrents reflected in the above comments; the goodness of the missionary influence as experienced by Ajay's family; and the discomfort with missionary efforts intended to "convert" expressed by Peter and others. It would be far too simplistic to see these crosscurrents as somehow canceling each other out, or that one is right and the other wrong. What the stories do demonstrate is that the interface of cultures is a complex and delicate matter, to be approached with great humility and genuine respect. Ajay's desire to share the new dimensions of the pacifist gospel he's learned with friends and possibly with his own people back in India seems to grow out of his glad and spirited experience of his family's "many missionary stories" from an early age.

Chapter 14
Relating to People of Other Faith Stories—II
(Group Interview)

"God and the world become more complex"

As we've already seen, many young adults are asking questions that grow out of their encounters with people of other religions and cultures. They wonder what their responsibility toward people of other faiths is on behalf of Jesus and the gospel, and how to find their place in a complex world that offers a multiplicity of good ways of being.

Since these questions frequently showed up in the individual interviews, we decided to make them a focus for the group interviews. Below are the newly framed questions and their responses.

Group Interview Questions

Mennonites, while remaining a somewhat distinct faith community, have been enriched by interaction with other Christians, people of other religions, cultures, and even popular culture. Yet sometimes what we've learned has conflicted with or contradicted our assumptions about God and what we think we ought to believe and practice as faithful Christians.

After listening to several comments from other young adults, reflect on the core beliefs that are most central to your life, those about which you are most confident. What do you think is an appropriate way to interact with people who have a different worldview, primary narrative, religious heritage, or cultural reality from the one you are most rooted in?

Derek: "I remember a comment Myron Augsburger made, that we should know enough about people of other faiths that when we are in dialogue with them, we could almost be convinced. I think it is good to interact with people of other faiths and viewpoints. But as soon as someone is going to be aggressive about how the world works, like about politics, I shut down. I'm totally open to and genuinely interested in talking to people of other worldviews, but if I lack the ability to claim my own truth, I render myself useless in that conversation. Christ is my truth, so when I am in conversations with people, I have to be unabashedly open about that."

Anita: "Most of my friends are non-Mennonites, and many are non-Christians. You have to approach them with an attitude of not trying to impose beliefs on them, not just assuming you are right. For these conversations to work and be productive, the approach has to be that your truth is not necessarily the only truth. At home I was in public school, so most people weren't Christians, and they were mostly against Christians because people were always telling them they would burn in hell. You have to approach them by being a good example and then gently showing them what you believe. Be careful because what you say can really throw them off."

Rose: "I feel like faith is very 'on-location' and you have to be doing, not simply talking. Also, you need a community of people with whom you can talk about faith, one where it feels safe to process what you are thinking about. If you are having conversations with people of different faiths or viewpoints, you need to have a community of people that shares your basic understandings to come back to. Otherwise, you become a floater that doesn't do any good. Sometimes I feel as though I'm just doing damage control for what other Christians have done, but I don't want to just be cleaning up damage. I want to be doing something constructive. And I think we need a community in order to do that."

Phil: "I agree. One thing I would add is an attitude of humility. We should recognize that our belief systems are constantly changing and be open to the possibility that interacting with people who are different will help us learn and grow. The community needs to be flexible enough that they can allow for that responsibility, and they can help you work through those things in a nonthreatening way."

෨෨෨

Jennifer: "This has been a major portion of my developing in the past ten years. I have only grown and been strengthened by meeting people of other faiths and worldviews. I believe in the broader understanding that can be gained by opening yourself to someone else's experience and journey. I try to learn to know about people's lives, their struggles and joys, and to be open to learning from them. And I've also learned to be as honest and open about who I am. I feel much more comfortable listening, but an ideal is to put my stuff on the table as well. This process of open listening makes me less sure of my own beliefs, but I derive comfort from allowing God and the world to become more complex. It makes me doubt myself and the way I live and think. That's a good thing."

Ellen: "You can't go wrong with love. No matter who you come across, interact from a basis of love. Christians operate out of having one right way of living. In such a diverse world, it's better to ask the right questions. You have to be honest and open to listening and sharing and be interested in the lives of other people. And go beyond that: walk consistently with people."

Karla: "One of the young adults quoted earlier talked about a 'biblical worldview.' I would hold to the biblical worldview no matter what context I'm in or what people group is surrounding me. Moving around, you naturally take on characteristics of the people you're with. Jesus held this balance that is just so hard. He loved people but also called them to other standards of life. The good news is controversial. It calls people to a whole new standard of life. That's the tension I live with. How do you hold to a controversial gospel? It means love and it means change."

Ken: "It's an era thing. We come into this newfound freedom to deconstruct everything around us and to leave it by the roadside if it's not working for us. Earlier generations inculcated me with a sense of duty, even though I'm so flighty in my current young-adult postmodernism. My young-adult years are tremendous testing grounds for the greet-everyone-with-love ethic.

"When I first started working with my home church after I graduated, I had the opportunity to work with a Muslim family—refugees for whom our church was providing housing. I spent a lot of time with them, praying with them, trying to build trust, and trying to help them interact with the greater community despite the huge barriers that stood between them and our church. My efforts weren't working. I started with love, but I became hateful of their distrust. I can't believe I'm saying that. So the 'love' answer is feeling too simple for me. This is serious stuff here. I'm still figuring this out."

Lisa: "I work at a domestic violence shelter. It is an underground railroad of sorts. For women running for their lives, we're one stop. When I first started working with the women and their relationships, I was tied to the outcomes. I rode their roller-coaster with them. But it's gotten better. I've learned to meet people where they are and walk with them consistently.

"Another story: When I was nineteen, in India, it was impressed upon me that the whole world is one, interconnected. I think of myself as one cell in this body, and I feel a responsibility to be aware of other cells in the body. We are all part of the whole. We are all part of a system. As a result of my Menno upbringing, I feel a responsibility to work toward the well-being of the poorest of the poor. I need to have a global consciousness. We all do start from different places. I don't have any expectations except for this understanding that we're all part of the same."

This sparked conversation with another interviewee, who asked: "What about when there is no shared pulse? You say we are all connected, but what about when that understanding that we're all part of the same just isn't there?" Lisa responded, "I spend a great part of time with people who are already working for change in their own lives, so the shared pulse is already there, I guess. It is clear that they want me there, walking with them, . . . so I don't know."

಄಄಄

Margo: "I think that for Christians our primary thing is that Jesus is God's Son, and through him we can have eternal life. So interacting with others is hard because I don't want to say that they are wrong or right. I don't know what God's plan is for the world. I think we should share what we believe but without judgment. Look for common values and work with that."

Don: "I would prefer not to use a judgmental attitude at all. In any encounter, we should first look for a relationship, then begin to dialogue about what we believe. And we shouldn't assume that they will only learn from us; it should go the other way, too. There should be mutual exchange, learning from each other."

Curt: "A book I was reading brought out that denominations have 90 percent of their beliefs in common; only 10 percent is what holds them apart. I think that commonality is good. We should come at our differences from that perspective, and be willing to experience and learn from other denominations. I think we should go and experience other denominations: Catholic, Pentecostal, and so on. We should be able to walk into a church without a thought in our minds of trying to talk to anyone about peace and justice. But we are open to talk with people and learn from them. If people are hungry for God, then they will ask, and maybe we'll have a chance to share about our distinctives. But we also should be willing to learn."

Josh: "I grew up in a Catholic school, and with Muslim friends and even grand-parents, so I was constantly exposed to other groups and the conflicts that can arise. In Ethiopia we have more problems with the Orthodox church than any other group. They really are quite different, and they don't accept the evangelicals and Mennonites. They sometimes become violent. My father translated a book, *Ishmael, My Brother*, and people even within the Mennonite church and more outside it have problems with this. I'd hear people on the street corner preaching against the concept: 'Ishmael isn't your brother; he's your enemy.' This is when I started to notice differences between cultures, denominations, and religions. What I learned from my father is at least to listen to other people. Respect what they believe."

Curt: "I think international experiences are good."

Don: "Definitely. Travel alone can break down any issues you have. It is not just about being hospitable and inviting people in, but you getting out."

Al: "I think it is important to have the attitude of a learner. You can always learn something from people. That is the ideal approach."

Greta: "And you always have something to offer as well, whether encourage-ment, a listening ear; there's always something to offer."

∽ ∽ ∽

Linda: "The cynical part of me says that everyone should 'mind your own busi-ness.' In our society it is politically correct to be tolerant, almost to the point of accepting everyone else's beliefs, which I can see people in the Mennonite church starting to do. Sometimes it's honestly hard to have theological discussions and not to walk away pissed off at each other. It's sometimes easier to talk to persons of other religions because the differences are greater. It's easy to say 'we're toler-ant,' but we're not always tolerant. At the same time, I'm rather open-minded. When I'm with others, I choose the approach of listening, nodding, and smiling, and while leaving say, 'Oh, that was nice!' I wouldn't want to believe them, nec-essarily, but I would say that it was interesting to listen to."

Tara: "For a while it was drilled into my head that this is the 'only way.' My approach is to acknowledge that there are a lot of beliefs out there, and I need to be nonjudgmental, open-minded. We need to have action behind our words. If people see you living out your faith, then it is a powerful witness. If we weren't so focused on our differences, how much more we would get done!"

Ray: "I don't have a good way to answer this question. There is no hard-and-fast answer. I would try to be respectful and to be true to Christ. I have to believe Christ would be good for other people too. That's where it's hard."

Tony: "It's easy to believe that you live out what you believe, but I fail to live out what I believe, for example, following Christ's example of service. I don't think you should push beliefs on others. You can only be who you are, and if it is something that appeals to others, then fine. I think it's important to live out and model your faith, to be kind even if others are cruel to you. God has to be bigger than we've ever imagined."

∽ ∽ ∽

Tim: "I don't understand how to answer about what's appropriate. I can't be scared to be in the world. I can't be scared of pop culture. Sometimes I feel pressured to share—evangelize—but how is that going to happen if we stay in our boxes? I think it's good that we go outside our boundaries and yet still stay true to ourselves, although we might change a little. It's how we mature."

Beth: "During my cross-cultural experience, it was good to see how different the Mennonite church was there. And my friends' experiences with cross-culturals led to conversations about what we grew up learning, or not learning. Sometimes I think my church community is ignorant. They just don't know. A church that recognizes other groups' realities is important. You can't evangelize until you address a person's real-life situation, their basic needs. I feel strongly about it. I also struggle with the quote that Christ must be the only way."

Tim: "We talk about this at least once a week, because of our situation [having a baby out of wedlock]. For my parents, it was hard. My dad's a leader, and he still struggles with it. In conversations with my parents, I feel judged. It feels like my parents are on our backs. I think you can't address spiritual needs until you address people's physical needs."

Beth: "My father and his wife went on a mission trip to Russia [evangelizing]. The conditions are horrible. All I could think of was the social situation. I could not imagine focusing on revival without addressing who these people are and how they live, what they have to live with. Other people want to go into an area that is dry and revive it. But there's a space and time for that."

Tim: "Before you chastise me, ask me how my day is. If a stranger comes up to you and says you need to be more spiritual, give him a strange look. I want a community that can do both things, meet the spiritual and the physical needs. There must be a middle ground."

Michelle: "I would say it is important to be open without being judgmental or condemning. There is something to be said about standing up for one's beliefs. There is something to sticking with your worldview and beliefs."

James: "That's really close to what I would say. You need to be kind, open, understanding, and at the same time willing to share your beliefs as well, especially with some prompting to share."

ᔐ ᔐ ᔐ

Sarah: "I don't feel any mandate to go out and convert people. I've chosen to put my faith in these things, but what assurance do I have that it's reality? I'm going to be really respectful of others' faith, because they've probably come to those beliefs in the same way I've come to mine. I would like to dialogue about it but not to convert everyone."

Aaron: "Dialoguing is the best way for me to keep exploring my worldview. It's changing all the time based on who I'm interacting with, where I am, what I'm doing. My work is fundraising for Children International. It's not government or religiously affiliated. In most cases, this makes people much more comfortable in supporting it. People don't seem to trust religion as much today. Maybe that's because of the conflict seen between different religions. Maybe people then think it's religion itself that is the problem. But really, people just need to be more open to dialoguing."

Ann: "I think that's something the Mennonite church has to offer. Right now I have the opportunity of participating in a Bible study at the school where I teach. It's composed of Seventh-Day Adventists, Baptists, and so on. I hear from all different perspectives. I like that."

Conrad: "Usually people have more questions for me than I do for them, such as explaining the whole Amish thing and so on. I don't always have the answers. I'm good at faking it."

Andy: "I've been thinking about this a lot, being a Christian and a Mennonite on a secular college campus. A lot of people are into secular religion, but not really participating in or caring a lot about it. I don't need to go and knock on doors, but I feel like it's my responsibility as a Christian to share the hope that I have since God has brought me through a lot of things. It's a gift I need to share. I agree that it's important to listen. People don't want to hear what you have to say until you listen to their journey. And that's part of my responsibility—to care about others. I don't agree with all the inclusiveness that's being talked about. I think that if I've found something that's really valuable and true, then it's got to be true or I don't want it. I believe what the Bible has to say about Jesus Christ as the Son of God."

> ### What I Hear
>
> I hear a lot of wisdom coming through these comments from young adults who are savvy, self-aware, humble, and wise in their understanding about what it takes both to own "one's own truth" and to be open to learning from others. They have a lot to teach the rest of us.
>
> Overall, I hear these young adults appreciating and even celebrating that "God and the world have become more complex." Their encounter with "the other" has been the occasion for personal growth and new respect for other people's realities and rich heritages. So many have grasped the significance of both respectful listening and honest sharing about their own "truth" and "stuff." They offer a strong resource to all of us.

Chapter 15
General Cultural Narratives

"I don't go out and shoot people when I listen to Eminem"

Clearly for those interviewed, the stories of family and faith have been powerfully formative. But there are many other stories that are vibrating on the airwaves, in the print media, on the screen and computer monitor. How influential have these other stories been? We asked young adults: Which narrative sources—books, TV, movies, music, the Internet, radio, magazines, newspapers—play a big role in your life? What is the relationship between an activity and what you truly value in life? How do these contribute to your ability to make sense of the world?

I find it intriguing that several persons, in reflecting on growing up Mennonite and then becoming more aware of other narratives, talked about the need to "play catch-up." Previously, Jessica remarked that she wished she would have been introduced to some basic awareness of pop culture in her childhood. She feels left out of conversations about what it means to be an eighties kid or what is happening on television. And Miguel and Jason talked about "what I missed growing up."

Apparently this isn't only a "Mennonite thing." Later we'll hear from John, who didn't grow up Mennonite or even Christian but talks about wishing his parents would have introduced him to more of the general cultural narratives in ways that would have given him clues for his behavior.

In our interviews, we didn't directly ask about the degree to which these young adults were exposed to pop culture during their formative years. But we did ask them to reflect on what they are choosing to read, watch, and listen to now. Listen first to

Will's story and then to an assortment of other responses on general cultural narratives.

Will: Will remembers how his mom read to him at night from a book of Bible stories. He looks back on this as being formative. His dad told stories about growing up as an oppressed minority in an occupied country. His dad's stories were vivid and especially formative of Will's pacifism. If anyone ever had a reason to not be pacifist, it was Will's father. Yet he came through his experiences of occupation and oppression with strong pacifist convictions.

Will read lots of books. He remembers his library having some kind of celebration for him when he read his ten-thousandth book from the library. His family didn't have television.

Will thinks that the Bible stories in his childhood instilled in him a deep appreciation of Scripture. He remembers being deeply offended in a fourth-grade Sunday school class when the teacher insinuated that some stories from the Bible did not really happen.

The books he read were primarily formative in terms of the amount of information that Will gained. Part of his identity was wrapped up in commanding a tremendous amount of knowledge. But with fiction, Will read primarily "from the outside in," without identifying with the characters.

Will generally feels positive about the wide reading he did, even though most of it was for information he no longer retains as explicit knowledge. He can even see a long-term benefit of the "negative stuff" he read, such as literature from other religions.

Will has read a tremendous amount of theological material, although he perused much of it for information and did not integrate it into his own view of self and God. He has read much fiction and enjoys it, although he does not retain it or movies he has seen several times. For this reason he doubts it has much lasting influence on him.

Will spends a "well above average" amount of time on the Internet. His main topics of interest are theology, health, and finance. His goal is to "learn enough to regurgitate [the information] effectively." He finds he is "more teachable" when doing research this way because he feels as though he is selecting his own sources and teaching himself, so he invests more authority in what he reads.

Will reads a lot, even now while he is in college. "Most of the reading I do is outside of class work." The most significant books he's read have been by Christian author Rick Joyner, and in the past, "Baptist stuff." Will says he's "picky" about what he allows to have authority in his life. Additionally, his chosen areas of fascination change from time to time. His motivation for reading is to learn about and be able to articulate his faith. He says there are many influences that help him to be a "nice, amiable person," but these are reinforced and confirmed by his faith.

When Will listens to radio it is mostly right-wing talk radio while multitasking. He doesn't feel it has too much influence on how he views the world, just as "I don't go out and shoot people and debase women when I listen to Eminem." Will does allow that what he listens to would reinforce views he already holds.

Will watches movies, but doesn't feel they are influential; mostly he does it to relax or pass time with his girlfriend.

Journal Comments

Will was excessively entertaining to interview and gave me enough colorful answers that sometimes I wanted to transcribe the entire interview. He does not shy away from saying things that might differ from the opinions of others. If anything, he goes out of his way to point out ways of thinking he holds to that others might consider unique. While in many ways not "typical," I wanted to include Will because he added variety to my sample on a number of areas, such as his ethnic heritage, a significant time away from Christianity, and charismatic influence.

—*Aram DiGennaro*

Interview Questions

There are many channels through which stories come to us—books, TV, movies, music, the Internet, radio, magazines, newspapers. Which of these plays a significant role in your life? What is the relationship between an activity and what you truly value in life? How do these sources impact you and contribute to your ability to make sense of the world?

Jeff: A television will not be found in Jeff's house. The only times he watches are when hanging out with friends to watch a particular show at someone else's house. His main news sources are radio, Internet, and newspaper. He began listening to NPR regularly after 9/11. Turning it on most mornings as he is getting ready for the day, he has found that it provides a small dose of daily news in a way that easily fits into his schedule. By being aware daily of what is going on in the broader world, he feels better able to relate to the people with whom he interacts throughout the day or week.

The weekly newspaper *The Economist* is his other regular news source. He began reading this when for a short time he lived in Holland on business. It gives an international perspective to the world news, something that is difficult to find in the United States. It is important to Jeff to understand the bias of the news provider so that he can make his own judgments on reality.

He spends about sixteen to twenty-five hours a week on the Internet and divides that time among e-mail, shopping ("looking for the best deals"), and participating in listserves in which people give advice and recommendations related to his areas of interest. Self-reflection reveals that these Internet activities give light to his value of being informed about the decisions he's making.

Books Jeff's read in the past year include *The People, Capability, Maturity Model,* and *Something New Under the Sun.* The former deals with organizational structures within the workplace; the latter is an environmental history of the twentieth century. Most books he reads fall into the history category. They are often related to an interest in infrastructures and how systems work, an interest that developed from his past work experience. Rarely does he read any light fiction.

When asked which book he's read has been the most influential in his life, Jeff said it probably is the big blue children's Bible he referred to at another point of the interview. The work of Edward R. Tufte, who studies the impact of visual display in relaying information, has also influenced Jeff. Tufte argues that the visual is extremely useful and can make all the difference in conveying truth.

Mary: When asked about what media she consumes, Mary said that she is traumatized by NPR, exposed to all the crazy, traumatic, unjust realities all over the world. Yet so many people work to close themselves off to the realities of others.

Stories that were influential for Mary include Madeleine L'Engle's writing, which had a magical quality for Mary; John Steinbeck's *East of Eden*; and the stories of E. Nesbitt. All of these authors write about core characters, especially L'Engle with her recurring, stable characters in a big geographical area. Mary says she craves stability when so many questions are running around in her head. She read these books over and over—again for the stability, for the known.

Magazines Mary reads are the *New Yorker, Harper's, Gaming, Cooking Light,* and the *Mennonite Quarterly Review* in order to "keep up in the cultural swirl." She appreciates *Harper's* liberal view.

A movie that has been most significant for her was *Chariots of Fire,* because the hero displays an ability to have regrets and yet believe so strongly in something that there is no doubt. As a character he is so sure, so driven, and at the same time so gracious and humble.

Sherri: While driving, Sherri listens to the radio a lot, mainly to country music because its content and lyrics are decent. Because of her work she is on the road from 6:30 a.m. to 4:00 p.m. and listens to the radio the whole time. Country music is a big factor in her life and job. She occasionally listens to praise-and-worship music.

She watches TV about five hours a week and always watches *Everybody Loves Raymond* because it's funny and family-oriented. Sherri doesn't spend a lot of time on the Internet except to e-mail friends that live far away.

Sherri reads mostly Christian books, specifically Christian novels. No one book stands out for her. She reads her local city paper, particularly the local section to see who had a baby, who died, and so on.

Alisa: "I've come to realize," says Alisa, "how much TV has influenced me, and not always in a good way. I just had a long chat with God and said, 'OK, I got it.' So I completely gave up on TV for a week.

"I had felt this tug from God for a while. I would come home from work and just flip on the TV. I'd come home from the Neighborhood Learning Center really drained from the kids. I'd sit in front of the TV, it would finish draining me, and then I'd go to bed. The dishes were piling up, and the house was a mess. I realized that I was using TV to avoid the silence and avoid hearing God."

Alisa said that after that TV-free break, "The house got really clean that week! I felt more energy. I didn't have thoughts of this world so much in my head—people living together, fighting, all this crazy stuff."

Alisa listens to praise-and-worship and gospel music. Influential books have included Frank Peretti's *This Present Darkness* and *Piercing the Darkness*—novels about the spiritual realm and powers that are trying to influence the world. "It's a fight against these powers," Alisa reported. Also influential was C. S. Lewis's *The Screwtape Letters*, about "how Satan can twist the things that are good for his own advantage."

Alisa enjoys Francine Rivers' series about women of the Bible. "Maybe [women] do have a different place, but it's a wonderful place, and God can use us in deep ways."

Matt: Matt says that he sees an average of three or four movies or videos a month. He enjoyed *Good Will Hunting*, the story of a professor seeing potential in a young man. The professor reached out, showed unselfish care, and demonstrated tough love toward him. It is also remarkable that the young man never turned his back on his friends, even though they were "losers" to society and not well-educated. The young man is pushed beyond his comfort level. He is sitting on a winning hand—his potential—and afraid to play it. Matt feels that it is a good movie for young adults.

When in the car, Matt listens to radio. He watches TV occasionally, sometimes *Seinfeld*, and falls asleep on Sundays while watching a game. He counts TV as recreation and generally selects shows that are funny. The music Matt chooses is based on the occasion. For example, if he's going to work in a truck or milking in the barn, then he listens to country. If he is taking a long trip in the car, then Counting Crows, Ben Harper, James Taylor, and Full Table are some of his favorites.

Matt usually checks e-mail daily, about fifteen minutes a day. He goes to washingtonpost.com to check for more detailed world coverage to supplement the local paper. He usually reads *Newsweek* and *The Mennonite*.

Matt's favorite book is *The Brothers Karamazov*, by Dostoyevsky. He was introduced to it by a high school teacher who used to read excerpts in class.

Amy: Of all the media sources, Amy thinks the newspaper is the most important. She "likes to know what is going on in the world" and finds the newspaper especially helpful since she and her roommates have decided not to have a television. She laughed as she told me that the first thing she reads when she gets the paper are the obituaries. As a nurse in the emergency room, she is often concerned about what has happened with some of her patients.

Amy also reads because she wants to be better informed about politics. "I feel naive," she says. "I'm not a politically minded person." She recounted a recent experience in which she was pictured on the front page of a newspaper after participating in a peace rally in Washington D.C. Many of her co-workers saw the picture and made comments about it, asking her questions about why she felt the way she did about the war. Amy feels that since she takes a stand for peace, "you need to know enough about politics to back it up, or you'll be slammed down real quick."

Another concern that Amy has is that when she does talk about her convictions regarding peacemaking, she wants to make it clear that her pacifism comes directly from her Christian faith. She is committed to peacemaking because that is what Jesus calls us to as Christians.

Amy reads some Christian fiction and nonfiction. Her older brother and sister were "very much into eighties rock," and she found herself listening along with them. But eventually Amy sensed dissonance between her faith and the music to which she was listening, so she began trying to think of ways to relate the songs to her faith and sing them to God as a way of managing the guilt she associated with secular music. Finally her sister decided to switch to Christian music only, and Amy also did so at that point. She does not now have a problem if there is secular music playing when she's around, but on her own she only listens to Christian music.

Brian: Brian watches five to ten movies or videos a week and always has movies at home. He can't, however, think of a movie that has impacted him in the last few years or one that has had an especially powerful impact for his peers.

Brian listens mostly to sports on the radio and thinks that some athletes do amazing things. He himself has played sports his entire life, so he spends a lot of time listening to sports news. He also spends a lot of time instant messaging (IM) and e-mailing. Brian values communicating with friends and the type of community found through IM, with more than one friend at a time.

Brian is a music major in college, so music, especially gospel music, plays a huge role in Brian's life. He says it's at the top, next to piano and God. He enjoys playing gospel music on trumpet and piano. His career focus is on trumpet playing.

Brian regularly reads his city paper, *Ebony*, *Sports Illustrated*, and the local paper for the small town where he lives. He mostly reads the auto classifieds and the sports section.

Christina: Music has a huge role for Christina and is one of the most constant aspects of her life. She expresses emotion through music more than words. She likes to listen to instrumental music, like Enya, Italian, and Latin American music, and some Christian artists.

Ajay: Movies like *Schindler's List* and *Bowling for Columbine* are influential for Ajay. In addition, as he says, *The Simpsons* has "good social implications."

Dave: Dave recently read Catholic Worker Movement founder Dorothy Day's biography, *The Long Loneliness*. He talks about his frustration as a voluntary service worker, not having money and having to turn down invitations, but the Catholic Workers are "a breed of their own." They live on so little money.

Dave reads theology; thought-provoking, left-leaning books like Eric Schlosser's *Fast Food Nation* and James Lowen's *Lies My Teacher Told Me*.

He's still a news junkie, reading the paper and listening to NPR, as well as scanning his little hometown newspaper online. He watches almost no TV but loves watching movies. Ones that have played a big role for him are *The Mission*, *Jesus Christ Superstar*, and *Dead Man Walking*.

Ben: The Internet is the media source that Ben spends the most time with. A lot of the work he does on it is related to his schoolwork, and in this sense it is a source of information. Ben also uses it for finding news. He likes to be aware of what is going on in the world, to be more cognizant of himself and where he fits in the world. The Internet is also a place of recreation, finding and reading jokes and humorous articles.

Newspapers are probably second place after the Internet. Again, Ben likes to maintain a grasp of current issues: what is happening in the Middle East, politics, social issues. He considers keeping abreast of these happenings to be part of his faith. "These things should matter to me, and they do matter to me," he says.

Ben's ultimate goal is to learn how to make the world better. He feels that by keeping up with the news and current issues, he can better know how to do this. The most concrete example of this was a time he was living in a city neighborhood, and he and his roommates were working to "learn to be Christians on our block." Ben saw an article about a man who had been stabbed and sustained some brain damage. As a result he was also heavily in debt. Ben noticed the man's address and was surprised to see he was literally a neighbor. So Ben paid the man a visit, and even though the man refused any monetary help, Ben found the experience meaningful. This is a concrete example of the ideal that Ben says he wants to pursue by keeping abreast of current happenings.

Hannah: Hannah said that she now feels disconnected from the world, with "no idea what's going on." Her family watched the news every evening while growing up, but since college, she is more unaware than ever before. She and her husband intentionally have no TV, but they watch movies on a daily basis to unwind after work. One that has had a strong impact: *Dead Man Walking*, since she was quite involved with death-row issues in high school. One of her favorites is *Good Will Hunting*, which she sees as the most real portrayal of a human story she's seen on screen.

Jason: Jason was a history major and likes stories of immigration, global poverty, European history, the stories of revolutions like the French Revolution, the Bolshevik Revolution, and even the Renaissance. Significant changes in society are intriguing to him. He's interested also in alternative histories, and histories that haven't previously been told.

Jason likes anything that's a good conversation stimulus. Conversations are important to him. In first-year colloquium in college, students had to say why they came to college. For Jason, it was because he wanted to have better conversations—about religion, social and political theories, and history.

Jason reads a lot of existential stuff about creating meaning through interaction in a world that is meaningless when you enter it. He also likes postcolonial literature, books dealing with identity such as Salman Rushdie's *Satanic Verses*, on issues similar to what Jason has experienced, "imaginary homelands," and how people deal with their own ideas after leaving what is comfortable. Jason generally favors books with ideas about what it means to be human.

He likes movies that offer an alternative mode of thought. *Fight Club*, for example, offers a view of minimalist existence, with little emphasis on owning things. Someone in the movie says something like "People always work to make money to buy things they don't need."

Jason likes magazines that are literary, full of ideas about which he can have conversations and develop relationships. He had seven magazine subscriptions last year: *Harper's, New Yorker, Atlantic Monthly, Foreign Policy, Foreign Affairs, The Wilson Quarterly,* and *Rolling Stone*. Music he appreciates includes U2, with its lyrics about the search for meaning. The band is spiritual and working for good in the world but not too up front about it. Jason suggests that you should be "praying in a closet" and showing your faith through how you live your life.

Craig: Movies have not been very formative for Craig. He watches some, but thinks that most are poorly done and do not have much of importance to say.

He reads the *Washington Post* a lot, mostly front-page, world events and editorials. He reads some just for stimulation, but also to keep up with what is going on. Craig likes to read analytically, trying to make sense of what is happening in the world and why. His main use of the Internet is to find alternative news sources. Craig enjoys reading, and some books he's read have been formative. He named John Grisham's *The Chamber* and *The Runaway Jury*. Presently he is reading Bruce Feiler's *Walking the Bible*.

Renee: Renee uses the Internet daily for e-mail and "relationship-building," following current events, and educating herself on topics that interest her. She recently read an online article on the ethics of vegetarianism.

She reads the *Washington Post* daily. She also reads *Sojourners, The Other Side, The Mennonite,* and the *Mennonite Weekly Review*. Renee reads some Mennonite history and also a lot of books by women—fiction, womanist writings (Alice Walker), and writings by Latina women.

John: As a young adult, John gained an interest in narratives of the future, especially optimistic science fiction like *Star Trek*. He watches little TV, listens to little radio, "largely because I hate commercials." While growing up, he listened to some NPR, "at least nominally sanctioned in my family of origin," because of its liberal slant, of which his mom approved and his dad disapproved. He uses the Internet for "self-exploration," looking into things of interest to him, especially photography, so he can see what others are doing. On the Internet and elsewhere, he has also done some research on issues of interest, such as feminism and the social conditioning of gender roles.

Tom: Tom says that he tries to limit his movie watching to one per month. He claims that there is nothing really good to watch, and he admits that movies too often influence him.

"I'm impressionable when it come to movies, so I stay away from them. I try to make my own stories by reliving Bible stories in my life." He wants to "relive" what happens in the Bible, not in a literal but in a more symbolic way.

Tom claims that for his Christian friends, *The Matrix* and *The Lord of the Rings* have been two of the most influential movies recently released. He says many Christians claim that these films have Christian parallels. Tom agrees that they might, but questions whether we should watch them because they are so full of violence.

Television plays a big part in Tom's life. He can watch fifteen to twenty hours in a week. "It's easy and mindless for a few hours," he says. The TV is on a lot in his home, and when he walks by he often sits down to watch. He has no particular program that he watches, but he admits that it affects his "thought life" after he's done watching. Later in the interview, he said he didn't want a TV in his house when he got older. Tom pointed to the fact that sometimes he can be rather lazy, and that laziness can get in the way of doing what he knows he should be doing.

As far as television shows that speak to his generation, he named *The Simpsons* as the number one influence. He likes the show and states that the writers often speak about truths of God in everyday life. He also said that *The Simpsons* helps him get his mind off the world. The Internet is a place where Tom plays online bridge to relax. He also uses it for research for school.

Music plays a large part in Tom's life. He plays multiple instruments and even writes his own music. Writing helps him remember and express his experiences. He has recorded his songs on tape and listens to them in his car. He listens to "meaningful music," like praise-and-worship songs and music with words that engage him. "Music engages the mind and the emotions. When both happen at the same time, it is awesome."

What I Hear

I can't help but wonder—when with a couple keystrokes or the flick of a button or two, we can access more information and more kinds of narratives from around the entire world than ever before—how in the world particular people make decisions about what to watch, read, listen to. Why aren't we completely overwhelmed by the glut? Most of the young adults show some discrimination and are able to say why they value one medium over another, or one film over another. It would be fascinating to know a lot more about how individuals make these decisions. While Will can say, "I don't go out and shoot people and debase women when I listen to Eminem," there are plenty of people who do go out to shoot and debase, not necessarily because they listen to Eminem, but because they're "listening" to something. What makes Will different? How do the narratives we "listen" to form us in our basic character and imagination? I wonder which narratives compose the song we sing, the story we become.

Part 3
Practices

Chapter 16
Formative Childhood Practices

"My parents lived the narrative"

Now we shift focus a bit, to an emphasis on "practices," the concrete things we do together to feed, heal, pray, plant, build, and wash up. As we've seen all along, the stories and practices of our lives are inseparable; stories may be the inspiration for practices, and practices often reenact, ritualize, symbolize, or tell the stories. They are distinct in expression but interconnected in vital ways.

In *Anabaptist Ways of Knowing*, I discuss at some length how revitalizing core practices contributes to the renewal of community life. I am not talking about a legalistic imposition of authoritarian dictates from the past but about a quality of life that promotes human flourishing, generosity, mutual respect, and the celebration of our faith stories. In our desire for such a quality of life, many of us are energized to think about specific practices we'd like to reclaim or adopt. We sense the strong relationship between down-to-earth practices like eating and singing and "the abundant life" (cf. John 10:10).

When people are invited to talk about practices from their childhood or in their faith community, they are often eager to offer vivid memories of strawberry picking, birthday celebrations, potlucks, baptisms, funerals. . . . Conversation about remembered practices generates strong feelings, both about the disappointments and the creative possibilities.

In this section of the book, we will hear more formative narratives, but these stories illustrate the way people use practices to give shape to a way of life. Eric and Mike's stories tell about practices formative for them as children and ones that they choose to engage in now as young adults. And then we will hear from several others.

Eric: Eric heard most of his formative narratives through the church since his dad was a pastor. Eric remembers sitting alone in the front pew of the church to listen to his dad preach. At Christmas the family read the Luke account of Jesus's birth.

Eric commented that both of his parents "lived the narrative" for him through their professional lives, faith, and vocations, which were deeply integrated in the everyday. He appreciates that his parents encouraged him to grow at his own speed. Through his parents and the church, he learned that his family was enlarged by the church family. He saw this modeled especially through foot washing, which had a great impact on him as a child. The church family gave him a sense of identity beyond himself, and he felt well accepted in a way that was deeper than family bloodlines. The broader church family showed him that God is warm and welcoming. The good, positive atmosphere showed him a comforting, nurturing God. And through travel he has been exposed to the larger story of God's global people.

Eric finds that reading both the Old and New Testament Scripture is important. In high school and college, he saw the importance of the Old Testament for faith, but that the Bible "is not flat." Reading the Bible is like loving God with his mind. He also reads theologically oriented books, which then lead him into Scripture. He doesn't do as much devotion-oriented Bible reading.

Like his parents, Eric finds himself applying biblical learning to his daily life. He believes he is part of the biblical cause, which includes living out of this example, living out the Bible through his church work and his work within a Christian college. He observed that his faith is quite rational, like his biblical reading, and that he has not had any "trauma" in his life yet that has tested his faith.

Eric watches movies about three times a month. One movie of significance for him is the independent film *The Three Colors Trilogy: Blue, White, and Red*, which explores equality, fraternity, and liberty while drawing on life's gray issues. He enjoys films that tap into the big issues.

He watches about ten hours of TV a week, including shows like *NYPD Blue* and *The Practice*. He also watches sports, reality TV shows and the Food Network, and enjoys shows that play to his critical side and are interesting to analyze. Eric spends about ten hours a week on the Internet, reads the *Philadelphia Inquirer* online for sports news, and checks out university Web sites. While driving, he also listens to radio.

Music fulfills a significant role in Eric's life. He gets an emotional high from music that inspires him and takes him to a higher place. He listens to British or Irish music groups, like Coldplay and the Cranberries and really appreciates Mennonite hymns, especially in the past couple of years.

Eric reads the *Washington Post*, *Chronicle of Higher Education*, *Atlantic Monthly*, and he used to read *Newsweek*. He enjoys them because they present things in depth and attempt to integrate and account for all perspectives. He doesn't watch the news and is canceling *Newsweek* because there is too much "propaganda."

Eric works out of his home office in development at a Mennonite college. On an average day he makes coffee, reads the paper, cooks a nice dinner in the evenings, and spends time with his girlfriend. He takes evening classes, does course work on the weekends, and exercises. Eric thinks his daily practices show that he values recreation and sports, which feeds his competitive edge. His practices also show that he values good conversation, both in work and during meals. He values friendships and puts effort into relationships. Eric has some misgivings about watching sports and reality TV too much. As a perfectionist, he views these practices as lacking lasting value in his life.

Other current practices include his work and church participation. Eric says he finds his faith through his vocation. He feels he is not accountable to any person or group for his personal, interior faith, but that his faith is practiced through his outward work and his church involvement. Eric would like to fit twenty to thirty minutes a day into his life for meditation and Scripture reading. He wants to give more room for the Spirit within himself, but he is very horizontally oriented, so he senses God through others, not alone or solo. Spirituality with a slower pace would appeal to Eric, one that has a separation from the pace of life that social and work life demands. He would like to find a spirituality that stops and listens to God's voice and is reflective.

Journal Comments

In discussing practices, Eric's lifestyle follows the urban flavor of his surroundings. He emulates a typified independent, driven, conquer-the-world young man of our generation. He has postponed marriage and family for his career, and his practices follow those commitments. With regard to spiritual life, he also has a quite horizontal understanding of faith within the Mennonite church. He views his faith and his livelihood as integrally intertwined. His faith is largely based upon action as opposed to being. He admits that he has not yet had any "crisis" of sorts in his life to challenge his faith, or to refine it in a deeper way. He approaches his faith from a theological, academic perspective, choosing to view Scripture critically and analytically. He chooses movies, music, newspapers, magazines, and so on, media that connote international awareness and that promote his own commitments to the Christian faith.

—Annie Lengacher

Interview Questions

I'm going to shift focus a bit and ask, in addition to narratives, about the practices and activities of your daily life. Dropping back in time, tell me a number of daily, weekly and other practices that were typical of your childhood experience.

Mike: Mike talked about how he disliked school as a child. He cried almost every day at school until about the third grade. His mom gave him a little pin with a mirror in the back and told him that whenever he felt like crying at school, he should take the pin out of his pocket, look in the mirror, and remember that "Jesus loves me."

He said his mom was a source of comfort. "When I would cry," he said, "she would pray for me, and I would feel better." In prayer, Mike still finds that image apparent—God as a source of comfort.

Mike says that his dad did not like show-offs. As the youngest of three older brothers, Mike often took the role of show-off and was reprimanded for it. He says that they were never to brag about success, that pride equaled cockiness or arrogance, and these were considered quite negative qualities. "We were to do things quietly," he said. "If we were good at something, we were just to be good at it, not tell everyone that we were good at it."

In his opinion, humility was stressed too much, and this now manifests itself in a lack of self-confidence in himself and his father. He wonders if this is a Mennonite thing.

In eighth grade, Mike read the Bible a lot and says he delved deeply into it. In high school he read the Bible for thirty minutes every morning. His mom read the Bible while driving tractor on the farm. When his dad got up in the morning, he spent time with the Scriptures.

Mike had mentors: a high school teacher who pushed him to look at faith intellectually and nurtured interest in social issues. His older brothers' friends were cool, fun, and Christian.

Mike said that his mom was and is quite spiritual and charismatic. She believes that if you pray, God will answer. Mike acknowledges that she's aware of things in the spiritual realm that he doesn't understand. She has always looked at everything in the world as having a spiritual definition. Mike says that it's sort of an illogical way of looking at the world that he doesn't embrace like she does. He acknowledges that "my Christianity looks quite different than my mom's," and "I'm not sure how you can go through college without" questioning her viewpoint. But he respects his mom, and it's not as easy for him to brush off charismatic Christianity as it is for many of his college peers because of the experience he's had with her.

Ultimately for Mike, God equals safety. "This is my reality more than anything the Jesus story gives," he said. The safety concept is what he was raised with, sort of this "macro thing" in his formative years that has never been shaken. It occurred as a "whisper rather than a big storm."

A Bible verse that has a lot of meaning for Mike is, "I believe. Help my unbelief!" (Mark 9:24). He believes that God accepts gray and observes that I can say anything I want and he's still God. God doesn't fit in a box; there's no formula. Mike reported that many of his friends who went to college and had their faith challenged would no longer call themselves Christians or go to church.

"I still call myself a Christian, and I still go to church," he said. Why? "I was raised in a family that showed me a Christianity that was not generic. I grew up going to a church where people were sincere."

Journal Comments

I was intrigued with Mike's experience with a charismatic mother. As a child, her beliefs and worldview were a comfort. Now as a young adult, Mike thinks her reality seems skewed, out of touch, and so distant from his own. Yet, he wants so much to understand how to respect her, despite the distance. He has acquired a bit of cynicism about it all as the result of a liberal arts education, among other experiences, but he has not let the cynicism harden him or turn him away from the faith in which he was saturated as a child. What allows him to continue to find comfort in it, to continue to go to church without thinking and truly enjoy it when so many of his peers can't bring themselves to find peace in that practice or spirituality?

—*Melody King*

Peter: Every night when Peter was a child, his mother prayed with him before he went to sleep. They had a card with the names of all his friends, and they prayed for each one. His family prayed or sang before meals. Singing together was important. After they came home from Ethiopia, their church programs often included singing. They celebrated Advent every year with a calendar and wreath.

After his mother stopped tucking him in at night, Peter did his own devotions, which became increasingly more elaborate until his year of SALT in Uganda. Each evening there, he would record something he had learned and something he was thankful for. And he would pray for a long list of friends and relatives. After a while, though, it became "too much work."

Rachel: The various travels of Rachel's family members left her feeling like she could do most anything. They had all started "by gathering eggs in the chicken house." Growing up on a farm and watching how her dad treated the land taught her a huge appreciation for it, the seasons, and what it meant to rely on the land for food. She learned a work ethic. Her grandmother used to say, "If you're tired, work. If you're sad, work. If you're depressed, work. If you're happy, work. . . ."

Ajay: Ajay remembers being a devout child. "When I was a little boy, I thought of God as someone rather big and out there, but still very personal. Before I came to the USA, my dad would wake me up early in the morning, and I would spend time praying. I loved doing it."

Greg: Greg remembers bedtime prayers with his mom or grandmother, but in general he feels that there was a lack of childhood practices. There were no meals together, for example. It was a family that was so unstable.

Alisa: The "practice" that's nearest to Alisa's heart is "togetherness." When she was a child, her family did devotions together, ate meals together, played together, and baked together. "And Mom didn't make just one kind of cookie; she'd make three or four. Especially at Christmastime, it was a family affair."

Now Alisa loves getting together with friends to play games. "Just being together,even if you're not having deep discussions—just being together for the sake of being with other people."

Jeff: Jeff remembers that when he was a child, his family had breakfast and dinner together. A prayer was offered before the meal began. His weekly chore was to mow the lawn and daily to walk the dog.

Jason: Jason remembers going to church on Sundays, eating together as a family, playing a variety of sports and card games and board games, and going to Bible school, sporting events, and concerts. He prayed by himself. His dad used to pray with him before he went to bed, and his family used to pray before meals, but that has become less important.

Amy: Amy's family always went to church on Sunday morning and Sunday evening. Her parents always struggled with her older siblings (and to a lesser extent with Amy) to go to the evening service, but they always ended up going. This pattern continued as the children grew older, and even through most of high school for Amy's siblings. The conflict decreased for Amy when she was in high school and became more intentional about nurturing her own faith, at which time she became more eager to go along.

Hannah: Hannah loves music. She came to love hymns she learned from an Old

Order Mennonite high school teacher. Hannah remembers standing in her room at home, leading music, and talking about how much she loved those hymns. On family vacations, she said, the rest of the family would be reading. "In the back of the car, I would be sitting with the hymnal and singing." For Hannah, hymns have been one of the main draws to church.

Miguel: Miguel recalls that when he was a child, his parents wouldn't let him and the siblings leave for school in the morning without laying their hands on them and praying *la bendición*. Every night and morning his parents prayed together, and they still do. "Anna, my wife, talks about how we want to raise our kids like we were," he said. "I want my kids to see us praying together. I trust the way my parents raised me."

Kate: When Kate was a child, her family attended church every Sunday, prayed before meals, read and told stories, and sang lullabies and ballads before bed every night. They picked cherries together every Fourth of July and read the Christmas story every Christmas Eve. Before she went to sleep, Kate would say good-night to every doll and pray for everyone in her family.

"I was a very disciplined child," she said. "A little neurotic. I had to free myself from that. Now I realize that these practices are things you choose to give your life context and depth."

What I Hear

Kate says it well: Practices are things we choose to do to give our lives context and depth. The formative childhood practices that these young adults remember include a variety of daily, weekly, and yearly events. It is striking that nearly every person interviewed in the one-on-one conversations mentioned hearing and being read stories as a child—Bible stories, family stories, folk stories. Prayer is another frequent practice that shows up—usually at mealtime and bedtime.

There is frequent mention of going to church together, and how the church functioned as an extended family. Some cherished church practices like foot washing. And there is that subtle but more profoundly formative practice of parents and other mentors who "live out the narrative," demonstrating by the integrity of their faith and practice a way of life that rings true.

Chapter 17
Typical Daily and Weekly Practices

"Getting away from the 'party' attitude"

One can think of practices in several different ways. Certain practices express something profound about what we believe and what we most value. Communities intentionally cultivate some practices to give a particular kind of character to their life together. And families deliberately choose certain practices to express something special about their ethnic heritage, family story, or faith commitments. We'll look more at some of these in the following chapters.

There are also practices that may simply be a typical part of our daily or weekly routine that we haven't critically examined to consider how they express what we truly value or how they relate to a chosen way of life.

Below, we'll see first Mark's description of a typical day and the kinds of things he normally does. Then others will describe a normal day for them. They discuss faith-related practices and misgivings they have about some of those practices.

Mark: On a typical day Mark gets up at 6:45 a.m., eats breakfast, and goes to school for student teaching until 3:30 or 4:00 p.m. He works out on Monday, Wednesday, and Friday, and goes for a run on Tuesday and Thursday. He eats dinner with his family. He goes to see his fiancée. In the evenings he does schoolwork and relaxes, watches TV, or reads a little. Mark says that his activities show that he values relationships with people, family, and self. He also values time alone.

Mark identified some of the practice that he said are related to his faith. These include going to church on Sundays, praying before bed and before meals, and going to chapel sometimes at his Mennonite college.

Mark normally watches one movie a week. *Good Will Hunting* has impacted him. It is a powerful movie in terms of relationships among friends, and between a man and a woman. The film examines the impact that one person can have on others, especially in the bond between counselor and patient. That bond is stretched in the film to the point where Will, the patient, finally breaks.

The Green Mile was a film that also impacted Mark. This story, about a man who did small miracles but was a prisoner and wrongly executed, stands as a metaphor for Jesus.

Mark listens to the radio, mostly in the car, usually light rock, occasionally Christian radio. He watches TV about an hour a night, watches a lot of sports and reality TV shows like *Survivor*. He chooses his TV watching for relaxation, excitement, entertainment.

Music plays a big role in Mark's life. He really "feels" music spiritually; it affects his mood, and he just enjoys it. He listens to some Christian CDs like *Caedmon's Call*, *Jars of Clay*, some praise-and-worship music. He also listens to contemporary rock, including Live, Coldplay, Dave Matthews Band.

Mark says he's not a big reader. In the past year he's read part of the Lord of the Rings trilogy, Lois Lower's children's book *The Giver*, and Philip Yancey's *What's So Amazing About Grace?* Mark enjoyed Lord of the Rings because he likes fantasy books and sees their parallels to a good-versus-evil Christian perspective. He also reads *Time* and *Newsweek* because he wants to find out what's going on in the world, especially in Iraq.

Mark said that he's aware of praying at least once a day, plus at meals. He acknowledged that prayer isn't very significant for him. He feels like he needs a reason to pray, as when something is either drastically wrong or right in his life. He hasn't had any "trauma" in life to pray about.

Mark would like society to place a greater emphasis on sexual fidelity and purity in life. Among his peers he finds a mixed reaction. It's mostly "not a big deal" to them, he said. He has some misgivings about watching inappropriate TV or movies that have a lot of sex or violence. In general, though, he would like to see his peers getting away from the party attitude and away from purely social relationships to deeper ones.

The Jesus story is more important now to Mark than it was in his childhood. In his younger years, it was just like any other story from his childhood. Now he notices a pull toward Jesus and feels Jesus nudging him. Earlier it never really sunk in, but now it is the most important part of who he wants to become. Mark wants to respond to that nudging and find a deeper connection with Jesus.

Mark is involved with a practicing congregation of believers. He has attended there his whole life and is committed and involved in Sunday school. He would like to see the practice of Scripture reading retrieved, to give added meaning in life. Mark would feel at home in a church with people from similar lifestyles, who could communicate at a similar level. He is attracted to smaller congregations. Five years from now he would expect to be a member in a church, actively involved in the congregation, and undertaking some leadership in the youth group or Sunday school.

Journal Comments

Mark exudes a warmth from being raised in a loving, caring community and family. He came "alive" when he spoke about his grandparents and family and their impact on his faith. As a young adult, he seems to connect his faith with movies and finds movies with relational lessons important. He admitted the lack of impact the Scriptures have had in his life, where he seems to pick up more about the Gospel narrative within the movies he watches or books he reads. From listening to him, I gathered that he is not very literary, and so his channels for experiencing God are through auditory or visual modes.

Mark's daily practices now also reflect his close ties with his family, and he has definite ideas about what he wants his future family to look like (mentioned elsewhere). Many times he mentioned that for the first time in his life, he has been experiencing a tug from Jesus. He described a new yearning for God that is more vertical than horizontal. He seems dedicated to exploring this and answering that tug, and he reflects a desire for greater spiritual intimacy and growth.

—Annie Lengacher

Interview Questions

Tell me about a typical day in your life now. What do you do on a regular basis every day, week, or month? These practices may relate to self-care, to work, study, to your social or your religious life. What do you think these typical practices indicate about what you most value? Which of the practices that you do on a regular basis would you say are directly related to your faith? Do you have any misgivings about some or all of these practices?

Rachel: Rachel's life now involves work, work, work. She works ninety hours per week as a medical resident. The hospital brings her close to the pain and joy in the lives of others. In the past forty-eight hours, Rachel has talked to a patient who is dying of cancer and has been neglected by her family because she's a lesbian, seen someone in the ER who was raped, and delivered a dead baby. She talks with her fellow residents as a way of processing all that she encounters on the job.

There is thrift-store shopping and housework. She cooks regularly, but not much meat. She never eats fast food, eats out only occasionally, eats with her husband and her housemate when they're all home. Rachel knits at church or while watching TV, and she talks to someone from her family daily.

During premarital counseling, Rachel and her husband talked about the importance of establishing traditions in the home, but they have yet to really do that since they are so transient and so busy with school and work.

Rachel claims that her daily activities show she values relationships in her life. She likes people, talking with them, hearing their stories. She values family and her relationship with her husband—though they don't see each other enough. She values hard work, using her brain and her skills at work, and doing what she can to make the world a better place.

Which of her practices are related to her faith? Rachel stumbled over that question. She may have a hard time making a distinction between parts of her life that are faith-related and parts that aren't. She mentioned getting out of bed in the morning in the hope and belief that things can change for the better. She also mentioned her neighborhood, the working-class Germantown section of Philadelphia, where as a white person she's in the minority. She likes the neighborhood and knowing her neighbors, but wishes she was more involved with them. She's not sure how that's related to her faith, but it seems to be the way Jesus would live.

Rachel mentioned parts of her life that reflect what she calls "Mennonite culture": cooking her own meals and eating together, using an old TV, her husband taking the train and then biking rather than driving to and from Lancaster, and their thinking about adopting.

Rachel regrets driving her car to work and thus contributing to pollution. She has misgivings about not spending time with her husband because of work, about not going to church because of work, and about being part of racist systems. She also has misgivings about setting up abortions at work. She doesn't participate directly in them but she has to arrange them. This is tough, and it saddens her that a potential life is ended. She wishes the parents would think about letting the baby be adopted. She wonders what life would be like if the birth mothers of her adopted brothers had chosen abortions.

Journal Comments

Rachel spends most of her life at the hospital, where as an ob-gyn resident she works about ninety hours per week. That schedule doesn't leave much time for "practices" outside of work. As a result, the practices and values reflected by her time on the job came out more strongly in the interview: working hard, listening to patients' stories, treating all people equally, hating institutional racism, coping with immense suffering by balancing it with the stories of joy, knowing the names of the cleaning people and techs. If she had time, she would talk about other practices more. She would be out meeting the neighbors and having them over, volunteering at Habitat for Humanity and the Victim-Offender Reconciliation Program, reading, hiking, rock climbing, and definitely spending more time with her husband.

Even with so little time on her hands, I watched Rachel act out some of her practices and lifestyle choices while sitting with me. We sat in the kitchen so she could take dinner out of the oven when it was done. She sat knitting through the whole interview, making a baby sweater (that's all she makes) to give away. When her housemate left the basement light on, she got up to turn it off. When he left it on again, she asked him if he would mind turning it off.

—Deborah Good

Jeff: A typical day for Jeff includes getting up, showering, making breakfast and cappuccino, rushing out the door, and riding his bicycle to his job of working with information systems. For lunch, he bikes home and values this time away from the office at midday to get some rest, nourish the body, and gain some perspective. He negatively recalls a past job environment where it was rather standard to work straight through the lunch hour or grab something at the desk. After work, he returns home, cooks some supper, runs errands or reads, checks e-mail, and so on, before turning in for the night.

Weekly practices include church on Sunday, happy hour with a group of friends at a local restaurant on Friday evenings, and running three mornings a week with a friend at a local park. Saturdays are designated as Jeff's day to do leftover chores and errands and also something relaxing or physically healthful, like taking a bike ride.

Jeff suggests that the practices that compose his life indicate that he values taking care of his body. His weekly participation in a church service provides a time and place to "reset or reorient [oneself] for the week."

"Getting hammered on weekends" is a practice that Jeff has some misgivings about. The misgivings come from the overall unhealthy feeling that Jeff is left with when it's all over. In addition, it affects his ability to be effective in school and work.

Miguel: Miguel's most important practice is getting together with his extended family. "We congregate at least once a week, and we're eating together. Mom says, 'Did we pray?' and I say, 'Don't you think this is prayer—laughing, talking, being true to one another? Don't you think we're being true to our Creator?'"

Regarding prayer, a blessing before meals is important to Miguel.

"Even though I do feel that we're praying without ceasing, [I value] the practice of stopping and acknowledging that some people don't have anything to eat, and that I'm eating. Let's keep it real, man. There could be a day when you don't have a meal in front of you."

Miguel and his wife, Anna, teach the youth at their church on Wednesday nights. "But when we go to youth group, we hardly ever get time to do the Bible story. We talk to them about the importance of relating to one another. Where is God in your life this week?"

"Spending time with my wife, having lunch with a friend—these are spiritual disciplines that matter way more than being at a church service."

However, even though relationships come first, church is still definitely important to Miguel. He preaches when the pastor, his father, is absent. Miguel also moderates the church council and serves on the district leadership board.

"It's still important to go to church. I don't care if it's mundane; I need to go to church. Can we gather as a body there? Can we sing, however out of tune we are? Can somebody get up there and practice the antiquated didactic service? Can people give testimony to how God works in their lives? I mean, who am I? I'm twenty-six years old! Through being broke, through having nothing—this church practice has carried my parents, the elders through! I want to find strength in that outdated church.

"Everyone talks postmodernism now, but part of me wants to go to church and hear a sermon that I don't agree with. I just want to hear that God is in control. I spend a lot of time with people who think critically in academic settings. Sometimes I just want to go down home and do church. You know, afterward we can have a conversation about how bad it was, but this is good stuff."

Kate: Kate's current practices include praying before bed, cooking and eating with friends, remembering to be thankful when she eats, and observing Lent—a practice she learned from non-Mennonite friends in college.

"In college at Lent, people would always ask me, 'What are you giving up?' And I'd say, 'What are you talking about? I'm Mennonite, I'm not giving up nothing.'"

Now Kate, who often tends to daydream, uses Lent to try to pay attention, to be aware of what's around her while she's walking to school in the mornings.

"And I fail every Lent. But that's what Lent's about—at least I think so. I've never really heard a good sermon on Lent."

Her next "practice" goal is to keep Sabbath regularly, to have friends over for meals on Saturday nights, and then to attend church and rest on Sundays. She says it will help her keep good perspective while she's in law school.

"If an institution has certain goals, it's easy for me to subscribe to them. Sabbath will help me think about why I want to do well in school and what I want to get out of it."

Jessica: Jessica sees all of her practices as in some way impinging on her Christian faith, even if at times the connections seem unclear. Her work, for instance, often seems rather mechanical and pointless. Surely serving is good, but does it really matter to anyone else, or to her faith? Often it does not feel like it. Other practices seem contradictory—listening to certain kinds of music or watching violent movies, for instance. In these cases, Jessica feels guilty, but she also tries to rationalize that that practice has some remote connection to her faith. It might, for instance, educate her to be able to converse with and influence another person. In any case, the goal is to relate everything back to her purpose and to serving God.

Studying is easier to connect with practices because Jessica has a sense that her education is leading her toward her purpose. Friendships are an important avenue for serving and inspiring others, and she takes them very seriously.

Ben: Although he "hates to admit it," Ben spends a lot of his time studying and reading for classes. He lives in a community house and likes to spend time interacting with people. This helps him to "reduce stress and relax," but also is a means of "challenging myself spiritually and mentally," through dialogue and hearing the viewpoints and experiences of others.

Sports, camping, and occasionally reading are other activities that Ben enjoys and does for recreation. Ben regrets that he cannot spend more time in those activities.

Jason: Jason's current practices reflect that he is in transition. He uses the Internet and newspapers to look for a job. He sleeps in, then makes and drinks coffee in the living room while reading magazines or something else he picks up. He enjoys games and movies with housemates and occasionally a few other friends. He drinks alcohol at home and while out (at home when trying to save money). He eats at the house or grabs something on the run. He reads, often in the same room while other people are doing something else, such as watching TV. He enjoys going out to bars, coffee shops, and restaurants, having conversations with friends, sometimes meeting new people, having good conversations wherever he is, depending who he's with. He does some running in the park for exercise, smokes pot with friends on occasion, has a travel bug, and sometimes writes down thoughts, but not as much as he'd like.

His practices suggest that he values relationships, friendships, conversations, and the pursuit of knowledge. He is breaking from the strict rules of his upbringing by drinking, smoking, and having a "good time." He also values being a global citizen—not "American." Jason has some misgivings about pot, not because it's wrong, but because it affects him by making him slower in his reading and processing and lowers his self-confidence.

Mary: Mary said she doesn't like getting up in the morning, probably because she dislikes her job right now. She goes to work with her boyfriend, and they come home for lunch together. They lie on the futon together and read or talk. She tries not to dwell on the fact that she doesn't like her job. Evenings are for relaxing, shopping, cleaning. She often forgets to eat. She and her boyfriend read to each other in many environments—while one does the dishes, while lying in bed at night, and so on. She dreams with her boyfriend about grad school and the future. They go away a lot on the weekends to visit friends or families in nearby cities.

Reading is her lifeblood, sitting side by side and reading with her partner and talking. She is curious, likes to do research, and wants to know how things work. She acknowledges that she doesn't take care of her health very well.

Mary has misgivings about living with her boyfriend. It's like baptism, she says, "which I was made to believe was right. I was made to believe this practice of living together is wrong, without being presented with any good reason. Yet I know myself well, and we so much enjoy each other's presence."

She commented that it also doesn't feel right that she dislikes her job; she doesn't respect what she does. She is doing something so far from filling her own needs, which feels quite rotten.

Dave: Most days, Dave reads the newspaper over breakfast and is often late to work. He works late, then sits around and debriefs with his housemates and often eats dinner with them. Occasionally he goes out, sometimes for beer and "bad bar food," and sometimes for an actual dinner. But he doesn't go out as often as some since he's an introvert and doesn't have the money. He reads, sorts mail, and does other "boring" stuff alone in his room, always with the music on. He prays before he eats (less often at work), and often prays before he goes to sleep. He goes to church but dislikes that he doesn't have a church home in the city where he now lives. Instead, he alternates among several congregations.

Dave has misgivings about spending too much money on happy hour when he should perhaps be more productive. But going out does build relationships, and that's not bad.

Renee: Renee's daily activities include reading the paper, going to work, eating lunch, walking home, processing the day, and praying as she goes. When people ask for money, she doesn't give any but tries to acknowledge them, to look into their eyes and say "sorry." When people harass her on the street, she tries to carry herself confidently. At home, she debriefs the day with her housemates.

Other activities include eating with her housemates at least once a week; sitting in the chair in her room, by her window, sometimes reading, journaling, talking on the phone, or simply being; going to church every Sunday; talking to her parents on the phone about once a week; drinking coffee and reading the paper with it; meeting friends at restaurants or for coffee or drinks.

She attends free concerts and goes to free museums around the city because she's frugal and doesn't like the uppity, selfish feeling that she often finds at places that cost money. She drinks alcohol about once a week with friends, either at someone's home—her preference—or out at happy hour. She spends time on the roof, by herself or with others.

Renee said these practices indicate that she values time alone for personal reflection on faith and how it interconnects with her life, and for cultivating self. She values friendships and people in general, being connected and known, learning from others, and taking care of her body. Community is quite important, though she's introverted and sometimes can only give so much. Church and the larger community of believers are important to her, along with her family and open lines of communication with them. Renee also values being countercultural.

Renee has some misgivings about her TV watching because it is not productive. She wants to use her time to better herself and to learn as much as she can, and she therefore dislikes "wasting" it. Renee also wishes she read the Bible more and memorized more Scripture. She also wishes she had more exposure to organizations doing good things.

Tom: Tom's daily practices include morning prayer and Bible reading, student teaching at a local high school, planning for the next day's classes, coming home and unwinding in the garden as plants and nature relax him, eating a snack and watching TV till supper, then working on lesson plans, meeting with friends, playing guitar, and sometimes going on a walk before bed.

When asked to reflect on his daily life and what it says about his values, he mentioned that he thinks he values sleep, relationship with God, quiet time, and his relationships with people and family.

Tom says that he has to work quite hard at relating with his family. He is now spending intentional time with each member and trying to connect with each one. He is "learning to value them now because the past wasn't so good."

Mike: Mike's daily practices include a devotional before breakfast. He occasionally prepares something for supper that evening, like a Crock-Pot meal, then heads to school. When he returns home, he eats dinner, watches a movie, or does homework. He says that a good day equals a productive day, a work ethic he learned from his dad. He attends church weekly, spends time with his girlfriend on weekends and evenings, and every Sunday watches football and takes a nap. Sunday was and is always a time to relax.

Mike values meeting with other Christians. Church is a norm; not to go to church is not necessarily an option, he says. He goes and enjoys it. He values productivity, getting things done.

Will: On a typical day Will spends lots of time sleeping, eating, breathing. He figures he spends close to an hour a day smoking. He reads as much as possible and spends "way too much mindless time with my girlfriend."

In identifying faith-related practices, Will said that "standard fundamentalist practices" like praying before bed, fasting, reading his Bible, and going to church are quite important to his faith and life.

Will doesn't believe that time spent on activities necessarily correlates with what one values, in his case especially. Many people have values that they don't live by. If time and values did correlate for Will, he observes, it would seem that he values sleep, his girlfriend, and feeding his mind intellectually. Will says that the practices he has misgivings about are mostly sins of omission. If anything, Will wishes simply that he did more of the things that he knows he should do.

Hannah: Hannah wishes she had more sleep so she could take more peaceful time in the morning for grounding herself. Her goal is to eat breakfast together with her husband; it doesn't happen yet. At work she manages fifteen to thirty minutes of quiet time in the classroom.

Hannah participates weekly in two small groups, one through church and one with friends from college. One to two nights a week are taken up with social gatherings of some sort. She needs downtime during the week. She rotates cooking responsibilities with her husband, and they often eat dinner in front of a movie. She doesn't like this fact, but frequently she needs something mindless in the evening. Hannah has misgivings about watching too many movies, which she does sometimes on a daily basis. She would like more balance of other activities in the evening.

She comments that these practices aren't the ideal she's working towards. She is learning to slow down her life and seek more places of rest.

What I Hear

In one form or another, "time with friends and/or family" shows up more often than any other "practice" in these descriptions. Whether eating together, debriefing at the end of the day, joining others for "happy hour," recreating together, spending the evening with a boyfriend or girlfriend, relaxing with a spouse, meeting with a small group or Bible study, going to church, or just gathering for conversation—many of the practices mentioned above indicate a high value placed on friendships, relationships, and interaction with others.

I enjoyed the somewhat ironic comment from Miguel, for whom church is so important: "Through being broke, through having nothing—this church practice has carried my parents, the elders through! I want to find strength in that outdated church. Everyone talks postmodernism now, but part of me wants to go to church and hear a sermon that I don't agree with. I just want to hear that God is in control. I spend a lot of time with people who think critically in academic settings. Sometimes I just want to go down home and do church. You know, afterward we can have a conversation about how bad it was, but this is good stuff."

It would seem that there are more ways than one to "party," or as Mark says, to "get away from the party attitude."

Chapter 18
Typical Faith Community Practices—I

"Nice Mennonite men didn't do that"

Theologian and philosopher Nancey Murphy suggests that the Anabaptists were a particularly creative bunch in their day when it came to renewing and generating new practices such as believers baptism, community-based interpretation of Scripture, and "the rejection of the sword." It is especially among the Anabaptists and their heirs, she suggests, that we find the expectation that the Holy Spirit will be present in recognizable ways within our community-based practices.

Many practices are typically present in Mennonite faith communities today. They are familiar to those of us who grew up in Mennonite communities because we've seen them in our own homes and churches. As we saw in chapter 4, there were practices that A. D. Wenger, as a forward-looking Mennonite young adult of his day, observed a hundred years ago. I think it's fair to say that most of the practices he identified continue to be present in some form in the Mennonite communities where many of us grew up. And there are significant differences.

Practices are gifts that have taken shape over centuries as people respond to their experience of God, suggest Craig Dykstra and Dorothy C. Bass in *Practicing Our Faith*. Practices are ancient and larger than we are, and they "bear standards of excellence," which means, when done well, they contribute to human flourishing. But practices need to be continually evaluated to see whether they serve a life-giving function, whether they need to be reshaped to more nearly express the "truth" of God's presence among us. Reflecting on the value of familiar practices is essential for the ongoing vitality of communities shaped by those practices.

Below, Laura reflects on her formative childhood stories and the many, many practices that fill her busy young-adult life. And other young adults comment on how they regard a variety of typical Mennonite practices.

Laura: Laura's dad grew up Catholic and her mom grew up Mennonite. Her dad "didn't really feel fulfilled" with the Catholic church. He had grown up as a farm boy in New York, ended up in Lancaster County, met some Mennonites, and joined the Mennonite church.

Laura's dad shared stories about his childhood, mostly funny ones, the kind that you weren't sure whether they were true or not. One time he messed up his knee with a pitchfork, and while he was still healing from it, he was walking down the aisle at church when his knee gave way and he fell down. [Laura laughed as she told this and other stories, clearly stories that were laughing matters at home.]

She learned something that didn't fit her understanding of the world: "I found it interesting that my mom's dad smoked and that he died of emphysema which, you know—I thought that nice Mennonite men didn't *do* that." Immediately following this comment, Laura talked about her grandpa's faith, reiterating the disconnect she sees between Christian faith and smoking.

"I don't know if he was—I mean, I think he was a Christian, but I don't think he was maybe as devoted as my grandmother." Her grandmother was "a big old round lady who always had candy. I remember sitting in her lap."

Laura observed that her parents' families were quite different. Her mom's side was Christian. She saw this difference in several ways. Parents and church were more a part of her mom's stories than her dad's. Her dad says he's realizes now that his family was rather dysfunctional. He has one brother who is quite bitter. Her mom's family's approach to life is much more joyful, but on her dad's side, there's usually someone who's not happy with someone else.

Sometimes, Laura said, she has a hard time seeing how her dad came from such a family, but she now understands that "Christ can change lives." Through their stories, Laura inherited her parents' good values, including the value of hard work. She often heard, "When you're asked to do something, you do it and you do it well."

Laura listens to contemporary Christian music because of its positive messages. She likes singing in church, observing that some songs have amazing words: "It is well with my soul," for example. Recently a tragedy occurred in Laura's church. A young man killed himself on his honeymoon, leaving behind a young widow. This woman's faith through the experience has made an impression on Laura. She has come to a peace about it and has used those words, "It is well with my soul," which has changed that song's meaning for Laura. She also enjoys praise songs and says that it's important to give praise to Jesus for what he has done.

Laura does Bible reading and journaling in the morning. Every day she drives alone to school, sometimes with music, sometimes not. She fasts one day a week. At school, she often eats by herself. She enjoys the time by herself. Sometimes after school Laura helps at a youth center run by area churches. It has a Bible study, basketball, Ping-Pong, pool, and other activities. She mentors a seventeen-year-old girl who recently became a Christian. They try to meet once a week. Once or twice a month, she also meets with two girls from church who are preparing for baptism.

Laura and her parents usually eat together about once a week, and always for Sunday lunch, when her brother and sister-in-law sometimes join them. Laura writes letters and birthday cards to friends, people from church, from high school, and even to people who live close by.

"I'll crank out like a dozen at a time, and that will be it for a couple weeks." She meets with the youth group on Wednesday nights for three times a month. She spends time with friends sitting and talking, bowling, shopping, toilet-papering others' houses, playing cards. Once a month she meets with a missionary support team for a girl at church. Laura prays, sometimes with Bible reading and devotions, but often in the car, or in the middle of the day, whenever. And she attends a Wednesday morning prayer group at church.

Laura values simple living. She remembers going down the street to another girl's house when she was young and being fascinated with this friend's "whole entire dresser full of makeup!" Laura's mother doesn't wear makeup. Part of living with less has to do with their income level, but also with the principle that having lots of things isn't important. Valuing people and relationships has sometimes meant that she's been showing up to class late because she doesn't want to cut a conversation short.

Laura values her relationship with the Lord. She has a future goal of becoming a missionary. She values being content with life, and she values family. There are no practices Laura has misgivings about, and there are no practices she wished she knew more about, though she wishes she prayed more and read the Bible more.

Journal Comments

Laura has a quite strict understanding of what behaviors should be practiced by Christians. Smoking is out of line. Divorce is out of line. Homosexuality is *definitely* out of line. But when Laura began talking about the young man in her church who recently committed suicide, she admitted that she was no longer convinced of her belief that suicide was a sin. She admitted that knowing someone who killed oneself changed her perspective. My own experience in Mennonite liberal arts education was that I learned to be critical and ask questions about the world around me. I am grateful for this. But there's also something beautiful in Laura's unquestioning "okayness" with how things are.

—Deborah Good

Below is a list of practices that I have observed as typical in many Mennonite homes and communities. It's not a comprehensive list by any means, and there are many more practices we could add. The twenty-eight young adults we interviewed one-on-one seemed to recognize the practices listed below as typical Mennonite practices, but they frequently wanted to talk more about what a given practice really entails. In addition to commenting on the practices listed below, we invited them to rate the importance of each practice. Those responses are tallied below. Not everyone rated every practice.

Interview Questions

A whole variety of practices have traditionally characterized Mennonite faith communities. Which of these practices do you think is important for the life of a faith community to which you already belong or may want to belong?

How important?	Very	Somewhat	Not
simplicity of lifestyle	15	5	3
nonviolent love of enemies	17	6	
forgiveness and reconciliation	21	2	
truth-telling	20	3	
nonswearing of oaths	5	12	6
integrity of being and doing	22	1	
Sabbath-keeping	10	10	4
hospitality	19	7	
regularly meeting with others for worship	19	5	1
singing together	13	8	1
meditation and prayer	18	5	
reading and meditating on Scripture	13	6	2
community discernment for making decisions	13	8	1
sexual fidelity (intercourse only in marriage)	24	3	1
tithing	14	5	1
service to neighbor	20	2	1
mutual care within the community	21	3	
modest attire	8	10	4
care for nature	17	5	
testifying/speaking publicly about one's faith	12	10	3
eating together	12	10	2
cross-cultural mission and service	19	6	
rituals: baptism, Lord's Supper, foot washing	14	8	2

Below are comments from some of those interviewed. Not featured here are comments on prayer and on sexual fidelity, described in the next chapter.

Laura: When asked further about the characteristic Mennonite practices listed above, Laura commented, "These are the values I was raised with." When asked about specific ones, she said: On nonviolent love of enemies—how can you love and show violence? On tithing—because it says to do so in the Bible, and I believe in sharing a little of what God has given you. On modest attire—how you dress determines what people think of you. You shouldn't cause someone in the community to stumble or be distracted.

Rachel: Rachel commented that nonswearing of oaths isn't really important in a court of law, but in community we should take each other at our word and not have to swear oaths to each other. Reading and meditating on Scripture isn't important, but looking for truth anywhere is very important.

Rachel said that testifying or speaking publicly about one's faith isn't important. Acting on it is much more important. She said that cross-cultural mission and service is quite important, even if the mission is just outside your door.

About the rituals of baptism, the Lord's Supper, and foot washing, she commented that foot washing especially is important. The others have less meaning for her. And a bit more on hospitality: While she was growing up, Rachel's household was certainly open. There were always people over, always people borrowing things. It's important to make sure people know they're welcome, she said. Rachel told a story of how her parents recently took a stranger in for the night because his car was stuck in a nearby ditch.

Miguel: Miguel said simplicity of lifestyle is quite important "if it's defined differently for different communities." He observes that some Mennonites who "wear Dockers, plaid shirts, and brown shoes" have visited the churches in his area, and the members say, "Oh, he's one of those *simple* Mennonites." Miguel also considers most of the other practices as very important, with eating together getting a "very very."

Somewhat important were Sabbath-keeping and modest attire. He reported that in his local culture, "it's important always to wear your best for church." On cross-cultural mission and service, Miguel says, "As the church has defined it historically, it's quite problematic. I'm hopeful that the church is figuring out new ways of doing that." He listed nonswearing of oaths as not important.

Jessica: Jessica regarded most of the typical Mennonite practices as important. About Sabbath-keeping, she remarked that it's important at least in the sense that some day should be set apart for worship. "I'd be lenient on rules about what can and can't be done."

Will: Modest attire, Will said, is important but not in a traditional Mennonite way. Will commented that he can see the value of simplicity for himself personally, but he doesn't see it taught in Scripture. He finds nothing meaningful related to Sabbath-keeping. He likes having a day for ministry and worship, but thinks that should happen every day, and does not find it particularly restful. While Will would not want to "impose" hospitality on all Christians, he has greatly appreciated and benefited from Mennonites' practice of hospitality in the past, and thus considers it valuable. Will feels that service to neighbor and mutual care are important, but he did not see that practiced in his home church to nearly the extent that he felt it should have been, given the Mennonite tendency to talk so much about it.

Kate: Kate said that cross-cultural mission and service are definitely important "if you take out mission." Asked why she reacted to the word "mission" and what she felt was her "mission" in the world, Kate responded: "I want people to realize the love, joy, and peace that are already around them, and to connect with their communities. I'm part of the Mennonite community, then I'm American, then you make that global, and then there's the whole natural ecosystem. And not only am I a part of those communities; I also have responsibilities! I see missionaries coming in and saying, 'Oh, you have no hope. Well, look at this thing. This thing way over here. This is what you've been missing! It's been way over there the whole time!' And missionaries have brought a lot of hope to people—the Mennonite African churches, those are great! But I want to help people see what's already in their communities. I want to be an example of love and joy and peace, to be rooted in my multiple communities, to help other people connect with their communities *locally* and globally."

She said testifying publicly about one's faith is somewhat important, "if they do it right." Not important—modest attire. "I'm not going to go around all dolled up, but I want those people in my community."

Peter: Peter commented that testifying about one's faith experience is certainly important within the group but not necessarily to the "outside world."

John: John commented in particular on truth-telling and integrity: "We should know who we are, believe what we believe, and do it. Our beliefs should affect our lives." John also sees an emphasis on life *here* as important. "Heaven is out there somewhere, but earth is where I live now. What I do here is more important than saying 'I believe this or that,' though beliefs are important. Salvation does not depend on works, but that does not mean that works are not important." John rejects "a hollow faith that alienates a lot of people and makes a lot of proclamations without *doing* anything." He observed that singing together is quite important, mostly because he enjoys it, and that community discernment for decisions depends on the decision. About mutual care within the community, he recommended "not being a busybody."

Mike: Mike acknowledged that he doesn't personally connect closely with many of the practices, but he believes that all are important for community.

Amy: Among various practices that Amy identified as significant for her are hospitality, which she sees as "a way of showing Christ's love to others." She also flagged corporate worship as important for teaching, for providing support to each other, and for reminding us of what perspectives we should have as Christians. Amy considers testifying about one's faith as quite important, especially given her recent experience of being in the newspaper (mentioned previously). She commented that it is definitely important that we are willing to "be bold [and] stand up for what we believe."

Greg: Greg commented on several practices from the list. Hospitality, he said, is definitely important. "We need to push ourselves to find what hospitality truly means. It means making self more vulnerable than just hosting other Mennonites. Hospitality means a stranger eating in your house."

In response to cross-cultural mission and service, Greg said: "[The apostle] Paul would hate me for saying this but—somewhat important. Cross-cultural mission and service is secondary to community. Small towns that used to be strongholds of faith are being depleted because we aren't putting our energies into them. Our focus is shifting from having strong immediate communities of faith to going overseas. If you don't come from somewhere, represent a specific people, what do you take with you when you go anywhere else? So many missionaries are displaced and don't care about where people come from. And Christians have a horrible record of destroying any place they go."

Christina: Christina offered several qualifications about practices she thinks are quite important. She feels that a lifestyle of stewardship is more important than tithing. She questioned the definition of modesty, and she remarked that the importance of testifying or speaking publicly about one's faith experience depends on the context.

Jason: Jason commented that reading and meditating on Scripture aren't important, but looking for truth anywhere is very important. He also maintained that cross-cultural mission and service are definitely important when mission isn't defined in the traditional sense of mission. And a practice worth retrieving, he said, may be foot washing.

Mary: Mary doesn't like the legality of things, like nonswearing of oaths. The internal aspects are more important than the external, such as integrity of being and doing, as opposed to modest attire.

Jeff: In going over the list of practices characteristic of Mennonite communities, Jeff was adamant about the unimportance of testifying or speaking publicly about one's faith. He has seen how evangelism can be mishandled. It has the potential to separate and harm people. He believes instead in living by example.

Hannah: Hannah commented in particular on the following practices: "Sabbath is very important but at this point in our lives, we're doing so much traveling on weekends that it's hard to create a routine for ourselves to set a day aside."

Hospitality is quite important—outside the congregation but also within the congregation. "I don't attend a welcoming church," she said. "People don't know I've been coming there for a long time. I take part in a small group but it's not as intimate as I would like it to be."

On public testimony, she commented, "I have baggage with that"—only somewhat important. About eating together: "Eating together *in the service* is fellowshipping. We need more of that!" As an example of this, she mentioned the Moravian Christmas service, in which hot rolls are passed around during worship. Cross-cultural mission and service are somewhat important—building relationships within the church is what needs emphasis.

And foot washing is very important. The practice is a powerful image of Jesus and his example of humility.

Craig: Craig commented that sometimes Mennonites are too "zealous" about simplicity for its own sake. It should be expressed as faith in "kingdom treasures rather than earthly treasures," solidarity with the poor, and so on. And he said that nonswearing of oaths isn't important, if using bad language is meant.

Mike: Mike acknowledged that he doesn't personally connect closely with many of the practices, but he believes all are important for community. Nonviolent love of enemies, Mike said, doesn't feel close to his personal reality right now and is not something that he has passionately lived out. He sees it as more of a political discussion.

Tom: On simplicity of lifestyle, Tom claimed that he is trying to be faithful with what he has. He is a "poor college student" who just bought a sports car that was broken down and doesn't work so well. So he stated that even though the exterior of something may not look simple, the inside and the motivating reasons behind buying it may be.

On keeping the Sabbath, Tom says that he tries "to practice a little bit of the Sabbath every day."

On tithing, Tom stated that he has no money to tithe right now, so he tithes himself and his life to the church. He believes that the church has had too narrow a view on tithing, constricting it only to money. There should also be tithing of things and abilities. "Our whole life is a tithe."

On testifying on one's faith experience, Tom feels that living by example is more effective. From his experience in Germany, he saw that day-to-day living and meeting with people worked better than outright evangelism.

Renee: Renee commented that simplicity of lifestyle is definitely important. With an awareness of the consumption and materialism in our society, it's important to make the countercultural decision to try to live differently. Materialism is idolatry, she said. Consumption is taking away from the general welfare of the rest of the world.

On truth-telling, Renee said that she values honest friendships and friends who can challenge her on things. Sabbath-keeping is quite important, not rigidly on Sunday, but rest is important. Hospitality is very important, a good way to hear and tell stories and learn things about people.

On modest attire, Renee said that she feels like she doesn't quite fit in among Mennonites. She's not "the best Mennonite" because of the way she dresses. She likes looking nice. She grew up with an awareness of looks and shopping.

On testifying or speaking publicly about one's faith experience, Renee said she shirks away from anything with an evangelical element. She would love to talk to anyone about how her theology has developed, but she's seen evangelism, which she defines as sharing a testimony and then expecting something from the listeners, as destructive. She's not sure how to respond when the opportunity arises to share about her faith. Her tendency is to affirm where others are at but to say nothing about her personal experience.

Singing is an important form of worship for Renee, a way of expressing gratitude toward God. She loves singing hymns and hearing voices without instruments. The MCC house hosts a monthly hymn sing for young adults in the city, a practice that Renee sees as countercultural. She laughed when I asked her why: "People who are twenty-something don't just get together and sing hymns in four-part harmony. Anytime I tell somebody about it, I get a mixture of looks—like you're kind of weird but a little bit cool too. 'It's kind of admirable that you guys know how to sing like that.' I love telling people about hymn sings to get that look that says, 'You're different.' It often opens up to good conversations."

What I Hear

Most people chose to report where they would place a practice on the range of "very important" to "not important." Those who elaborated on their choices seemed to do so for one of three reasons: either they considered a practice extraordinarily important, were adamant about its unimportance, or sought to qualify the meaning or expression of the practice.

The simple numerical tally of responses puts sexual fidelity at the top of the list of practices thought to be important. Since in follow-up questions the interviewers often asked specifically about sexual fidelity and prayer, there were many comments made about those two practices in particular. These are collected in the next chapter.

How many times have we heard a comment like Laura's? "Nice Mennonite men don't do that." I used to hear it often, in one form or other, but much less frequently now. In recent memory, our communities had clearly defined expectations about how we were to behave in the practical dimensions of our life together. For all sorts of reasons, the expectations now seem to be much more relaxed. We've embraced a many-textured diversity of practices, and some would say we're busily assimilating into the mainstream. And yet some practices persist.

I wonder what the core practices embraced by the young adults of this generation will be. How will they provide cohesiveness and integrity to communities of the future? Will there be any reason to say, "Mennonite men, Mennonite women, don't do that"?

Chapter 19
More Faith Community Practices
—Prayer and Sex

"Looking out for yourself and others"

It would have been wonderful to have had more time in the interviews to explore each person's experience with practices more fully, to hear more stories, more description of how and why practices are important or not.

We were able to follow up with further questions about several practices in the one-on-one interviews. Two of those mentioned in this chapter are the practice of meditation and prayer and the practice of sexual fidelity. Since there were so many responses on these two practices, they are grouped here.

Some of us on the research team were surprised to see sexual fidelity come in as the most frequently rated "definitely important" practice. Meditation and prayer was moderately high on the same list. As the next chapter with the group interview results will show, meditation and prayer came in second among the practices people said they want to do on a regular basis.

Here is Matt's description of a typical day and the practices that he intentionally chooses to give meaning and shape to his life. Included are his thoughts on prayer and sexual fidelity. Following his contribution, we will listen to the comments of others.

Matt

On a typical day, Matt wakes up at 5:00 a.m., packs his lunch, and reads during breakfast. He prays while driving to work, works during the day with a building crew, shares stories with the crew at lunch, comes home, jogs or walks, has supper, works outside in the evening with parents or does things with friends, then watches TV or reads before he goes to bed.

In reflecting on his daily activities, Matt says they indicate that he values spending time with people, but he also values downtime and having space for solitude between moments of socializing.

Matt says practices that directly relate to his faith include praying on the way to work, singing while walking, hearing songs in his head while working, and thinking during work about things he has read. He talked about attending church and then discussing the sermon with his father on Sunday afternoons. He is an active listener and generally takes notes during the sermon, and he will refer to these during his discussions later that day.

Matt would like to spend more time reading the Bible. He also would like to take a class to study the Bible more academically.

He would like to pray more throughout the day, but finds it difficult to focus his thoughts. Matt misses college roommates and their discussions about faith. He would like to find that type of community again.

From the list of characteristic Mennonite practices, Matt can't distinguish which are important or not. He feels that all are integral. He believes, however, that the ultimate motivation for any practice should come from following Jesus. He finds some of those listed to be a result of a larger practice. For example, from meditation, prayer, and reading Scripture come practices that include hospitality and tithing. He believes that some of them are ambiguous. Thus, simplicity of lifestyle can have a number of motivations, including to be religious or to save money.

When asked specifically about prayer, Matt commented that he prays at meals, at church, and on the way to work. He often prays aloud, rambling to God. He finds that praying and thinking flow together.

Matt believes it is very important to abstain from sex until marriage. He sees it as looking out for himself and looking out for others, spiritually, socially, physically, and psychologically. He has watched the way premarital sex has affected others' relationships and their personal well-being. He thinks that many of his peers believe in abstinence but are unsure of the biblical basis for it and are ill-equipped to support their beliefs.

Matt currently belongs to a congregation of believers. His commitment is not extremely strong because of changes in his life. He is at a point of transition that affects his commitment, but he plans to commit to a congregation when he settles in one place and is more stable.

Matt says he has never felt like an outsider in a church. He has always felt quite welcomed and comfortable. Even during his college years, he felt that congregations were invitational to college students. However, during college the central place for spiritual connection was not in the church, so he didn't expect to be "plugged in" and overly involved.

Journal Comments

Matt had a solid belief in grace and hospitality that was reflected in his daily life practices. I appreciated watching him unintentionally and humbly demonstrate a lifestyle of discipleship and consistent being and doing in his comments. He took his faith seriously and with a depth that amazed me, and he was able to assess his spiritual life in a way that moved beyond convention. His language was fresh and original as he spoke about his faith. I could intuit that he knew how to be comfortable in God's presence and spoke out of that experience, not out of an embedded faith or spoon-fed perspective. His words showed his autonomy from his parents' faith and his feeling of being at home within the Mennonite church.

Matt also demonstrated his spiritual maturity in the ways he experienced God, describing a life of prayer as a fusion between his being and doing. He allowed his daily activities and thoughts to be a time of prayer and noticing God. He found ways to practice the presence of God and remain attuned to God's movement within him and within others throughout his day. As Matt described his faith, it did not have a marked dichotomy between the sacred and secular times; instead, it had an infused quality throughout his life.

—*Annie Lengacher*

Interview Questions

Let me ask you about some specific practices. How often, for example, are you aware of praying in an average day? How significant is prayer for your daily life and well-being and why?

Craig: Craig wants to learn more about praying regularly, especially when he does not feel a connection with God or feel like anything is being achieved. He'd like to do something about the state of being busy, which interferes with his awareness of God.

Craig said his prayers tend to be "unstructured and irregular," occurring in small portions throughout the day. His prayer life has varied greatly at different periods in his life, depending on how close a connection he feels with God. Craig also questions what might be his motivation for prayer. Simply to obtain blessings seems selfish and perhaps simplistic. He wonders, Does God want to bless me because I'm faithful? He'd like to learn about fasting for a longer period, learning to listen carefully to God, especially regarding direction for his vocation.

Jessica: Jessica's daily routine has developed themes that began to emerge even in her childhood. During her school years, she would always complete her homework as quickly as possible after school to allow for personal time in the afternoon. In those days, she would write stories, draw pictures, and generally be an introvert for a few hours before spending the evening hanging out with friends or family. Now in college, Jessica gets home from work or class in the afternoon and takes personal time for Bible study, prayer, a nap, or writing. Around suppertime, she makes a shift to spending time with her boyfriend, mutual friends, and activities.

"Time to be an introvert" is quite important to Jessica's life. Without it, she feels her life becoming shallow and unfocused. Prayer and reflection help her to value her experiences, to guide and empower her interactions with friends, and to nurture creative expression. Going a time without praying makes her feel guilty, but just as much, she feels she is missing something terribly important.

Peter: In his senior year of college, Peter took a class called Spiritual Path of the Peacemaker. It explored traditions and practices from other world religions as well as Christianity. "At that point," Peter remembers, "I was still leery of trying other ways. Even though I was into thinking that maybe Jesus was not the only way, I had a little bit of inner resistance. I have a tendency to defy whatever's around me. In a conservative setting, I tend to be more liberal, and in a liberal setting, I want to provide some counterbalance."

Peter tried meditation for a while, as an assignment for the class, but "despised it. I couldn't sit still." He also tried yoga, but as he says, "I get bored with most practices. The more I do them, the less meaningful they become." For two or three months, he was faithfully writing "morning pages," an Artist's Way practice that involves covering three pages with handwriting without a whole lot of thought every morning.

In a transitional home for homeless men called Christ House, where he volunteered for two years, Peter had discipline forced on him by his housemates, who mandated house prayer at 6:00 a.m. every morning. Peter mostly remembers being tired all the time that year. But he cites it as a positive time for learning the value of consistency. Interestingly, even though he despised meditation in college, the practice that Peter has settled on currently is centering prayer, twenty minutes a day, four days a week.

Sherri: When asked about prayer, Sherri responded that she believes prayer is very important. She prays because it brings her peace and relieves stress. She thinks her praying and talking kind of go together. Sherri would like to have more scheduled devotions and quiet time with God. She defines this time as alone in her room, intentionally reading or praying. She feels that she would grow closer to God if she practiced it more. She would also be more willing to share her faith with others.

Greg: Before meals, Greg and his wife sing and/or pray together. They kneel beside a chair and hold hands. It's not a practice either of them grew up with, but they're trying it out. They don't do it when guests come because they're not sure if they'd be comfortable with it.

Greg says he wishes he did "a more intense devotional, but I don't." He doesn't set aside the time. "I keep God's standards in my head as a way of praying ceaselessly—keeping these in mind in interactions with people at work, with my thought processes always resonating." As he learns more, Greg says he adds to the constant stream or "standards" in his head.

Ajay: Current spiritual practices for Ajay include taking time in the evening to read books or the Bible and to pray.

"Praying for me isn't always sitting and closing my eyes and saying something, but just sitting silently and letting God's Spirit work. I find a lot of strength in that.

"I'd like to learn more about fasting, even prayer—you know, when you pray, it's not always exciting—and more about meditation." Ajay adds that he'd also like to learn more about "drawing from the Bible for how I live my life."

Amy: While Amy is still quite faithful in going to church, she has come to realize that "you don't just meet God at church or while reading Scripture. He's there all the time."

She finds it meaningful to be by herself in order to read the Bible, pray, or sing with a guitar or hymnbook. This is something she would like to do more often—every day or every other day. Music is a meaningful part of Amy's faith. She enjoys singing hymns and songs and feels it helps her to focus on God.

Amy struggles with how to fit her faith in with her work. She wants to be able to show Christ to others in her workplace, but often finds that the pace of work and constant business makes that difficult. She feels it is important to be in prayerful conversation on a continual basis throughout the day. This has become a habit and is her most prevalent experience of prayer. She often offers short prayers when a need comes to mind for someone else, or when she realizes that she needs guidance or wisdom in a situation.

Tom: Tom states that he prays to God throughout the day. It's an off-and-on kind of thing. He prays as things come up. He also prays during the Pledge of Allegiance and the minute of silence at school. He stands during the pledge but does not say it or cover his heart. Instead, he mouths a prayer and then prays that he will be a witness for Christ to the culture in which God has placed him.

Eric: Eric is aware of praying twice a day, usually at night and sometimes before meals. He is aware of his pride if he goes too many nights without praying.

Ben: Ben "would like to pray more than I do" and says he does it less than previously. This is largely because he has less free time, and also because of the stage he was in. The years between high school and college were quite spiritually formative and intense for Ben, and thus prayer was a bigger part of his life. Ben's experience of prayer now "emphasizes the listening aspect" more than before. "Asking for stuff" seems to be self-focused, and Ben shies away from it for that reason.

Mary: Mary said that at night and morning, serious thinking goes on, synthesizing the day, trying to incorporate its lessons into a worldview. God is never far from my mind, she says. People are representations of God. She tries to bring thoughts of the day down to a relational level. Working in the business world also leaves her unsettled about questions of morality and faith.

Mary says she prays every other day, if not daily, and that prayer is definitely important to life. She says it keeps her in line and helps her retain a perspective on things. It serves as an affirmation of belief in God, keeping that channel open.

Alisa: Although Alisa sees prayer as important and is currently reading books on prayer to learn more about it, she has some questions.

"Does God really want me to tell him the same things over and over again? If I don't have anything new, do I really need to pray? I don't tell my friends the same things over and over, and God has a better memory than they do!"

In addition, although she remembers being surrounded by God's presence during her mother's illness, as a young child she understood her prayers as unanswered. "When my mom got sick, everyone said, 'We need to pray.' There was a faith there that God was going to take care of us, take care of that situation. For me, I saw it as 'God's going to make her better.'"

Mark: When asked specifically about prayer, Mark said that he's aware of praying at least once a day, plus at meals. He acknowledged that prayer isn't very significant for him. He feels like he needs a reason to pray, as when something's either drastically wrong or right in his life. He hasn't had any "trauma" in life to pray about.

Will: On meditation and prayer, Will commented that they're important, especially intercessory prayer.

Jeff: Prayer is also a practice Jeff wishes he did more of and thinks it would give some of the same benefits as the Taizé service at his church, which leaves him with a sense of calm and collection and feeling better able to handle challenges. Currently he prays about every two or three days.

Brian: Brian remarked that he is aware of praying in the morning and before every meal. He usually prays for God's provision and another day to live.

Hannah: "Every day at school I pray during the Pledge of Allegiance," Hannah quipped. She prays before dinner. "The Taizé services are the most meaningful thing my current congregation does. Their clean, organized steps are cleansing, and Wednesday night (the regular time for these services) is a perfect time. I find so much to pray about midweek! I also pray for my students."

What I Hear

Many young adults describe prayer as a practice in which they participate, usually on a daily basis or at least several times a week. Fairly often, praying occurs at set times throughout the day, like morning and evening and mealtimes. But others talk of praying on a continuous or irregular basis and of wanting prayer to be part of an ongoing conversation. A fascinating shift from thinking of prayer as "asking for stuff" to prayer as "listening" seems to have taken place for several people. Many frequently referred to prayer occurring during times of solace and solitude, during intentional personal time.

Most often in reference to prayer, people spoke of the personal benefits they experience from listening prayer: strength, a sense of calm, regained perspective, renewed creative expression, empowerment, guidance, wisdom, peace, stress relief, an open channel to God, help with discerning one's vocation. A couple of people spoke of prayer as also something done on behalf of others.

Interview Questions

How important is the practice of sexual fidelity, traditionally defined as the expression of sexual intimacy only within marriage? What behaviors do you observe among your peers related to this practice?

Hannah: About sexual fidelity, Hannah commented that it is very important! In the church she thinks there is a lack of openness about sex, which is frustrating. People need a space to talk about it. People are going from singleness to marriage without much guidance from the church, she said. In college, she was somewhat open with girlfriends, but we need more discussion about all the dynamics involved in a sexual relationship. Her friends have known what she thought about it, but not until she was in a relationship did she really have to define the lines.

Craig: Craig's parents have recently divorced, which makes Craig feel much more strongly about sexual fidelity than he has in the past. He is uncomfortable with his own lack of purity in thoughts and discussion, and that of his peers. That lack of purity is something to which he tries to give attention.

Mike: Mike commented that sexual fidelity is definitely important. There is a skewed idea of sex in our society, he says, that ruins many lives. But sex is powerful, "enigmatic," and has the potential to be such a positive thing within a loving relationship. He suggested that it's important to surround oneself with people who have similar views on the importance of sexual fidelity.

Laura: Laura commented that sexual fidelity is so important. People end up with babies. Sex can cause pain, and committing such sin can lead to guilt. You can't get that part of yourself back. And there are always sexually transmitted diseases.

Tom: On sexual fidelity, Tom thinks that it is something that young adults don't talk about much. He thinks that most Christian young adults know that sexual intercourse should be saved for marriage and respect that. He also thinks that most non-Christians do not regard sexual intercourse that way. He says he practices behaviors that keep him from "being led away. You have to guard yourself" against the things that can tempt you. "Just because you believe in sexual fidelity doesn't mean that you can't be tempted."

Rachel: Rachel said that sexual fidelity is definitely important within committed partnerships, but she's not willing to say "only within marriage," because lesbians and gays can't legally marry most places.

Kate: For Kate, sexual fidelity falls into the "somewhat important" category. "It's very important for me personally," she said, "but I have some friends who, . . . well, that's all they see in church." Kate also specified that people who are lesbian or gay should be welcomed in the church.

Peter: Peter cited sexual fidelity, along with many other practices, as quite important, but also commented that it should include all sexual orientations.

Greg: Sexual fidelity is definitely important, says Greg. In particular, he commented on his disagreement with homosexuality. "It's not my right to judge, but if somebody's critical of my lifestyle, they're critiquing a whole umbrella of standards. That's how you live in community, sharing standards."

Greg is thoroughly convinced that God sanctions sexual fidelity. His peers are on the same page in believing it's very important. It's helpful to end up with friends who share the same desire to restrain their physical selves and be in support of each other in that effort, he said. He remarked that sex is a mystery. He doesn't understand why we're given so much power to create life, but to treat that power loosely is to disrespect the Creator.

Sherri: Sherri also believes that sexual fidelity is very important, especially for Christians. She feels that some of her non-Christian friends just do whatever they want. She doesn't talk about sexual matters with her peers.

Christina: Sexual fidelity is important for Christina, but it is not upheld among her peers in general. Only among her closest friends is it valued.

Brian: Brian strongly believes in sex only in marriage but finds the exact opposite among his peers. A few of his Christian peers feel the same, but others disagree with him.

Mary: On sexual fidelity, Mary remarked that marriage is an unnatural thing, and she doesn't think that's acknowledged nearly enough. Fidelity is difficult and somewhat also unnatural, but much more important, she says. It goes beyond a romantic relationship. Faithfulness to a partner isn't limited to sexuality, she said. She's heard peers do a lot of line-drawing. "We did this but didn't do this, so we're okay," they seem to be saying.

Will: Will said that he "abstains from drugs and sex more than I would if I weren't a Christian," and also from crime and other "desires of the flesh."

Mark: Sexual fidelity is very important to Mark. Among his peers he finds a mixed reaction; it's mostly "not a big deal" to them, he said. He would like there to be a greater emphasis on fidelity and purity in life in general. He has some misgivings about watching inappropriate TV or movies that have a lot of sex or violence. In general, he would like to see his peers getting away from the party attitude and away from purely social relationships into deeper ones.

Eric: Eric finds sexual fidelity important from a sociological standpoint more than a religious one; he's unsure of scriptural references in support of abstinence. He views it as a relational thing, and the fullest expression of intimacy can only happen within marriage. He thinks that most of his Mennonite peers share his view but that most other peers do not.

Renee: Renee thinks that sexual fidelity is very important. She was definitely taught this since she was young. This is one of the only things she has not allowed to be challenged since her move to the city. It's based in the Bible. Sex before marriage brings extra problems she doesn't want to deal with. This has definitely been reinforced at the rape crisis center, where she has seen the destruction caused by sex.

Jeff: On the issue of sexual fidelity, Jeff believes that pop culture negatively affects our society as it glamorizes infidelity. This leads to damaged families. People he knows who are or were promiscuous in their late teens and early twenties find it difficult to value a permanent, monogamous relationship.

What I Hear

Almost uniformly, those interviewed on the question of sexual fidelity consider it to be very important, though they have varied reasons for *why* they consider sex only within marriage to be important. Some put the emphasis on the negative effects they've observed in those who've engaged in sex outside of marriage. They recognize the pain it causes, the damage to the possibility of forming a lasting relationship, and the destructive effects to one's personal well-being and health. They spoke of how our culture glamorizes sexual infidelity, providing us with a skewed understanding of the power and potential of sexual interaction. Others spoke of the mysterious, enigmatic power of sex, which has the potential to be such a positive thing and to find its fullest expression in the intimacy of marriage.

I am struck by the unselfishness and maturity of the comments by Matt, who stated that abstaining from sex until marriage is his way of looking out for himself and looking out for others, spiritually, socially, physically, and psychologically.

Chapter 20
Typical Faith Community Practices—II
(Group Interview)

"Practical ways of showing love"

After learning from young adults in the one-on-one interviews how important they felt various "typical Mennonite practices" were for them, we wanted to test what we learned in the group interviews. We reframed some of the questions, revised the list a bit, and invited further response.

Included in the group interview was an invitation to identify the practices about which young adults want to talk more. This seemed to open up intriguing questions about the meaning and context of practices. Over and over, they energetically sought further discussion about practices in the church, and presumably elsewhere—as illustrated below. The questions raised will hopefully generate discussion in other settings and conversation about practices not on the list.

Before looking at responses in the group interviews, however, we look at Ben's story. He has fond memories of formative childhood stories, but he thinks that learning through personal experience and practice has been more important.

Ben

Ben heard Bible stories from an early age and remembers a storybook with the standard childhood Bible stories. There were also Mother Goose, Dr. Seuss, and some TV cartoons in his home. He said there weren't many family stories. But he feels that the stories he heard were meant to show how easy he has it compared with the previous generation.

Ben has fond memories of the stories of his childhood, especially the Bible stories, and feels he gained from them. He thinks "these stories are something that should be taught to kids, as one way to instill basic values and morals." While Ben learned "values and morals" from the stories, he learned even more through the example and instruction of his parents.

It's hard for Ben to pinpoint exactly what the childhood stories have done for him. But he feels his "own experience" since childhood has been more formative. He thinks learning through personal experience is more powerful than learning through story. For example, he commented: "If I take something without asking and get caught and punished, this is a more powerful lesson than hearing a story about it happening."

Ben feels his parents' example contributed to him understanding his identity and how he wants to live. He thinks his dad takes too much time away from the family, and that is something that he doesn't want to emulate. But he also sees how his parents are faithful and involved in church, and that is something he does want to mirror.

One of the practices most significant to Ben's faith is looking for ways to "learn from and work with" people. He wants to help people, but he realizes that he often ends up being helped and encouraged in his life and faith by the people he is aiming to help.

Ben spent a summer working in Chicago with a church that helps the poor and homeless. His goal became to "see the face of God in the city," and this effort became a meaningful experience. By interacting with people whose lives were much more difficult than his own, Ben could see courage, faith, and hope more powerfully than in his own life. To Ben, this meant that God was already at work in the people he had come to serve.

In looking over the list of characteristic Mennonite practices, Ben commented that the most important items on the list were "practical ways of showing love." "Love should be the motivation for our actions," he said, "and we should be actually doing things to express this love."

Attending church is a regular part of Ben's life. This year he found a congregation closer to school, one that has a good young-adult group where he fits in easily. Ben says his experience at this church is definitely "in my comfort zone," and he recognizes both benefits and dangers of that.

Ben wants to see churches more involved in serving and helping communities, especially the underprivileged. He'd also like to see his peers engage in more volunteering and "service-minded practices," and contributing more to the sense of church community, even if it's just being available to talk.

He would also like to see them work more with "the outside world" to change legal structures. On the other hand, Ben sees it as even more important to work within the church, to help the church promote justice and show compassion, rather than merely relying on the government.

Group Interview Questions

Here is a list of practices that some young adults have identified as very or somewhat important. As I read comments others have made about these practices, be thinking of five in particular about which you have questions and would be glad to talk more. Also identify the practices you either do now or intend to do on a regular basis.

Circle the five practices about which you are most unsure and wish to discuss more in church or other settings. Which ones did you circle and why?

Put an X by the practices you either do now or intend to do on a regular basis. Tell me about some that you marked and why they are important to you.

How might the church be helpful to you in the cultivation of these practices?

Here is the tally of the total number of responses, with comments following:

Number of	Circles	X's
simplicity of lifestyle	11	18
nonviolent love of enemies	8	20
truth-telling	4	19
integrity of being and doing	9	20
Sabbath-keeping	10	12
hospitality	5	22
gathering together for worship	4	19
singing together	0	16
meditation and prayer	8	22
engaging the Bible	8	18
group discernment/ listening to each other/Spirit	12	16
sexual integrity and fidelity	10	20
stewardship and generosity	6	26
service to neighbor	3	21
nonprovocative attire	5	7
eating meals together	3	19
mission and outreach	12	18
care for one's own body	4	18
rituals: foot washing/ Lord's Supper/other	8	12

Karla: "I have questions about these practices. Let's unpack these. Let's find out what they mean: Simplicity of lifestyle; nonviolent love of enemies—what do these mean in different contexts? Care for body; Sabbath-keeping—do these mean literally? Truth-telling—what does that mean? Does it mean exemplifying love or confronting?"

Jennifer: "These are the things that I have the most questions about how they work out in my life: Gathering together for worship—I'm not clear about what worship means or if I want to be a part of that. Sexual fidelity is a huge question in my life. This is important to me but only on nebulously religious grounds. I would be interested to explore that more within a religious community. Mission and outreach—are these valid? Sabbath-keeping—sounds great, but I don't really know what it means."

Lisa: "Nonprovocative attire—as human beings, it's important to respect anyone, no matter what. It should be irrelevant what they're wearing; and provocative is a subjective term. Rituals—I wonder about them in general. I would like to hear more about that. Sexual fidelity—Jesus was the ultimate human being, and he was [not sexually active]. That doesn't leave me much to work with as I make my own decisions."

Ken: "Simplicity of lifestyle—this seems idyllic. I am aware of the disparity between the ideal and what I see looking at my life. I own a lot and don't share as much as I should. Sexual fidelity—sexual integrity and fidelity were taught to me my entire life in such a simplistic way that when I actually got into scenarios and situations, I couldn't really understand myself, [or know] how to navigate them. How prudish my community is in talking about sex and human sexuality. Mission and outreach—'mission' is a dubious word; it so quickly falls into the same category as 'crusade.'"

Ellen: "Because I'm interested in what the church would say about these, because they seem open to interpretation, let's talk about them: Truth-telling—are we telling your truth or my truth or The Truth? Sexual integrity—I got absolutely no lessons from my home; I feel so unsure about what that means. [This sparked a discussion about how other denominations and ethnic groups talk more openly about sex.] Group discernment—I have really negative connotations with that. Nonprovocative attire—I'm going through this stage right now where I don't have a problem with it, so why should anyone else? But that's not good."

᠃᠃᠃

Aaron: "I want a lot of these practices to be part of my life; a lot already are. I love eating meals together. Engaging the Bible—I'm not doing that right now. The same with meditation and prayer and gathering together for worship. Nonprovocative attire—I don't feel like it's a huge issue."

Ann: "I circled nonviolent love of enemies and engaging the Bible. I'm not really doing that at all right now."

Conrad: "Sabbath-keeping is a source of discussion/disagreement with my wife. I grew up being taught that you didn't do anything on Sundays. You relaxed. My wife didn't grow up that way, so we sometimes argue about what should and shouldn't be done on Sundays."

Sarah: "The ones I circled and X'ed are the ones that are hardest for me to put into practice. For example, simplicity of lifestyle—I love entertaining, dressing nicely. But then I also want to be simple. So what really is a simple lifestyle? Same for nonviolent love of enemies—it's hard for me to think personally of my enemies. So how does that work out in life? Meditation and prayer—something I want in my life, but it's easier to say I want it than to actually do it or know what that means for my life. Stewardship and generosity—I think it's important and want to do it, but when it comes to the reality of paying bills and tithing 10 percent—those kinds of things are complicated. Mission and outreach—personally, I don't feel it's important, but I would have questions about it."

Andy: "I have trouble with nonviolence and pacifism. I'm not sure how that all works. Sabbath-keeping—I'm not a stickler [against] not working on Sundays. I believe it's important to rest with God and focus on God. Hospitality—I don't know how I would feel about hospitality to the point where I invite someone to live in my house. I need to think about that honestly. And I really enjoy singing together. But I don't rank that up there with meditation and prayer."

〜〜〜

Derek: "There's really a lack of rituals. I've been appalled at how Low-Church I am. I rarely did communion and never did foot washing until I was in SALT."

Rose: "I never found it important until I was in a context that took rituals seriously, and since then I have seen it as very important and really miss it. On mission and outreach—I think the Mennonite church needs to look again at this idea of mission. It needs to be an emphasis, but it's kind of stuck with the wrong kind of ideas in mind. We need to allow people to start doing missions in the area of gifts, life passions, and do that as missions instead of prescribing places and specific jobs."

Phil: "Mission is a passion of mine personally. A lot of that has to do with having seen it done very effectively. Other times the way it is done just makes me mad. Hospitality—I have thought a lot about that lately—we need to make church a welcoming place for those outside of the community. One of the biggest barriers for new people coming into the church is that people don't feel comfortable."

Derek: "Nonprovocative attire, care for body—they seem important, but they are too broad."

Rose: "I circled and put an X on simplicity. It's something that's really important to me, but I hope that we can expand that to the way that we operate in relationships. I shop at Goodwill and eat beans, too, but I don't want that to turn into a rule that everybody needs to follow."

Derek: "It's not supposed to be about rules, but if it makes anybody else stumble, I want to change it."

Anita: "Nonprovocative attire is a big one for me. Back in Puerto Rico, I would dress one way, and then I come here and everyone's like 'whoa.' So it really depends on culture. Same with alcohol. In the Bible they drink wine, but it also says don't be a slave to alcohol."

Derek: "And don't be a slave to nonprovocative attire. I'm really surprised by how much we all agree on all this stuff. There's nothing so far that I feel like I need to offer a rebuttal for."

භ භ භ

Linda: "I would like to hear the church talk about simplicity of lifestyle. The church is doing jack squat about this issue. Personally, I want to eat meals together. That's easy to do with people I know. I want to invite people I don't know, but I struggle with that."

Tara: "I would like to hear the church talk more about truth-telling. It's not always easy to point out things in people's lives to work on. We need a balance of accepting and challenging others. Personally, I want to practice missions and outreach, especially within the country and within the church."

Tony: "I would like to hear the church talk more about engaging the Bible and group discernment. The more you read the Bible, the more you can discern together. Personally, I want to gather together for worship."

Ray: "I would like to hear the church talk more about group discernment and listening to each other. Personally, I want to do all of these practices."

~~~

Beth: "The few that I marked go together: simplicity of life with stewardship. They have to do with lifestyle. I want them to be a part of my life. I'm not evangelistic, but how I act paints a good picture of how I'm feeling or where I'm at with simplicity. I think of the *More-with-Less Cookbook*, which is about just taking care of what you have, and being smarter and wiser and more economically friendly. It's a lifestyle.

"In the church, I'd like to talk more about group discernment, which fits back with my desire to be in a small-group Bible study. I'm learning how to incorporate things into daily life, like meditation and prayer. It's tough though."

Tim: "In the church, I'd like to talk more about group discernment and wanting to engage the Bible. I need interaction with other people. I'm an extrovert and need input from other people in my life. Integrity is the biggest thing for me. Some people are really Billy Grahamish, but I can live out my faith through my lifestyle, in how I interact. Hospitality is very important to me; I value my friends a lot."

Michelle: "I chose to circle group discernment. I don't understand the Holy Spirit or how to listen. I also chose service to neighbor. I want service to be a part of my life, but I want to know how to be a servant without being taken advantage of."

James: "I circled gathering for worship. I'm not sure how our standard way of gathering for worship is supported traditionally, especially since these gatherings are not how I feel or see God. I would be open to see the format and structure change. I would like to hear how others feel about this."

Michelle: "I put X's beside singing together and meditation and prayer. These are the ways I connect most now to God, so I want to keep doing them. I also marked stewardship because I feel it will be important in the future to be a good steward of money."

James: "I also put an X on truth-telling, which I think is important because … nothing functions well under false pretenses."

What I Hear

Many excellent questions were raised about what we mean by these practices. While allowing for differences in interpretations, and the differences in the two lists of practices (here and in Chapter 18), it is interesting to combine some numbers and see where agreement might emerge.

In response to the question of which practices young adults do or intend to do regularly, "stewardship/generosity" received the most responses this time around. We chose this alternative wording to replace "tithing" on the earlier list, which garnered only fourteen responses of "very important." The alternate wording of "stewardship/generosity" seems to surface as a core value for these young adults.

When adding the number of responses of "very important" from the first list in chapter 18 to the totals from the second list, there are six practices that emerge with scores of 40 or higher: "sexual integrity and fidelity" (44), "integrity of being and doing" (42), "hospitality" and "service to neighbor" (41 each), " meditation/prayer" and "stewardship/generosity (formerly tithing)" (40 each).

Two practices that were 20 or above in the first list but were dropped in the second list were "mutual care within the community" and "forgiveness and reconciliation."

Ben's comment sums everything up simply and powerfully. The most important practices on the list are "practical ways of showing love." "Love should be the motivation for our actions," he said, "and we should be actually doing things to express this love."

Chapter 21
Narratives and Practices for Future Family Life

"Family and children will be my career"

In the interviews we spent a lot of time inviting persons to reflect on the formative stories and practices they remember from their childhoods. But we also thought it would be interesting to invite people to imagine what stories and practices they might want to pass on to their children. We thought that asking people what they want for their own families might indicate their expectations and provide a glimpse into what they truly value. We didn't spend a lot of time on this question, so the answers are brief but revelatory.

First Greg, Brian, and Sherri share their stories. They describe how their vision for the future of their own families is directly informed by their own childhood stories and practices.

Greg: Greg's dad died in a farming accident in South Dakota when Greg was a year old. Throughout his childhood, Greg's mother and grandmother told Greg stories about his father. Many on his dad's side died while he was young, and this resulted in a strong tradition of stories that described the family's loved ones. The early deaths also caused Greg's mother to move a lot, as she sought a living for herself and her two boys.

"All of a sudden, I'm ten and everyone's dead and we've moved." Greg felt a lack of stability and roots.

Greg's older brother remembers his father and others who died when Greg was a baby. This left Greg with only stories to guide him, and he often wished for his brother's experiential knowledge of these family members.

He remembers bedtime prayers with his mom or grandmother, but in general he feels there was a lack of childhood practices. There were few meals together, for example, because the family was so unstable.

Greg always looked at the void of his childhood experiences as a weakness. But today he finds strength in it. He loves to hear people tell their stories. He seeks them out in a crowd. "I grew up thinking I had a very peculiar story. So I try and look for other peculiar stories. It's a way to hear others' stories that I'll never meet. The closest thing to real life is listening, and you can multiply that around the world."

As a child Greg had no stable church affiliation to provide narratives. He says he had no idea of who he was. He had a small idea of where he came from but was ashamed of what he knew about his past. He blamed God for many things that were not healed in his life.

"God was my enemy," he said. This negative perception of God seems to have come from the lack of a father figure in his life and the absence of an emotional attachment to a church or denomination.

When Greg was in the fourth grade, his mother married a Pentecostal Christian. "What the Pentecostal church taught about God was the farthest thing from what I needed for answers to all my questions," he said. The church to which his stepfather took the family seemed to be for social purposes only; people acted strangely, and there seemed to be a noticeable inconsistency in people's lives outside the church.

The life stories of Greg's friends in college were so different from his own that they comforted him. He remembers visiting a friend's grandmother's house and being captivated by sketches from the *Martyrs Mirror* on the walls. He couldn't stop looking at them and wanted to know the stories behind them.

"These other stories gave me perspective," he said. "I realized I'm not the only person in the world, and it helped me stop seeing myself as a victim of my circumstances."

In light of Greg's quite unstable childhood home, he places a high value on "stable family limits."

"Family and children will be my career," he says. "I want to work only part-time so I can work with our kids, teach them how to can, fish, chop wood, pray, and sing. Sports will not come before my family, church, and faith."

Greg wants to have meals together with his children and for them to see their parents reading the Bible and talking about their own faith. He wants the Bible to be presented in a way that meets each stage of their lives and brings it to them again and again in refreshing ways. He would use children's literature to foster their imagination and expose them to "outside narratives," observing that "Jesus never called himself a Christian." The way one lives one's life is what's important.

Journal Comments

Greg's story of losing his father at a young age and growing up without routine, without story, without ritual has affected him immensely. He took the first question of narratives and developed beautifully on it. He revealed painful and powerful moments of his life. I found it interesting to hear Greg's stories of not growing up in the Mennonite church but coming to it in college. Over about a decade, God changed from an enemy to one he can't box in, of whom he can't demand answers, but whom he can merely strive to understand.

Throughout the interview is a theme of wanting so much to be confident of his own narrative, to be confident of where he's coming from. He expressed appreciation to the person who thought to investigate these things in young adults, knowing from his own experience how important it is to sift through the narratives that compose us and deal with the baggage that may exist.

—*Melody King*

Brian: David and Goliath was an important story for Brian because it demonstrated how small people can do extraordinary things and accomplish goals, he said. He remembers his dad making up stories about a boy and his horses. His dad named the horse Smarty and the boy Timmy, and he would relate the stories to whatever had happened that day. The story always had a moral about God working things out in life as long as you trust in God.

One horse story was about Timmy falling into a river. The boy couldn't get out. Smarty was off eating apples and couldn't hear Timmy's call for help. But Smarty felt a small voice inside him telling him to go and check Timmy, and the boy was saved.

Stories helped Brian believe that he could do anything, like direct a choir in college, if he had enough trust to let God direct his path. The stories demonstrated God's faithfulness and that if you listen, God talks to you.

Brian's dad recently told him a story about his college experience that has had power for Brian. His dad sang in the choir in college, even though he can't carry a tune very well. This story impressed Brian because his dad had a lot of fun traveling with the choir and doing something he wasn't good at. The story showed Brian that he should get involved even if he doesn't excel at an activity.

As a child, Brian rode his bike a lot, played sports, and played with the neighbor kids. He had band practice every Tuesday after school and didn't watch a lot of TV.

A typical day for Brian now starts about 7:00 a.m., when he gets up. He eats breakfast, prays, goes to work at a children's camp by 8:00 a.m. After work he goes to see his girlfriend, eats dinner with her or at her home, sits down to watch TV, spends some time on the Internet, goes for a run at night, lifts weights, and finally goes to bed.

Brian works at his church, where he participates in the kids and adult choirs. He helps with a local youth group and does worship practice during the week. Brian said he would like to be more involved in the prayer group in his church; he thinks it would help his spiritual growth and his relationships in church. He would like to work on issues of trusting and showing faith in God.

Brian belongs to the congregation of believers in which he grew up. He has considered going elsewhere during college, but he is very committed to this body. He feels that his home congregation could be doing a whole lot more. The services could be longer, and he suggests that church revival meetings could occur more often. Brian would also feel more at home in his church if his background in gospel music was reflected more in the worship style.

In his future home, Brian will continue his father's Timmy and Smarty stories, along with stories like *The Three Little Pigs*, if they are reshaped to incorporate his African-American background—like *Slick Willy the Pig*, for example. Brian said he will try to set an example for his children at home with regular prayer times, talking to them about Christ, sharing Bible stories, and pointing out life lessons along the way. He feels that prayer within the home can give new meaning to family life.

Journal Comments

Brian views music as his form of prayer and worship. He experiences God through his musical involvement in the church. He also reflected a mission-minded approach in his view of the church's purpose and its need for revival and renewal.

Brian's language for God draws on the idea that he can do anything with God, and that God will always be there for him. Brian spoke of God's provision for him, helping him through rough times and defending him. He seemed slightly dissatisfied with his current experience of prayer, and he mentioned that he wishes he would pray more. Yet, he seemed unaware of the prayer forms within his music and the ways that he obviously prays through his musical gifts.

—*Annie Lengacher*

Sherri: Sherri remembers that as a child her parents read the Berenstain Bears books to her. At Christmastime they read the story of Christ's birth. She also remembers reading Frank Peretti's books, which scared her and exposed her to the idea of spiritual warfare. Now she sees that she has a new awareness of the spiritual realm from the Peretti books and that the Berenstain Bears stories helped to give her a set of values.

Sherri observed that stories tell her about God's continual love, that God is always there for you. She notes the value of Bible stories she learned in Sunday school, though she would like to have had more devotional prayer time with her family.

As a child, Sherri always helped in the barn with the morning and evening milking. Supper with the family was normal. She participated in Future Farmers of America in high school and worked at her family's produce stand.

A typical day for Sherri now unfolds something like this: She wakes up between 6:00 and 6:30 a.m., calls in for work, takes care of her puppies, talks to her fiancé on the phone, and has breakfast. Sherri is in the profession of breeding cows. She visits between fifteen and twenty farms a day. If she's close to home, she stops by for lunch. She returns home about 4:00 p.m., helps with milking on her farm, eats supper with her family. In the evening she works on her wedding plans and listens to the radio before going to sleep.

Sherri values the independence of her job. She knows that working alone requires honesty and trust, and she has learned that being honest with farmers in her work is important, since no one is "looking over her shoulder."

She belongs to a practicing congregation of believers but isn't overly committed to it. She serves on the Bible School committee, which keeps her involved. But she would enjoy church more if there were greater numbers of young people attending.

Five years from now, Sherri probably will be fully involved in a church, especially if she has children. She would participate in Sunday school and a mothers' group.

Sherri would like to see families spend more time together, playing games, taking vacation, and having meals together. She plans to tell stories to her children about hard work and life on the farm. And she would tell them Bible stories, such as Joseph and his brother, and Daniel in the lions' den. Sherri would regularly pray before meals and have a daily family devotional time. And around the house she would like to have magazines and devotionals such as *Our Daily Bread*.

Journal Comments

Sherri openly discussed her faith, and I appreciated her genuine presence in the conversation. I found her interest in the spiritual realm, end times, and the

Apocalypse intriguing. Her image of God largely centers around an almighty God who rules over all realms of reality. She spoke of God with words of enormity and breadth, not ones of closeness and proximity.

Sherri rarely strayed from the language typically taught by the church. She admitted that she "should" have devotions every morning to improve her relationship with God. She only considered "devotion" time as being alone in her room, set apart with God, focused on prayer and reading Scripture. She maintained a division in her language between her God time and the rest-of-life time, instead of seeing God's work in every part of the day. She upheld honesty, community, and hard work as key elements of faithful living.

—Annie Lengacher

Interview Questions

What narratives would you be most eager for your children (if and when you have children) to hear and use to construct meaning? What practices would you expect to regularly incorporate into your home and church life?

Mark: Mark would expect to read Bible and children's stories to his children. He would also watch good movies with moral applications and listen to music with his children. He would model respect in his relationship with his wife. He'd have his family attend church, have daily devotionals, and promote a general openness in the home to talk about faith.

Ajay: Ajay wants to raise his children as he was raised—with regular Bible stories and prayer. "I also want to pray regularly with my wife. I think that's important."

Christina: Christina wants to tell her children stories of people in her life, in their family's life, as well as selected Bible stories. She wants to practice hospitality in her future home and church life. She will have a commitment to the church setting and the practices of the church. She wants to connect her family with a genuine spirituality, not just practicing "family devotions."

Amy: Amy would plan with her family to attend a Mennonite church and participate in her community and the congregation, and to interact with extended family.

Matt: Matt would like to see family visits on Sundays revived, with renewed closeness of the family unit. He thinks the former custom of making Sunday-afternoon visits with extended family would be beneficial today.

In the future Matt would want to tell his children about their grandparents. He would tell Bible stories, Mennonite history, martyrdom stories, acts-of-grace stories, and stories of his experience in Guatemala.

Matt would be involved in Sunday school. He would want small-group participation for social and spiritual purposes, and he would like to instill the importance of holidays.

Will: As his mother did when he was a child, Will would read bedtime stories to his children. He would want to live a simple lifestyle and would probably not want his kids to have too much. He would want to relate to the community around him and to follow a biblical order for his home.

Jason: Jason would want his children to hear stories about Jesus's life, Greek and Roman mythology, the history of Buddhism (he admits he'd have to educate himself more), stories of historical figures like Gandhi, Socrates, the Hindu narrative, the Renaissance, people's movements such as the Cuban revolution, and the end of apartheid. He would like to eat together as a family, but he hasn't thought much about it.

Mary: With her children, Mary hopes to share Dr. Seuss stories and narratives that develop from growing up in different places but still feeling rooted in something. She wants her children to learn a variety of languages.

Dave: Dave would like to raise his children similarly to how he was raised, but he would like to be a little more emotionally involved than his dad was. He doesn't want to shield them from the world and hopes to emphasize that faith is a choice. Dave wants his family to eat together, spend time with extended family, have church as a regular part of life, talk about faith, and communicate hopes. But he would leave room for choice and have family time. He wants to have a work life that leaves evenings and weekends free.

Alisa: Alisa wants to pass on to her children "mutual love and care and respect for each other. How important it is to take people where they're at, to love them where they're at. That's one of the things I admire about [my fiancé]. I didn't feel like I had to be part of a conversation about some theological thing that I don't have any idea about; he just loved me for who I am."

Eric: Eric will hope to read Old and New Testament stories to his children. He wants them to read secular books and see secular movies and TV without highly stringent monitoring. He likes to encourage exploration. But the biblical narrative will be most consistent for his family.

Eric wants to eat together as a family, be involved in a small group that would include his family, be involved in a church body, and encourage youth-group involvement for his children.

Renee: In her family, Renee wants there to be a lot of dialogue, an openness to talking about things and hearing different perspectives instead of setting laws and rules.

Laura: Laura would hope to tell her children missionary stories—hers and others. Since the United States may be foreign to them, she will tell them stories from her life in the States. She'll also tell Bible stories and stories about her family.

Tom: In his own home, Tom would like to have daily devotions with his family in the morning "to start the day by giving it to God." He wants to have mentors in place for his family and himself to "bounce ideas off of and to keep me accountable." His vision is to "bring the kingdom" of God by being involved in people's lives, praying for people, and finding out where God wants him to be.

Rachel: Narratives Rachel would like to include in her family life? All of them. If she adopts, she would tell her children the stories of their adoption over and over. She would want to include practices such as eating together, gardening, putting up food for the winter, visiting people, working together.

Mike: Narratives Mike would be eager for his children to hear are the Bible stories. Because of his own personal doubts about faith and since his parents never explained the ambiguous aspects of faith and religion, he would value honesty and questions and want to make space for this with his own children.

Practices he would expect to incorporate into his home and church life would be talking about the day as a family, being aware of each other's lives outside the home, being part of a church, and eating together.

What I Hear

The above suggestions for future family life provide a fascinating glimpse into the stories and practices people remember fondly from their childhood and want to continue, and also some changes they intend to make in their own family life. Most people mentioned their desire for their children to hear Bible stories. There was frequent mention of the desire for open, honest conversation about faith, for eating meals together and visiting extended family, for regularly participating in church, and for praying together. Greg's story seems to show that being deprived of a relationship with his dad and experiencing the overall instability of his family life contribute to his determination that "family and children will be my career."

Chapter 22
Practices to Do More or Know More About

"Spirituality should address life in its entirety"

Pastor and postmodern author Alan Roxburgh, in his book *Reaching a New Generation: Strategies for Tomorrow's Church* (Downer's Grove, IL: InterVarsity, 1993), describes how a longing for "wholeness" emerges in many conversations he has about spirituality—a longing to reconnect with the mystery and sacredness in nature. Many of us, Roxburgh observes, have lost an awareness that God is revealed in the natural world.

The world was never intended to be just "material" matter devoid of life, he writes. In fact, the "new physics" confirms that the material and spiritual are inter-related. The world is a web of relationships that can't be broken down into sub-ject-object, mind-body dualisms. The world is a single, holistic organism that can't be split into separate, autonomous parts. "It is the sacrament of God's pres-ence," he writes. "It is food. Everything that exists makes God known to us and enables communion with God." Here is a spirituality that brings "mystery, con-nectedness and unity back into the relationship between humankind and nature. The world is the incarnational locus of God's meeting with us."

Many of the young adults speaking in this chapter seem to confirm Roxburgh's assertions about a pervasive longing for a more integrated, whole spirituality. They are seeking practices that enhance their sense of well-being and at-homeness in the world, and those that connect them with what they care about.

In one-on-one interviews, we asked young adults what practices they would like to see their peers taking seriously and performing more often. What practices add richness and meaning to life? We also asked more broadly about which features of spirituality appeal to them. First, John gives poignant insights into a "whole" spirituality.

John: Bible stories were not an influence in John's family. Around age ten, he heard some fairy tales. There weren't many family stories, either. About all he knows of his family is that grandfather or great-grandfather emigrated from Bern, Switzerland.

The guidance of John's parents is a kind of noninfluence. They didn't try to instill religious values; neither did they hinder their children from taking them on. There was religious influence in elementary school—a Bible study in an off-campus trailer.

"Everyone was kind of expected to go, unless you were a Jew," John said. "If you weren't a Jew and you didn't go to Bible study, you were in big trouble."

John was one of those who "didn't go" and experienced the resulting ostracism and vindictiveness from other students. Their attitudes gave him no reason to want anything to do with the Bible or with Christianity.

John was home schooled at first, so he and his sister "kind of created our own world." He and his sister were "good" kids, so their parents left them to figure a lot of things out on their own. It was hard to fit in when they went to public elementary school, where social circles began forming in kindergarten. John's parents were not very involved, though they sympathized in the negative experiences and "helped me to cope" but not to become more integrated.

John wishes his parents would have accepted and introduced him to more of the general cultural stories, narratives that would give him clues for his behavior. John said the "permissiveness" of his parents was too extreme.

John engaged more closely with Christian narratives when he began part-time at the Mennonite college he has attended for several years. These narratives are gaining importance for him. He attends chapel regularly, "mainly because I felt like I was supposed to." He met people and began to hear theological discussions, although he "kept his mouth shut" for quite some time for fear of being called into dialogue. He came to see a quite different side of Christians and Christianity from what he had experienced in elementary school. "People were actually nice," he said.

John now realizes that his appreciation for Mennonites stems from the conservative Mennonite friends of his parents. "Religion never really came up, but I knew they went to church, and that they were friends of my parents. They weren't pushy, but they had their beliefs, and they weren't afraid to live them, even though it made their lifestyle quite different."

Now John goes to church every week, attends chapel regularly, prays "before mealtimes and in unstructured ways." He is intrigued by the ascetic orders, like Trappist monks he has heard about. He is interested in such a lifestyle, at least for a short while. He likes the monks' deliberate use of time.

John wants to be deliberate about interpersonal relationships, too. He sees them as having a purpose, and they move toward that purpose by getting past small talk and gossip.

He would like to see more respect for people regardless of their background. No matter where people have been, they deserve to be listened to. He would also like to see an increased respect for nature and the beauty of creation, and a recognition that we are not independent from it. He would like to see technology used critically and as a tool, not as an end in itself. We should be in control and define how we want to use technology, not see it as a must-have, he said.

John also values simplicity of lifestyle, stripping away what's unnecessary. He would relate all of the above elements to God, so that God is seen as active in all things, that God is the undercurrent and the overarching pattern to everything we do and experience. In a word, "holism." Spirituality should address life in its entirety, not just one specific sphere or one day of the week.

Journal Comments

This interview was a very pleasant experience. I was glad to be able to include someone who did not grow up in a Christian family. While we had known each other, the interview actually opened good opportunities for me to relate to John on a more extensive basis.

—*Aram DiGennaro*

Christina: Christina didn't have a TV until age ten, so TV wasn't a big source of narrative in early childhood. She remembers seeing a lot of Disney movies, like *The NeverEnding Story* and *Honey, I Shrunk the Kids*. At bedtime, her mother would tell her stories about growing up on her farm in a conservative Mennonite community. It was an interesting contrast to the city in which they lived. Her parents read Bible stories to her and books like The Chronicles of Narnia. Stories were given a big importance in her family and were told on a daily basis, usually before bedtime. Christina grew up as a missionary kid in a foreign country, surrounded also by people's stories of that land.

Christina values stories from her extended family about their family network and their younger years. These give her a sense of identity and show the imperfections of her family, which adds to her identity.

Christina reads the Bible every day, or every other day, especially since she's taking an Old Testament class right now in seminary. She currently finds her perspective shaped by academics, which provide her a new lens for reading Scripture. She thinks that Bible reading, which she had to do as a child, shapes who she is becoming, especially in understanding God's character. Christina thinks of the Bible as the most important book in her life.

Practices related to her faith include church involvement, times of quiet, journaling, and living in an intentional community. Prayer plays a significant role in her life. She is aware of conscious prayer three to four times a day, though she feels she is continually praying.

Christina would like to know more about a contemplative lifestyle, which would bring balance and wholeness to her life. She is very committed to and connected with her congregation of believers. She would like to revive the practice of spending Sunday with people, from the afternoon into the evening. Christina thinks this would promote an unhurried and free life.

She would like to see more times of silence in church life. She thinks there is more freedom in silence without definition or structure. And she would like to see her peers practicing more communal discernment. Individuals too often make decisions on their own, Christina thinks. People should share about life more with others.

A spirituality that appeals to Christina would have a balanced combination of contemplation and expressive faith.

Journal Comments

Christina's faith spoke to me, particularly because I share her appreciation for contemplative spirituality. She has a depth to her faith that seems quite rooted in solitude and meditation. Her prayer life reflects an awareness of God's presence at a variety of levels and a seamlessness of prayer throughout her day. She yearns for more silence and space in the modern church and has some reaction against the evangelical climate of her childhood.

She has a thoughtfulness and introspectiveness that she carries in a very calm and peaceful way. I intuit that she is exploring the silences of God and experiencing this presence pervasively through her life. She mentions wanting a slower lifestyle that takes time and space for intimate relationships and rest in God.

—Annie Lengacher

Interview Question

What practices would you like to see your peers taking seriously and doing more often?

Peter: Regarding practices his peers should take more seriously, Peter said: "More people should practice war-tax resistance." Peter would also like to see the church "responding to people in need when we see them, not just brushing past them and ignoring them; being aware of how we can use our privilege to pay more attention to people who are being taken advantage of. That's as much for myself as anyone else."

Known at his church for his love of vermicomposting, Peter added, "There should also be more composting."

Ajay: Ajay wishes that his peers would take nonviolence more seriously. "Not just nonviolence on a one-on-one basis, but also in the sense of how the government affects the people—how all of these things are connected. Not just looking at war in Iraq and saying it's because Saddam is such an evil man, but saying, 'Why did the U.S. really get involved; what was the reason?'"

Jessica: Jessica is concerned that her peers do not pay enough attention to basic practices such as attending church and praying, especially together. Both in her home and at the first college she attended, praying with friends became a natural and quite meaningful part of her life, but at her current college few people are at all open to this.

Will: When asked what practices he would like to see his peers do more of, Will mentioned prophesying and waging spiritual warfare. Will feels it's important to practice "all the spiritual gifts," and he feels that Mennonites his age usually completely ignore these, despite Paul's admonition to "seek the best gifts."

Will would like to see his peers "taking Scripture seriously" and be more engaged in evangelism. He does not feel the Bible is at all irrelevant but that we need to obey it more literally.

Eric: Eric would like to see his peers adopt a simpler lifestyle and make more conscious choices on how they spend money. He would also like to see his peers have an appreciation for the corporate side of worship and faith.

Hannah: Hannah would like to see her peers practice more hospitality outside the chummy college stage. And she would like them to learn to pray together and discuss intimate things, but there's no forum for this.

Hannah remarked that the "postcollege transition is ten times harder" than her college cross-cultural experience was for her. "Where's the preparation for that?" she asks. "All of a sudden we are faced with so many concrete decisions regarding lifestyle and occupation. I respect my friends who strive to live simply, but I also want respect for a personal decision to live a middle-class lifestyle."

"How do I now achieve community with my postcollege friends?" she wondered. "Lifestyle decisions now influence our times together more than during college. What does fellowship mean? My family always spent money on fellowship, such as going out to eat. Mennonites aren't comfortable with spending money to be with people. My family spent money on the arts: food, travel, film. This for us is fellowshipping. I get frustrated when a lifestyle choice is done at my expense or if I'm not treated with hospitality. I don't care what is served; I just appreciate the expression of hospitality."

Laura: Laura would like her friends to take the practices of sexual fidelity and simplicity of lifestyle more seriously. "I think it's easy to get caught up in the American dream of having money," she says. She also mentioned modesty.

"I'm amazed by clothing choices. I think that some people don't realize the negative effects clothing can have, and they're trying to get attention. They need to respect themselves."

Mike: Mike would like to see his peers valuing a spiritual relationship with God and also valuing some balance of social justice awareness and activism. He observed that so many of his peers have one or the other. Often social issues are taken on at the expense of the spiritual relationship with God or any form of evangelizing about one's faith, he said.

Rachel: Rachel would like to see her peers complimenting and encouraging each other more; listening more and talking less behind each other's backs; knowing the names of the cleaning people; living more simply and not doing things for the money.

She would like to see people relying more on the land and appreciating it and the seasons more. We lose touch with why it's raining and where our food comes from. She would also like to see people living together in communities and neighborhoods, not isolated in suburbia.

Amy: Amy would like her peers to be more committed to and involved in local congregations. She feels that young adults often are "lost" in the church during college years and soon afterward. It is hard to know where to fit in. She feels that churches could pay more attention to helping young adults find a place, but also that young adults could be more intentional about getting involved.

Amy would like her peers to be more intentional about adhering to Christian lifestyles rather than copying those of the people around them.

"Many times we get corrupted in how we dress, what we watch on TV," through the materialism around us, she said. She has chosen not to have a television and feels that this type of choice should be more common. "I think we need to stick out more, to show who we are, and stand up for what is right."

Interview Question

What are the features of a spirituality that would appeal to you?

Matt: Matt would want a spirituality that is genuine and full of integrity. He appreciates a spirituality that is holistic with God and people. He would stress community and care. Matt admires a steady spirituality, not stagnant. He's not very interested in charismatic spirituality.

Matt found that completing his voluntary service application helped him articulate his faith. One experience he had that relates to how he articulates his faith occurred in high school. A group of students began emphasizing a more fundamentalist, experiential, evangelical wing of Christianity and used a lot of "saving souls" language. Matt reacted strongly against that and found himself wary of the "hyperspiritual" language to describe faith.

Greg: Features of a spirituality that Greg values are humility, patience, lots of grace, not being a dogmatist. You "must be confident of where you're coming from. If you don't know where you're coming from, it's okay to be honest and share that with others."

Mark: A spirituality that would appeal to Mark would be gentle, loving, not pushy, not very evangelical. It would be built on listening with open communication and not being judgmental.

Jeff: Included in a spirituality that Jeff would find appealing were silence during worship. So often in worship services there is such a set agenda or a particular time crunch, and no time is left for reflection after a sermon or other important moments. It's easy to let it just wash over without being processed. More time is needed to process, both individually and with others after the service, either in homes or in a casual conversation time after the service.

Another spiritual feature Jeff emphasized is respect for others' experience and avoiding a prescriptive spirituality. Jeff also emphasized overall wellness, bringing attention to the mind-body split that so often occurs in understandings of spirituality. He longs for a more whole and integrated spirituality.

Mike: Features of a spirituality that appeals to Mike would include a balance between his mom's spirituality and his own current spirituality: a bridge between the evangelical literalist and the questioning soul.

Amy: A spirituality appealing to Amy includes generally "believing in Jesus and making that a part of your life." She believes this makes one's life much more meaningful and healthy, for one's self and for the community. She rejects traditional definitions of success. Having a decent job and a living wage is "okay," but not the driving to excel and get ahead.

Sherri: Sherri is not exactly sure what spirituality would appeal to her. But she would like more praise-and-worship songs, and wishes for young, energetic groups of people with whom to seek fellowship and encouragement.

Jason: Jason says he is not a spiritual person. No features of spirituality that he's tried have worked, and he's never really thought about what *would* work. He might possibly be interested in Buddhism. He doesn't know. He would like to do meditation and yoga because it would help him get away from everything for a bit and sit with his own thoughts. He wants to know more about Judaism for the knowledge, not to participate. Jason would like his peers to take new and alternate ways of living more seriously.

Mary: On spirituality Mary wonders, "How can you feel so close to something that is basically your imagination?" To say you've experienced God seems very unnatural, she thinks.

Eric: Eric would like a spirituality that stops and listens to God's voice and is reflective, a spirituality at a slower pace than what social life and work life demand.

Rachel: What are the features of an appealing spirituality? Less talk, more action, says Rachel. Beyond that, "I don't know. I have a lot to learn in life," she acknowledged.

What I Hear

What I hear most clearly, expressed in a multitude of ways, is a longing for the experience of a spirituality that invites us toward becoming whole. This is described as a longing to know God as active in all things and as the undercurrent and overarching pattern to all we do; to reconnect with nature;

to overcome a mind/body dualism by embracing life as an integrated whole; to experience a spirituality that is genuine, full of integrity, steady, humble, patient, full of grace, gentle, loving, not pushy. There is a wariness about "hyperspirituality." John summed up the longing apparent in these responses when he talked about a desire for spirituality that addresses life in its entirety, not just one specific sphere or one day of the week. He called it "holism."

Part 4
Vision for the Future Church

Chapter 23
What Do You Want in a Future Church?—I

"How will we ever know what God is?"

We now turn to the third and more future-oriented purpose of our conversation: imagining the future. Here young adults describe the stories and practices that should characterize communities of faith to which they might want to belong.

Alan Roxburgh, a prophetic voice on behalf of the languishing church in North America, talks about our widespread search for community. Many people, he observes, are concluding that the churches have nothing substantial to offer them. Yet many want to believe in something other than themselves. They want a compelling vision of life's wholeness, and they want to experience a transformational reality. Their search for community is a quest to heal their fragmented reality.

The church that has shaped its life around the needs of the individual has sold its birthright, he says. Instead, Christians must recover the biblical core of our identity as the people of God and a covenant people joined together in pilgrimage toward the wholeness and healing of creation in Christ. This recovery is central to the witness of the gospel.

Getting there is not so much about bringing the Word of God to the people, he says, as it is about finding the word among the people and bringing it forth. It's about showing hospitality to people who come to church looking for spiritual connection, about drinking coffee and going for walks together, about bringing our real stories into conversation with the biblical story. It's not about giving answers so much as it is about tasting, seeing, and exploring the connections. It's about joining together in spiritual practices of prayer, breaking bread, and caring for the poor. And as we are resocialized into the stories and practices of the gospel, we will rediscover the delight of a soulful community and a loving God.

The young adults we spoke with repeatedly talked of their longing for genuine connections in a community that welcomes their questions and invites them into a more transparent relationship with each other and with God.

Mary's story below offers an eloquent, poetic, and heartbreaking plea for more connection and for more genuineness in our communities of faith. We listen first to her, and then to the dreams and longings of others.

Mary

Mary remembers as a three-year-old realizing that her mom was a person within herself, not just a mom. After she would finish reading the bedtime story, her mom would wander downstairs and keep doing things, keep thinking things, keep being an individual. Mary realized that people are so much more than you ever knew and so much more than they could ever show you.

Mary loved *Anne of Green Gables* and identified with Anne's search for a kindred spirit. But Mary realized her own "gap between people" and wasn't quite as trusting as Anne.

Mary remembers that baptism happened for others at her church around the seventh grade. People were baptized as a class. Mary, however, declined and has not been baptized. There were too many questions she felt the church couldn't answer, especially regarding behavior and sexual boundaries.

Mary spent her childhood in a large city and in a rural area of the Midwest. She loved the city because she felt others were taking care of the world. She believed that if you stuck your head out the window and screamed, someone would come. In the rural Midwest, she felt suffocated.

Mary found attending church at times stressful. "We're all supposed to be very candid about our spirituality, and I didn't see how this was possible when we in the church knew so little about each other.

"There are questions I'm afraid to think about and confer about because their findings may turn everything upside down. Dealing with a mass religion is like walking through a huge bookshelf at a library and saying, 'I'm going to read all of them.' It's very overwhelming. Sometimes it's easier to ignore the issues and questions and go back to God as a 'controller.'"

Church life often felt disconnected and petty. Mary felt that the church's concerns—for example, whether to buy a dishwasher—were so much less than the big questions in her head. Yet she never spoke to anyone about those questions. She was intimidated by the largeness of many churches and felt that they were not good places to share differing viewpoints.

"Church feels very unproductive and lonely because you can never really converge or hear everyone's stories," Mary said. "We're all just going along in a parallel fashion with our own ideas rather than sharing and mixing and learning from each other's different beliefs."

There must be room for the latter in order for church to be a church, she asserts. "How will we ever know what God is if there's no close-knit group that meets?"

Mary relates more to an image from the work of poet William Blake than from anything she's heard in church. He claimed that God splintered, and pieces of God went everywhere and to everyone and everything.

She is also influenced by Emily Dickinson's later poetry, in which she writes of finally knowing God by feeling God's absence.

"God is not only presence," Mary said. "God is absence. And I know the absence, so I can more fully understand God. And that gives me goose bumps."

Mary says she has tried to go to church. She stepped into the foyer of one church but was overwhelmed by all the people. She would appreciate church community within a small-group setting. She didn't want that intimacy in college, but now she says she's digging up questions that might be answered in that setting. Mary does not belong to a congregation right now.

She would like to see more sincerity among her peers. She wants to be able to talk about things people believe in. This openness leads to practice and to a decision on going to church and participating in rituals.

Mary talked about post-structuralism, language games, post-Freudian feminism, and the ways that words mean different things to different people.

"A community needs to reflect reality," she said. "We have communities in the church that talk about God, but we also need to have communities that talk about *not* God. Right now, the people talking about the latter don't participate as equals. We need to find a common, safe language for discussing all parts of our personal stories within the church. To keep minds together, we must have room for all thoughts. But it's *hard*!"

Mary appreciates the Quaker practices of a group of people making decisions and taking time to discuss big questions within a small group. She would like in five years to regularly participate in a church that is challenging enough.

"I like the Mennonites," she said. "I don't think I'll ever not be Mennonite."

Journal Comments

Mary's voice spins pictures of childhood, of mortality, of a splintered God found in all persons, and of a relational community as a necessary result. Many themes surfaced, thanks to Mary's naturally poetic language and way of thinking. Mary knows the absence of God and thus knows that a God must exist in order to feel the absence of such a God. At times I found myself disturbed with her depressed focus on the morbid nature of so many aspects of this life. She shared about the sleepless nights and social phobias she tries to overcome that are a result of her mind's preoccupation with the weighty questions of a world that doesn't make sense to her. Mary wants answers to questions but has yet to find a safe environment in which to voice them. She longs for this in the church, but cynicism and fear of prescriptive narratives or trite answers keep her away.

I wonder where individuals like Mary will find themselves in the Mennonite church of the future, or if they will find themselves quite far away from it. I want to grant her peace, but her questions haunt me after she is gone. There's nothing simple about faith. Practices, too, are complex when they are broken down into questions of purpose and value. Light bulbs come on, voices alter, pauses manifest themselves into revelations or misgivings.

—*Melody King*

Interview Questions

Do you belong to a practicing congregation of believers? How would you describe your level of commitment at this point? What features of church life would you most like to see change for you to feel ownership and at home in a community of faith? What practices, if creatively and imaginatively retrieved, would add richness and meaning to life? What practices would you expect to regularly incorporate into your church life in order to construct meaning and build community?

Kate: Kate's a member of a Mennonite church in which she grew up. "But do I feel like that's my church? Not so much." She attended a Mennonite church while in college and now attends one in the city where she's in grad school.

Regarding her ideal congregation, she said, "This is hard. There's what I intellectually want, and what I know I need at this point for worshipping. Theoretically, I think it's very important to be in community with people of different backgrounds, places in life, life experiences, ethnicity, and age. Then you can come together and realize the enormity of God. But at the same time, I need hymns in four-part harmony and thoughtful sermons."

Kate emphasized that she'd like to hear sermons from many people in the congregation—not just the pastor, though the pastor would be there to provide context and background for the difficult stories in the Bible and the troubling aspects of faith.

She also appreciates the rituals of communion and foot washing. "Let's have communion every week. Forget that! Let's have meals together every week!"

Kate's struck by the words: "'Every time you break bread, every time you lift this cup . . .' This is a very spiritual thing that we do, eating together. Food is important to me, along with sharing food and eating something that someone else has made."

About foot washing, she said, "It's a physical reminder that you should be getting down on your knees, but also have someone get down on their knees for you—it's very powerful."

Kate anticipates a high level of church involvement for herself five years from now. At that point, she guesses she'll be finished with law school and working either for MCC or another nonprofit organization.

"I need accountability," she says. I ask her for what, and she jokes: "Oh, the drugs, Bethany. The drugs and the sex!"

Seriously, she says a church community will "help me recenter and figure out what my priorities are. The work that I do with my law degree could be a losing battle, helping to guide people through systems, helping to reform these systems. Some of the activist lawyers that I know—these people are not healthy. It's hard not to be cynical, not to hate the system, or not to make an idol of your work. I'm going to need perspective, and I want the church to help give me that perspective."

Journal Comments

In her ideal church, Kate wants to preserve the communal aspects that hold the most meaning for her—communion, foot washing, hymn-singing, shared teaching and preaching. She wants to leave behind things that are typically divisive or that leave people out of the community, such as rules about sexuality. She holds MCC in high regard, as well as her grandparents' work, and she seems to put higher value on living out faith than working through one's theology.

—Bethany Spicher

Peter: Peter was baptized at his home church in Virginia, but he now attends a house church in the city where he works. Peter's ideal church includes "people who are geographically close to each other, who come from a variety of backgrounds, but yet agree with me on everything. I'm kidding."

Peter emphasized that racial diversity reflecting the demographics of the area is important to him. "At our house church in the inner city, why are we all white except for the kids who are adopted?" Peter added that his ideal church would be "a church that's involved in the local and global community in terms of witnessing for what Jesus calls us to be, a church that has fun together, has good discussions, has potlucks, goes out to the woods from time to time."

Peter expressed some dissatisfaction with his current church experience, saying that it's difficult for him to establish deep relationships with the other members. "But I wouldn't want to start my own church. It's too much work. Maybe I'm lazy."

Journal comments

Peter is very aware of the privileges his race and class have brought him. He says he's never really had to work toward goals. He's always had enough resources. While he wants racial diversity in his ideal church, he wants everyone to agree with him. And I'm not entirely convinced he's kidding.

He longs to use his privilege to do good—along with a church community—but sometimes the injustice overwhelms and sometimes it just feels like "too much work." Since he has grown up in the church, he values practices that hold people together, such as regularly meeting for worship. But he's not quite fully engaged in his congregation at this point.

—Bethany Spicher

Jessica: Jessica would appreciate more contemporary worship. While she is growing to appreciate hymns, she misses this form, which for her is very meaningful. On the other hand, during a Taizé service, she experienced the mixture of solitude and corporate worship, the freedom from the familiar conflict of music styles, and the joy and intriguing lifestyle of the monks. It was very meaningful.

But for Jessica, church is not something that must change to fit her. Rather, she understands that fitting into a congregation is her responsibility. She has had to adapt to the hymn-singing congregations of the area where she currently lives, and this seems an acceptable price to pay for involvement. She maintains close ties with her home church in Ohio as well as a congregation in her college town. She serves on a worship team in both places and hopes that her level of involvement will continue to rise.

While congregational ministry may not be in her future, Jessica is quite interested in serving the church full-time, perhaps with some kind of writing assignment, or some conference-wide responsibility. Meanwhile, she continues to appreciate the narratives given to her as a child and hopes to continue their outworking in her own life.

Hannah: Hannah talked of her father, whom she called an incredible storyteller, relating farm stories. He grew up on a farm with four brothers. His father was a minister and a farmer. He's probably the person Hannah's dad respects most in his life. This is apparent through the stories told of his great character. One of grandfather's famous phrases was, "You go to church to serve, not to be served." This attitude shaped a mentality for viewing the church that Hannah still appreciates. For Hannah, hymns have been one of the main drawing cards for church. She's involved in a small group and some music, and she would expect in five years to be a more regular attendee than now.

Will: Will states that while church participation is one of his values, he is currently "not involved at all." He did say that he has superficial involvement with his girlfriend's youth group. He attends that church every other week and visits other churches in between.

In the future Will would like to be very involved in a congregation. His dream is traveling and relating to a number of congregations, but he thinks it is more likely in five years that he will be with a single church.

In a church of the future, Will would like to see "simple childlike obedience" to Scripture. He mentioned unity and thinks the emphasis should be on the kingdom of God rather than on the church. Will also stated that "the church should be more worldly," doing things that are life-giving to the whole community, not just "doing church stuff."

Sherri: Sherri would like to see groups more comfortable with talking about faith. She feels that the preacher preaches, then people socialize and go home. There are no deeper discussions about personal faith. Sherri believes that fellowship with people her own age is very important. She would like to attend a church with more young adults at a similar place in life with her. She wants to know what's really going on in others' lives. She's not interested in megachurches.

Greg: Greg tried being part of a small group as an intentional place to talk about questions and concerns with peers in a more intimate setting. It's not happening as regularly as he prefers. In the future, he would like to attend church in the community where he lives.

In general, Greg "leans heavily toward tradition." He sees many things in the Mennonite church today that show greater assimilation to the mass culture. As an example, he offered permissiveness regarding foot washing, letting anyone participate, as opposed to the traditional view of seeking some accountability before people could take part in the practice. This leads to a decreased level of intimacy within the church, Greg thinks.

He sees people looking to books for direction and manipulating biblical language. It "seems like we want more of a show, want to go to church and have a staged experience of God. Jesus did very simple things with his disciples."

Greg wonders how the church will address each person's personal story, which he says is important to gaining and understanding of one's self.

He wishes there were more rituals to make church feel less like a spectator sport. He thinks a strength of the early Anabaptist church were die-hard practices that necessitated a level of intimacy among a group of believers. He commented, "If your whole tradition is four-part harmony and now everybody wants a praise band, what do you have left?"

Greg wondered how we might modernize the ancient practice of fasting. One possible way: no fast food. He reflected on breaking bread, which he sees as a way to bridge the gap between each other, not necessarily just "saints with saints." Greg sees "breaking bread" in itself as a way to witness.

John: When John thinks of what he would like to experience in a future church, he mentioned having contact with the community on more than one day of the week. He now goes to church regularly every week. He would like to have people within the community "who will ask me hard questions" and hold him accountable. John would hope for a community that addresses true needs, not just felt needs.

Ben: Ben would like church to be more than a Sunday morning event. Churches should offer their building to be used by the community. Members should ideally be together more. The church should place more concern on community and service, and less on getting doctrinal issues exactly right.

Amy: Amy would like the church to offer more accountability and support. Often young adults are able to lead whatever kind of lifestyle they want, and no one will confront them, she said. "Many times we make assumptions about where people are before God." Or young adults may go through a period of struggle or difficulty, and no one will ask them about it or offer to help.

"We need to know we are not alone in failure, but that we can work through it together."

Regarding worship, she said she wouldn't change much, but "I like variety a lot." She would like more often to see variation in worship formats.

Dave: Dave was commissioned by his home church to do voluntary service, but he isn't very involved in any church right now. He expects greater involvement in five years.

Dave would like to see the church have a little less ethnic-Mennonite focus and more grace for each other.

"We're drawing too many lines," he said. "Let's agree to disagree more often.

We should put more focus on the basics that we have in common."

Dave wishes his peers would go to church more regularly and talk more seriously about faith with one another.

"We get caught up in living life without being intentional in our choices. We become too busy individually and don't spend enough time together as a congregation. We should have smaller congregations." Dave wants the church to be small, friendly, and intimate, and to include retreats, communion, and lots of sharing time for open and really honest sharing about struggle in life's journey.

Jeff: When asked about faith-based practices he would like more of in his life, Jeff immediately thought of the Taizé services that take place monthly at the church he attends. After these services, he is left with a sense of calm and collection and feels better able to handle challenges. He feels that more of these would lead to better decision making and greater clarity as he goes about discerning parts of his life.

Jeff attends a local Mennonite congregation. This year he is becoming more involved as a part of two committees. However, he realizes that while in school, he chooses to give priority to classes and work, which take a lot of time and energy and make it difficult for him to become involved in a congregation.

He sees himself giving more time and money to the church in five or so years, when his time commitments and priorities shift. His lack of involvement thus far has more to do with time commitments than it does with dissatisfaction with the church. Other than wanting more open-mindedness in the conference of which his congregation is a part, Jeff is "rather satisfied with the current church."

Jeff does hope to see more young-adult involvement in the church. He believes it is a part of a healthy lifestyle—physically, psychologically, and spiritually—that he hopes all his peers can find. He did not wish to specify any particular practices that he thought might be helpful to the church as a whole to incorporate or emphasize. "Different practices suit different people." But speaking for himself, he mentioned wanting to continue to emphasize the practices of eating together with family and church members, helping each other, using our individual gifts, and participating in small groups within the larger congregation.

Eric: Eric regularly attends a congregation and is considering transferring his membership. Eric would enjoy seeing foot washing revived. He finds that it speaks loudly and powerfully. He would also like to see more regular gatherings of the church body beyond once a week. He feels that this would cultivate a greater feeling of community. Eric would like to see the church more accepting of diverse viewpoints and have greater transparency and openness.

Craig: Craig suggests that churches could do more to acknowledge the complexity of the world and the issues of faith about which Christianity makes claims. They make it look too simple, paint over incongruities, rather like "the public relations world" does. Unfortunately, people in the church who have questions about Christianity's truth claims can feel that they don't fit in, or that their perspectives are not valid.

Craig sees his spiritual understandings as something of a "roller-coaster" and would like to have the difficulty of his journey acknowledged or even affirmed by the church.

Renee: Renee attends a church regularly and exhibits what she feels is more than average commitment. She would get more involved, but she knows she'll be leaving in two years.

Renee would like to see her peers living more intentionally in community, depending on each other more, eating more meals together. She wants them to talk more about how to be a Christian in the world, "how to live counterculturally, how to live ethically and responsibly." Renee wants them to talk about how to be more inclusive of people from other cultures, races, and socioeconomic backgrounds, and to spend time with people of other religions. She wants them to talk about money.

She would like to see discipleship programs that encourage intergenerational relationships. She favors reviving a greater use of liturgy and rituals, something her current church does rather well.

Renee desires more time for sharing about lives in the community. She would like smaller congregations and a greater inclusion of all people, regardless of where they are. She is not sure how "truth-telling"—confronting one another on places where we think the other is wrong—should happen within a community. Perhaps confronting one another one-on-one and then following the pattern outlined in Scripture would be best, she thinks.

Renee sees herself being just as committed to church in five years, maybe a little more. But until she knows she can commit long-term, she doesn't want to become too "entrenched."

Laura: Laura is quite committed to her church but would like to see some changes. The church members should show more vulnerability, be better at sharing with one another, and show greater acceptance of each another.

She also commented that the church should take firm stands on issues and not be "wishy-washy." She mentioned in particular the issue of homosexuality. People try to please every side, she said, but there are absolutes.

Laura would expect her involvement in the church to look very different five years from now because she will probably be overseas. She expects to be supported by the church here, but she would not necessarily be part of a formal church there. She does hope to meet regularly with other missionaries.

Mike: Mike said that he attends church regularly and leads hymns once a month. He'd like to see more organization in church life. His current church feels very unplanned and unpolished at times. He would appreciate more structure. Mike attended a liturgical Methodist church during his first couple years of college and liked its structure.

One feature of church that he appreciates is the sermon response time, which gives the congregation an opportunity to be honest, vulnerable, real. He loves how this time lets you "feel everyone" in the congregation. He appreciates the hymns and the silent times. This slow pace of resting is a comfort in contrast to the evangelical, charismatic church that his mom currently attends, where drums and other instruments are played. He feels like he has to psych himself up for that worship experience. But at his own church, he can just come and rest and worship.

Five years from now he could see himself involved in committees, still leading hymns, and perhaps serving as an elder.

Rachel: Rachel is still a member at her home church. She attends a church in the city where she now lives when she can, though it is rare because of work. She would love to go more and be more involved if she had more time available.

Rachel would like the church to include people from diverse backgrounds worshipping together and integrating diverse practices such as dance. She likes that she can knit in the church she currently attends. She would prefer that the church avoided internal bickering and church politics, and she'd like to see less money spent on logistics, aesthetics, and buildings. In five years she hopes to be much more involved in the church than she is now.

What I Hear

I am animated by the vision to which young adults call us. They challenge us to move toward a more sincere, real, honest, and intimate way of being in community and in relationship. This rich resource sparks fresh energy and spurs us on to imagine new possibilities of being church. Over and over, these young adults described their desire for small, close-knit circles where they feel free to establish deep and trusting relationships. With all of their questions, failures, love for fun, potlucks, hymn singing, and storytelling, they want to be themselves and be accepted for who they really are.

I think Mary's observations sum it up well: "A community needs to reflect reality. We have communities in the church that talk about God, but we also need to have communities that talk about *not* God. Right now, the people talking about the latter don't participate as equals. We need to find a common, safe language for discussing all parts of our personal stories within the church." This openness leads to practice and to a decision: we can go to church; we can participate in rituals. "I would like to see more of church," Mary said. "At least a relational church. How will we ever know what God is if there's no close-knit group that meets?"

Chapter 24
What Do You Want in a Future Church?—II
(Group Interview)

"A place to be real in faith"

Most of the young adults who talked with us about the future of the church are calling for significant changes to be made. They want the church to continue because of all the "good stuff." But it must be open to change.

North American culture, including the churches, are in the midst of massive change, Alan Roxburgh observes, a kind of epochal change precipitated by factors like rapid technological innovation, globalization, pluralism as a way of life, staggering human need, ever-present entertainment, and a postmodern reassessment of what it means to know "the truth."

Change, Roxburgh says, is what happens to us. But transition is our inner response to change, and he has a lot to say about how to manage the transition. His suggestions include learning to "let go" of the old world and of the myths of the modern one.

Several of those myths come quickly to mind: an unbridled confidence in reason and progress; that science is the arbiter of everything; that the supernatural can't be known or trusted; that our bodies, minds, and spirits are disconnected and not of equal value; that the individual is the center of the universe; that all value is reduced to an economic calculation about its worth to me; that the gospel is a code of ethics, and saving souls is its primary goal; that unless the Bible is proven to be 100 percent scientifically and historically accurate, the whole thing collapses; that church is made up of people who've got it all figured out; that Christianity owns God.

Letting go of these myths may seem easy, but we are infected by them more than we know, Roxburgh says. We cannot move on, he asserts, until we identify and cure that infection, which will be a messy, painful process of dislocation.

We are now in the midst of tumultuous change, and we know that the church must transition in order to journey with us. It seems to me that this is what these young adults are calling for.

Following up on the individual interviews about hopes for the future church, we focused some questions more directly for the group interviews. Responses are below. But first, we consider Tom's story. He has struggled mightily with transitions in his own life and yet is finding ways to offer leadership in his congregation.

Tom

Tom has many stories from his childhood experience as a missionary kid in Germany, where he attended public schools. He remembers his family being the only Mennonites in town. He saw his parents take part in evangelistic crusades and street evangelism, and watched neighbors come to know Christ. As a missionary pastor's kid, he didn't have many friends and tended to isolate himself from others.

Being a missionary family had good and bad aspects for Tom's family life. He recalls that the family had to be close, especially since most of the people around them didn't speak English. At other times, family life suffered because of people coming to their door at midnight, seeking help.

Tom returned to the United States and completed high school in a Mennonite school. His only friend that year was another missionary kid. He said the other kids seemed to be a huge clique.

A definitive point for Tom was when he attended one of the Mennonite Youth Conventions. For the first time he saw the larger Mennonite church and was impressed by the challenges, calls, and speakers. "It was a cool picture of the church that I hadn't seen before."

Tom talks of how he struggled with many things throughout his life. In fact, he calls it "the Struggle." Issues of faith, family, and a communal balance seem to be the prominent themes in his struggles.

After high school Tom signed up to be part of Youth Evangelism Service (YES). He didn't quite know where he wanted to go, but the option to go to Hong Kong kept coming to mind. After praying about it, he signed up. YES initially didn't want him to go to Hong Kong because the trip was booked. But Tom insisted that it was the only option to which he felt God was calling him, and so he went.

Tom found Hong Kong to be quite exotic but also spiritually challenging. He came back to the United States frustrated with the experience and "torn up," he said. He then went to a Mennonite college to "fill some time." He was asked to be a ministry assistant and to help lead a worship experience on Sunday nights at the college. Tom seemed to latch on to leading worship, claiming it as something he really enjoys. He did it at school, in church, and during the summers while working at camp. He says that while leading worship, you "learn to give up."

Tom is very committed to his local Mennonite church. He says he'd like to be more committed, but his school schedule doesn't allow it. He is often a music worship leader during the Sunday morning worship. He also is very involved in young-adult Sunday school and is a leader in the young-adult Bible study. Tom wants to be committed, "no matter what." "God wants me to be there," he said.

He wants a church where ideally he can be himself and worship in a way that is comfortable, and he wants the same for others. He wishes for church to be an uplifting event rather than awkward, building up the community. He sees the church as a place that only survives when there is community. "People's attitudes sometimes get in the way, but I trust God to bring growth even in bad times."

Tom would like to see young adults in the church more involved in each others' lives, discipling one another, praying more, and exercising accountability and healthy challenges. Healthy confrontation is something that he sees missing from the church. Tom feels that our society is too busy, so we neglect each other. The church also needs to be pointing out people's gifts and be more open about what it means to worship. For Tom, worship is "where God speaks to us through another, where we express kingdom living, a place where we experience our gifts, and a place to be real in faith."

Tom thinks that he will move from the area in the next five to ten years. He has a vision of a little country church someplace where the people are real and down to earth. He'd like to be involved in worship and leading Bible studies or simply just visiting people. "There are lots of victories by getting to know people."

Journal Comments

Tom is still searching for answers to some of his faith questions. But at the heart of it all, his desire is to follow God. I think many young adults are searching for a church that is different from their parents' churches. There are vestiges of the past they want to hold on to, but there is a desire to try to make it more "real," not just a ritual but a daily life-affirming practice.

Tom is an interesting case. He almost resents his missionary upbringing and numerous times hinted about moving away from it. But he seems to be drawn back to it again and again, going to Hong Kong, working in the public schools, going to find a rural community where he can help out. Hong Kong seemed to be a bad experience for him, and mission work didn't seem to be where God was calling him. Is he still exploring whether God is really saying that missions are not for him?

—*Nate Barker*

Group Interview Questions

Young adults yearn for many things when it comes to community or church life. After I read you several quotes from what respondents said in the other interviews, tell me what you would most like to see more of in the church? What are one or more things a church could do to help you feel ownership and at home?

Derek: "More focus on our common denominator, which is Jesus. I'm really distraught by the fact that on this [college] campus alone there is so much friction. We need more of a focus on Jesus. That is our commonality."

Rose: "More focus on what faith actually is and less on tradition. This is one of the reasons we left the Mennonite church back home; they kept doing the same thing over and over, and it didn't attract anybody. The church wanted people to come, but they wanted to do what they were comfortable with. I want people to be more honest, more real, and I want that to be okay even though it's more risky."

Phil: "I'd like to see more humility. In general, that has a lot to do with the judgmental attitudes that sometimes come out of the church, the lack of honesty and all that. Church should be a community that can listen to each other and put the issues of the world aside, prideful arrogance and all that, and come together as fellow servants of Christ. There is a lot of pride and arrogance in the church, not just on an individual level but also in terms of beliefs. This has a lot to do with what I talked about before about missions and the link to hospitality."

Rose: "It's funny because this conversation makes me realize how passionate I really am about the church. It's easy for me to grow cynical."

Derek: "The church is a voluntary community. Membership seems to oppose that idea. It's set up to safeguard against people coming in and going out. When we are baptized, we need better teaching. We need to hear the stories about people who wanted to follow Jesus and then follow as a community, less as an institution."

Rose: "I would disagree. There's something to be said about commitments. And at their best, institutions are the vessels for what's important. Really powerful things have happened within structures."

Derek: "How will people feel more at home and feel greater ownership? Give people responsibility, find committees, and give people a job to do. That's why the church I am at is growing. When people come they are immediately given something to do, and that promotes a sense of ownership. People come because they are able to contribute."

Rose: "And out of gifts, not obligation. It's not involving youth to have one fourteen-year-old read Scripture on Sunday. That's not calling young people into ministry."

Anita: "The church definitely needs to give young people more to do."

Phil: "And old people."

Derek: "I agree. Sometimes the old people are even more left out by all the changing worship styles."

ॐ ॐ ॐ

Ellen: "I like to be plugged in. I like when people take an interest in me, invite me to their homes. That's what gives me a sense of, 'Oh, I belong here. They want me here.'"

Ken: "This question really gets at the heart of part of what I do in working with young adults at church. Invitations are good, but I think the church goes on a rampage with that. We have committees, and we want to fill these committees with young adults. 'Get in here, get in here.' It can be overwhelming. The effort to include people has to be authentic." ["Yes, authentic," echoes around the circle.]

Jennifer: "I want to observe for a while. I don't want any of that fakery 'Welcome to our church!' And then, after a while, I want people to be totally welcoming. I want to be asked to do things, but I want it to be okay if I don't do it. I recognize that I'm a total nightmare. There's no formula for making me feel welcome. Authenticity is big. I don't want cheesy, surfacy stuff. Large events are overwhelming. I need safe spaces to get to know people."

Karla: "Consistency matters to me. A lot of people have had negative experiences because of inconsistency and human failure. If we're going to say the Bible is the foundation of our faith, let's talk about what the Bible has to say about sexuality or money or war, and live that out, not just live out what you think is going to work for your life. I have visited lots of churches, for example, where their stance on war does not line up with the way I view what the Bible says."

Ellen: "I want a church that asks hard questions, that doesn't let me be a passive member. This relates to having deeper relationships—getting beyond the surfacy stuff to listen to one another's struggles and challenge each other, but not in an attacking way."

᥉ ᥉ ᥉

Margo: "I think my direct community is my friends here at school. One thing that draws me to my church back home is that sense of community—cooking together, eating together, talking and sharing our lives. I especially experience God through the relating that I do to those groups of people."

Greta: "I'm drawn to freedom in worship. Freedom to move and express yourself openly."

Curt: "I agree with Greta. I would like to see arts and creativity, not just music: painting and pottery, too."

Al: "How about hiring full-time worship and music ministers? We need to be putting our money where our mouth is. If we truly believe in something strongly, then we need to take action. And this doesn't just mean music, but expressing the importance of God's reign in all aspects of our lives, having church life and spirituality involved with all of our lives, not just on Sunday and not just in meetings."

Margo: "And accountability. If we are going off track, I want people watching out for me and being willing to call me back."

Curt: "Amen."

Josh: "Being a musician—where I grew up it is hard to survive as a musician. My brother was kicked out of the church for being in a band. It is not accepted. I would like to see more of the arts and have that be accepted."

Don: "I would like to see more diversity in North American Mennonitism. I want to see more accountability with stewardship, especially for those of us who are wealthy relative to the majority of the world. Maybe 10 percent [giving] is not enough."

Al: "Something that I have heard and felt is the need for mentoring within the church for people our age. [We want] people who would walk alongside us. For how mobile we are, it is hard to have the rootedness we need. So, to have a spiritual director or mentor is really important. That would be great. To set up a system like that would be a good asset for the Mennonite church and for its future."

Curt: "I agree. And I like the word discipleship. We need opportunities to feed people who are spiritually hungry. I mean, how many young believers are prayed for on a regular basis? It's all part of that discipling thing, and it needs to be more intentionally done for people our age."

Don: "I agree. As kids, we are supported. We are expected to grow up and then be MYF (Mennonite Youth Fellowship) leaders. But we still need to be growing! As a young adult, I would like to have a spiritual director and other forms of accountability. We need continued input. We are going off to places where a lot of change is taking place and we have to do a lot of growing, and I don't want to feel like I'm doing that on my own. I need some direction."

Curt: "Another name for that aspect of direction could be spiritual parenting. This brings in the aspect of intimacy—the love of a parent but also the discipline."

Don: "But I would also like to challenge and question the mentor or older person too. Help them question in their own journey, so it can be a mutual thing."

Al: "And I would like to take some ownership there too."

Greta: "I was at the GYS (Global Youth Summit) in Zimbabwe. Worldwide, there is a hunger for mentorship, and that is one thing that they said to the council people. If they are going to raise up young people, it would be good to have the mentors to help with that. We need to know what the responsibilities of leadership roles are going to be and how to be involved. Also, [leaders need to be] making things available and encouraging people to take roles within the church. The church doesn't really have things for young adults. When I am at home, I feel like I am floating."

Don: "We are displaced. Until we have kids or are married, we have no identity, and it is hard to connect to our churches."

Greta: "There could be more integration between generations. So even if there is no Sunday school class for young adults, someone should invite me to another class. Don't just let me drift away and do my own thing. It's a thing of invitation as much as program."

Don: "Have you ever been in an intergenerational Sunday school class? I am interested in that."

Greta: "There needs to be recognition and welcoming for young adults coming back from different experiences, along with help in being reintegrated into the life of the church."

Don: "I was fortunate to have the welcoming when I was in Charlottesville. It was a church of forty people, and as soon as I came in, it was like, 'Hey, do you want to be worship leader?' The offer was there right away, and that is cool. It helped me feel appreciated and connected."

Greta: "If we did bring that stuff up to the church, how would the church respond?"

～～～

Linda: "I want mutual accountability and support. It would be cool to have more young people in leadership. It would be nice to have more connection with the larger community. It's easy to become wrapped up in your own Mennonite community, your own building. I'd like to see the church making more connections with the larger, local community on a personal level, outside the Mennonite church."

Tara: "I'd like to see more interaction between members. The bigger the church gets, the more you can overlook people and just blend in. I wish more youth would be involved and more interested in church. Waking up on a Sunday morning [and] thinking about going to church isn't the most pleasant thought."

Ray: "I agree with the more interaction idea."

Tara: "And giving people more responsibilities, that would be welcome. But not everyone's gift is up front. I enjoy helping with potlucks, food. It's a daunting thought to give time to church, but in reality it's not that much time. Mentoring relationships would help!"

Linda: "I would like to see more young-adult leadership and participation in the church, older leaders involving younger persons in the congregation, such as helping out with Sunday school or reading Scripture. We should be tithing our time to church. If people invited us over for dinner, that would help. But that hardly ever happens anymore."

Ray: "I would like a church to have no paid leaders. Somehow that would show that everyone wanted to be there to make church happen. It is a turnoff when the life of the church isn't a priority, maybe because it shows me something about myself. I would also want to see more young adults involved in church, [with leaders] noticing what gifts young adults have and calling them out. I wish for a church that emphasizes the continuity across the centuries, which would help to bring unity to a very scattered and fragmented church.

"If I were to start a church geared toward young adults, I wouldn't meet on Sunday mornings. Not because we're lazy. Young adults are just geared toward evening things."

❧ ❧ ❧

Beth: "I would just like being part of a group on days other than Sunday with meals or Wednesday night Bible studies. I wouldn't even need involvement in service; just involvement with people."

Tim: "The church we attend is mostly students. That's kinda hard. I want more community too. More young adults and kids for our child would be nice. I want a range of ages, to be more a part of something that feels more like a community."

Michelle: "The church needs to be accepting. Churches tend to be homogeneous. They need to pay more attention to the younger people in church. For me to stick around and stay there, it would help if church members would seek to get to know me. Now they don't know anything about my family or where I come from."

James: "The church needs more realism and fun. They could take a Polaroid picture of me and put it up on the bulletin board. I admit, there are some Sundays I want to be left alone, but some weeks I think, 'Oh, they're cold,' because I got exactly what I wanted."

❧ ❧ ❧

Aaron: "I like the suggestion about going out to the woods together. I grew up in a suburban church. I don't remember seeing much outreach there. They would give their time sometimes to other organizations, but I would like to see things like barbecues on the church lawn and inviting the community, just to hang out together, without expectations."

Ann: "My job is quite stressful and involves interacting with people all the time. It would be nice to be able to go to church and just feel like I could rest there on a Sunday morning. At the same time I want a church that's engaging, listens to and talks about many views, and is open to questions."

Conrad: "I look at my parents' church and see a tight connection between groups of people, especially people of similar age-groups. That gives them more of a motivation to go to church on Sunday morning, to catch up with each other. I think this happens within our church, but more happens outside the church walls. It feels like a separate thing."

Sarah: "I would like to see more understanding between rural and urban churches, more of an understanding of how the place where we live affects how we see the church and how we see our faith. More rural/suburban churches need to come into the city—not to change it or see it as their mission field, but just to understand it. I desire for the broader church to be more open to the urban church as a reality, a true part of the Mennonite church.

The Mennonite church is not just made up of those rural/suburban centers like Harrisonburg, Lancaster, and so on. We [in the city] are a real piece, too. Thus, there needs to be more communication and understanding between these realities. I feel this for my own personal life—trying to convince others from my home community that my home here in Philly isn't just a temporary stint—it's my life. And I feel pretty at home in my church. No church is perfect."

Aaron: "I think, too, rural/suburban churches need to recognize that there has been a change in the church. The urban church is different."

Andy: "I'd like to see more self-examination: 'What are our core beliefs?' What do we keep coming back to every Sunday? And [we need] more of an application of Jesus and his teachings and what that means for our church. We are a redeemed people, and that turns everything upside down. How could I feel more at home? I want people to be shaken up. I want people to be friendly, invite me to their house, ask me to participate in things. I like a church to be transparent, so people know what the church is standing for."

What I Hear

The clear word coming through from many of these young adults is that the church must make a more intentional effort to welcome their energy, their gifts, and their leadership. They're not interested in being the recipients of a fake "Welcome to our church!" campaign. But it is evident in the comments above that these young adults are eager for invitations to our dinner tables and invitations to plug into church life, to be recognized and appreciated for their manifold gifts, and to receive guidance and support as they find authentic ways to contribute. To put it bluntly, in their own words: "The church definitely needs to give young adults more to do." It would be "cool" to have more young adults in leadership.

In Tom's vision for the church, worship is a strong theme. His description of worship summarizes well the visions for church expressed by many of his peers. Worship is "where God speaks to us through another, where we express kingdom living, a place where we experience our gifts, and a place to be real in faith."

Chapter 25
Should the Mennonite Church Continue to Exist?
(Group Interview)

"The church becomes your family"

When our team talked about what we were hearing following the first round of interviews, we observed that perhaps we were assuming too much about these young adults and their interest in the church's future. Perhaps they, like some of us, take the church for granted and assume it will be there whether or not they invest in its future.

We decided to ask a prior question, one we hadn't asked in the first round of interviews: Should the Mennonite church continue to exist past this present generation? Why or why not?

Before considering answers from the group interviews, we pick up an excerpt from Miguel's story, which relates to the future of the Mennonite church.

Miguel

Miguel went to a Mennonite college for his junior and senior years. "I loaded up my white Mitsubishi truck with high school memorabilia and pictures of my family—no insurance, no money."

Miguel describes the experience of walking into his first class on nature writers like John Muir, Terry Tempest Williams, and Annie Dillard.

"I was so scared. I did not know what the heck they were talking about. I was coming from a completely different world. [But when I got to school] All the kids were white, all of them had read C. S. Lewis as kids."

While at college, Miguel became involved in antiracism activism on campus. His college had a student body that was 20 percent people of color, and a faculty that was 95 percent white. After college, MCC aggressively recruited him to direct work in his home area.

"I'm still trying to figure out what it means to be Chicano and Mennonite. The literature is all about Catholics. But I live it with them as they tell the story. Spiritually, we were there all along."

Miguel and his wife, Anna, have been talking about the Catholic tradition of *padrinos*, godparents, and how they don't want their children to miss out on that tradition. As Anabaptists, not practicing infant baptism, they might invite witnesses to the child's dedication.

"We want to reinterpret those rituals and traditions to fit the context of where we are," Miguel said. "To bring them into our story. If we bring these together, there's a clearer understanding of who we are in God."

Miguel wishes his churches would take his ethnicity more seriously and "find healthy ways to incorporate our story as Mexican-Americans. I watch the way we make the disconnect when we're in the church service. During that time, it becomes this personal relationship with God. The culture's very alive in our rituals, food, talk, issues—where does the disconnect happen that we don't feel that the communal story can be shared in that [worship] time?"

Miguel wants his community to "define what it means to be a community of faith on the border."

When asked what he thinks the churches in his area can teach the larger church, he said: "I think of struggle right away. The larger Mennonite church has gone through its own struggles. Maybe it has forgotten about that. It needs to be true to its history of colonization, to its first contact with Mexicans. A lot of the stories of Mexican-Americans who are Mennonites have not been told. When *The Mennonite* did a feature on the most influential Mennonites in the twentieth century, there was not one Mexican-American, yet people of Mexican descent were the first ones to start the Hispanic church movement. That story itself has been marginalized."

In addition, Miguel wishes the larger church could learn from "the way we work here on the border across cultures, the level of relationship that is formed across the border here." Finally, he believes a strength of the border churches is that "the church becomes your family."

Journal Comments

Even though he's "enlightened," educated, and reading Marcus Borg, Miguel still has a profound love for the church traditions, a deep respect for his elders. He loves to hear sermons he disagrees with, singing that's not in tune, admonition from *los hermanos y las hermanas*. Even though he wants his church to change, he believes they have much to teach the northern, white affluent churches; he's not afraid to challenge injustice and ignorance wherever he sees it.

Miguel has lots of responsibility, which makes him different than my other interviewees. One year older than me, and he's a church leader—preaching sermons, teaching youth, serving on boards, working with MCC, negotiating painful and difficult antiracism processes in his region. I really wanted Miguel's voice in these interviews. I have a feeling that at the end of this century, his face will be on the cover of *The Mennonite* as one of the most influential Anabaptists of the 2000s.

—*Bethany Spicher*

Group Interview Questions

As you reflect on your relationship with the Mennonite community and how much it matters to you, listen to comments from other young adults. These comments show how people have different ideas about what it means to be Mennonite. In your view, should the Mennonite church continue to exist past this present generation? Why or why not?

Jennifer: "I feel some connection to Mennonitism. I spent many years trying to grind away that connection. Now I'm trying to reconnect. I feel responsible to be as honest as possible, to offer openness about who I am in order to change or help to shape the church. I offer myself as I am."

Lisa: "Yes, I think the Mennonite church should continue to exist, which is funny because I hardly ever go to church. It is kind of like how I relate to cell phones. I'm pretty anti-cell phone generally, but I appreciate when other people have cell phones. I want the church to continue in the same way I want people to continue to have cell phones. I call myself an 'ethnic' Mennonite as opposed to a 'religious' Mennonite. Ethnic food is something I value about Mennonites."

Ken: "Yes, I think the Mennonite church should continue. I think of a book like [John Shelby Spong's] *Why Christianity Must Change or Die*. The structures need to change. The church must change to continue. And it should continue because there is good stuff there. While it might not apply, let's not throw the baby out with the bathwater. The good: peace, service, foot washing, male leadership [lots of laughter]. Also, community is a strength. And we are globally minded. We have to expand our definition of community to be more international. I think you can continue to teach certain principles within the global community and not indoctrinate others."

Jennifer: "Yes, I think the Mennonite church should continue. In the last couple years, I have been drawn back to some form of spirituality. I think that the Mennonite church I'm involved in has offered me a kind of spirituality that is open. . . . I guess if my Mennonite church ceased to exist, I'd be left with either having to go to a random Christian church, kind of the lowest-common denominator, agreeing-on-the-basics kind of church, which wouldn't work for me. The Mennonite church offers something besides the standard evangelical American pop Christianity."

Ellen: "Yes, I think the Mennonite church should continue. My identity is in it. I want it to continue for those selfish reasons. Also, in studying other religions, the Mennonite church does have a role to play. It should always continue, open to the changes that come and confront the church, open to discussion. What it has to offer is this: incredible community, insight about an alternative way of living and seeing the world and interacting with people you have nothing in common with on the surface, a Christian faith with love at the front of its teachings rather than just the foundation."

Lisa: "I agree with a lot of the positive things mentioned, about what the Mennonite church has to offer. But I have had some incredibly negative experiences in the Mennonite community. Terrible things happened within my Mennonite college community. These things shattered my idea of community in general because if Mennonites can't do community, nobody can do community. My grandfather was president of a seminary for twenty-five years. My aunt was shunned for getting pregnant and was forced to marry. The Mennonite church has not always been accepting and open. I hesitate to latch on to the Mennonite world because of those things."

Karla: "This is a hard question. This has been my identity question all my life. I grew up out of the States until eighth grade and then came back and chose to go to an all-Mennonite high school. It was a major culture shock after Africa. Then I purposely chose a nondenominational university for college because I wanted to be in the midst of a Christian community, but I wanted to see how other Christians worshipped, and so on. Being in Africa, I was never socialized as a Mennonite.

"Mennonites—we mix our cultural background with our religious belief. So being Mennonite is no longer believing in Jesus Christ, but it's having a

Mennonite cookbook and going to MCC relief sales. I have wrestled with what it means to be Mennonite. Ultimately, our identity is first Christian, and then Mennonite.

"Each denomination has strengths and weaknesses. Mennonites have strengths: peace and justice, social conscience, people wanting to be involved with the poorest, most marginalized, a humble, simple way of life. One I would add: the call to discipleship. Other denominations would say it's vertical: it's me and God, a personal relationship with Christ. Mennonites are more horizontal. What does that mean for our money? What does it mean for my job next year? Faith plays into everything. *But* we lose focus on the vertical. We forget that Jesus is the foundation.

"I would claim being a Mennonite. We need to cling on to our religious beliefs, not [just] cultural [matters], if the church is going to continue. That's why the international church is so important."

Ellen: "We shouldn't lose the Mennonite culture. Those who define themselves culturally as Mennonites have a role to play even if they don't believe. *And* we have to open our community to other cultures of Mennonites as well. I don't think we should focus 100 percent on either culture or religious faith."

Karla: "I'm not trying to say we should lose the culture. But when the culture becomes a hindrance for new members, to the growth of the Mennonite church, it becomes a problem."

Ellen: "I agree."

Jennifer: "We should recognize the culture as valuable, just as we value any other culture. Valuing culture as its own thing but recognizing it's not the *only* thing."

Ellen: "And the Mennonite culture can also incorporate the community as it broadens. Now at some Mennonite churches, we still have potlucks, but they're becoming international."

Jennifer: "Yeah! That's cool!"

Ellen: "I think it's a goal that we open the doors to having other cultures incorporated into the North American Mennonite culture, and also allow them to exist and *not* be incorporated. They don't have to be the same as ethnic Mennonites, and ethnic Mennonites don't have to be the same as them."

Lisa: "But potlucks are not just cultural. They're so symbolic of so many things that are part of Mennonite faith, like this whole idea of community and everyone bringing something to the table, sharing together, and communing intimately with our environment through eating. The tradition of eating together can be a very spiritual thing."

Ellen: "I'm glad the Mennonite church merged because all I've seen in religious history is division after division after division."

Ken: "I'm so anchored in this Mennonite thing. It's inevitable that I'll be a lifer. But it doesn't mean I can't look at other denominations. The Quakers' commitment to silence, for example. I think we could aspire to be like Quakers."

෩ ෩ ෩

Curt: "It is not a question of 'Should it exist?' But 'How is going to continue to exist?' Will our generation choose to see ourselves as a limb on the body? I love my heritage, but I appreciate the heritages of other denominations as well. I would hate to see the richness of all that diversity go to waste. I am not saying that we are stuck in some pervasive arrogant attitude, but I think that we need to check what is our attitude toward our denomination, that we don't just assume that we have all the right answers and everyone else is wrong. I think it is more of a decision as to how much we want to go after God; the denominational stuff isn't so important."

Don: "Traveling and living abroad, you really fall in love with culture. When I returned home, I realized that America is really a mixing bowl. I identify with the Mennonite church and that culture. That is where I am from. This is my identity, so it is my duty to keep that going."

Margo: "As I declare that I am Mennonite, I am saying that I back the beliefs of the Mennonite church. These things have a special place in the world, especially pacifism. I like the identity of the Mennonite church because I love the heritage, but it is more that I agree with the Mennonite stances in society."

Don: "And these stances are not heard enough in the broader Christian community and world."

Greta: "Yes. I think we need to take hold and have our voice heard more."

Josh: "I think of what the world is going through. The only hope is to promote the nonviolent way of life. I think the Mennonite church in the USA does a lot of this. I grew up in the Mennonite church but I didn't know it was Mennonite until I came to America. Our churches are totally different. I went to church all my life and never heard the nonviolence thing. This was new for me when I came to America. Thinking about how my church at home relates to this, I find that it is only Mennonite in name. The Mennonites started my church back home, so I guess it is Mennonite, but in many ways it is so different. I have appreciated learning about what it means to be a Mennonite from being in the States. And I want to promote the nonviolence aspect."

Al: "In the same way that the Mennonite church in the USA has a place in the Mennonite world, the Mennonite church in general has a place in the world. I think that we need to keep our identity grounded. Menno himself was an ardent student of Scripture and was taking his stuff from the Bible. As Mennonites, we all need to have a passion for the Scriptures and a love for Jesus. Here in Virginia, I think we stress that a lot. Maybe it's not so much in other places of the country, but it is important to remember that what defines the Mennonite church around the world is different from one place to another."

Curt: "God has placed the heart of servanthood in the Mennonite church for a reason. If we look at Menno Simons and the quote that was at the end of every paper he wrote—if we lose that focus, we are cut off from the vine of life. I think that a lot of Mennonites have gotten away from that. We need our foundation on Jesus Christ as Son of God and not just on Jesus as a good teacher. This is not to say that service not rooted in the love of Christ is [necessarily] not good, but I believe that our service needs to be rooted in Christ. If we are going to consider ourselves Mennos and part of the church, then we need to keep the focus on the foundation as Christ."

Greta: "I would say, too, that the church in general and some of our teachings are not rooted enough on Christ."

Josh: "In my church it is more rooted."

෴෴෴

Linda: "That's a hard question. I think Mennonites offer a different perspective. I'm interested in Jason's comment [chapter 6]. I'm so glad he articulated being a 'secular Mennonite.' I've noticed many people who call themselves Mennonite but are not Christian."

Ray: "The Mennonite church is only important as long as it is an accurate representation of what it means to be Christian. If it doesn't connect, then I'm not overly concerned. It's just a nice history and all."

Tara: "There's a big spectrum when you say 'Mennonite.' Some are so conservative; some have lost what it means to be Mennonite. There was a time when I wouldn't have cared about the Mennonite church; now, after starting college, I've seen a lot of healthy Mennonite churches who don't say, 'We are the only way,' or 'We have the best.' It's a hard balance between keeping the traditional beliefs and reaching out. I see many Mennonites as conforming [to wider society] and not keeping integrity and remaining distinctive as Mennonites. I know people who are turned off from the Mennonite church because it's too exclusive."

❧ ❧ ❧

Tim: "I think it should continue to exist. I was raised with morals from a Mennonite upbringing. It should exist, but now it's stagnant. It seems not to want to expand its borders or become more diverse. It just has a whole feeling that there's no need to expand. I think for it to survive, it needs to push the borders."

Beth: "I agree, it should exist. We are who we are because of traditions and values we hold, and that's important. At the same time, we need to be open to change. Gays and lesbians are big right now. We need a balance as a whole church to figure out a way to incorporate who we are today with where we've come from."

Michelle: "Yes, I think it should continue to exist. No general reason, but personally because it is heritage and what I would want my children exposed to."

James: "Yes, I think it should continue because the core beliefs have validity in today's standards, and some of the nonconformity and the peace ethic."

❧ ❧ ❧

Ann: "Yes, emphatically yes. Mennonites have an incredibly rich culture that should be respected just like any other culture. This culture includes martyrdom, acts of peacemaking, community as a prominent aspect, and living simply. To continue doesn't mean it shouldn't change. I feel that as Mennonites, we have something to offer the broader church, just like any other faith has something to offer, for example, the nonviolent beliefs as well as the community aspect."

Conrad: "It should definitely continue. Mennonite faith has an important voice in the world for issues like the death penalty, war, and other things."

Sarah: "It's important that those beliefs are not just secular. It's important to have a spiritual component within the Christian community for some of those tenets of Mennonite philosophy and religion."

Andy: "It depends what direction the church goes. There's a lot of secularism that I believe is unbiblical. That should not be the core of what it means to be a Mennonite. What does the Mennonite church have to offer? I believe it's about what it means to be following after Jesus Christ."

Aaron: "I think the Mennonite church should continue. I don't have a clear definition of what that means for the next generation—more spiritually or secularly based. Cultural elements are important: hymn sings—I'm glad I grew up with them. Potlucks too. Community aspects of what the church represents are important to keep up. I agree with all the tenets the church stands for, but I don't have the understanding or commitment to take that to the next generation."

🙿🙿🙿

Rose: "I have taken 'that peace thing' for granted, but have been in contact with people who don't hold to it. I have to figure out how to relate that teaching that was really important to people in the past to me today. As I realize it [the peace teaching] is something unique, I realize that I need to be a little tougher about it. I hope that it stays intentional. The Mennonite church should continue."

Derek: "The founders of early Anabaptism based all on Christ. If the Mennonite church is going to exist, it has got to be founded on Christ. It has got to take seriously Menno Simon's quote from 1 Corinthians 3:11. If that is the foundation, then the Mennonite church needs to continue to exist. In a context where people come from all kinds of backgrounds, I feel like I teach peace all the time. But my faith can't be founded on that."

Rose: "It takes effort to combine the part of the church that is about Jesus and the part of the church that is about peace. It is easy to divorce those two, and then it becomes lukewarm both ways."

Phil: "We need to find the things that set us apart, claim those things that are uniquely ours, but keep that rooted in Jesus Christ. Make sure that is the center. Finding that balance is crucial."

Anita: "I agree with keeping Jesus at the center, but each denomination has different perspectives on interpreting the Bible, and that variety has a lot of beauty."

Derek: "The Mennonite church will exist if and only if it is founded in Jesus Christ."

Rose: "I hope that being Menno is more than ethnicity. We can think of the twelve disciples as a possible model. They go away and do stuff, then come back, and all test it out in a safe place. The Mennonite church should continue to exist as long as it remains a dynamic place to come back to, not just an old thing that you have to come back to and check just because it is there.

"This kind of discussion makes me realize that I really do care about the church. It makes me want to go out and change things. A hundred years ago, the people running the church were our age. It makes me want to mobilize people. There are so many people my age that care about these things. So why don't we get together and talk about this kind of thing? That's why I love my church in D.C. so much, because each week people get together and talk about their faith while they are cooking and doing other things."

What I Hear

Most of the voices calling for the Mennonite church to continue coalesce around the assertion that the church has a distinct role to play among other Christians and in the broader world. It is an important voice in the world, a voice that needs to be heard more and that offers an alternative way of living, seeing, and interacting. The special emphases that the Mennonite church has to offer are variously described as peace and justice, a nonviolent way of life, death-penalty work, care for the poor and marginalized, and a call to discipleship that impacts our money, our job, our lifestyle—all that we do.

There are many wonderful features these young adults associate with the Mennonite church: community, potlucks, a global-minded outlook, a wonderful heritage and sense of identity, hymn singing, living simply, washing feet, eating ethnic food, and an open spirituality. It is an "incredibly rich culture," and as Miguel says, "The church becomes your family."

Chapter 26
Do You Want to Be Part of the Mennonite Church?
(Group Interview)

"Maybe not all Mennonites think exactly the same"

A question that seemed to follow on the heels of "Should the Mennonite church continue to exist?" was a more personal question: "Do you want to belong to and participate in a Mennonite church?" Assuming many young adults want the church to continue, what personal investment are they themselves willing to make toward its health and well-being?

Kate, one of the young adults we interviewed, made an interesting comment earlier. "I'm part of the Mennonite community," she said. "Then I'm American, then you make that global, and then there's the whole natural ecosystem. And not only am I a part of those communities; I also have responsibilities."

Below, Alisa describes how being a part of the Mennonite church carried her family through tragic times, and how now she is choosing to contribute to the ministries of an urban Mennonite church far from her family home in significant ways. Following her story, we'll see answers to group interviews about belonging to and participating in the church.

Alisa

As a child, Alisa remembers often hearing stories about missionaries. Her family had a book of Mennonite missionaries from around the world, and there was a particular family with daughters named Alisa and Ruth that the family would often pray for. Alisa has a sister named Ruth.

"As a young child I remember thinking, 'Could I do that when I'm older?' I definitely had this concept of helping people."

Again and again Alisa emphasized the importance of family in her life. Almost all of her extended family lives in her home state.

"Until I moved far away, I didn't realize how unusual that was. And we didn't get together just for Christmas—it was Christmas, Easter, Thanksgiving, Grandma's birthday—everyone got together!"

When Alisa was ten years old, her mother died of cancer, and the family moved from their corn and soybean farm to town. Alisa considers the larger community in her hometown as family also.

"I think of all the times after Mom got sick and after she died, how the community and the church really embraced us kids. I don't know where I would be today if it weren't for them. My dad was working a lot. When my mom was getting treatment, they would go to the neighboring state, and people would take us in. They'd bring in meals and pray for us."

She was touched especially by the people who continued to pray for their family long after her mother died. "On my baptism, someone came up to me and said, 'It was so great to hear your testimony, because I've been praying for you.'"

Alisa was baptized during her junior year of high school, a time she recalls as very meaningful. She remembers every summer's campfires, when campers would be invited to make commitments to lives of faith.

"We could share them out loud," she remembers. "I was never that bold, but there was always something." Campers wrote letters to themselves about their commitments, and staff mailed the letters to them months later.

Alisa participated in church youth-group mission trips throughout high school. "In my senior year we went to Chicago, and after that trip I knew that God was calling me to the mission field. One night after I got back, I lit a candle and I was reflecting and I felt God saying, 'This is something I have for you,' and it was a really powerful experience."

After college, Alisa knew she wanted to work with MCC, though she "didn't feel ready for something overseas." She now sees her work "with inner-city kids" as her mission, though she's still open to working abroad. "I'm not one to say that's not going to happen, because I know how God works."

Living in the MCC service unit in a major American city was an important time of growth for Alisa. "I realized that maybe not all Mennonites think exactly the same! This whole realm of doing advocacy work was a new concept to me. [I was] hearing more about world events and how people are actively trying to change them, and trying to discover for myself what it means to be a pacifist. It's not being passive. While growing up, I questioned pacifism a lot, and that's not what it's all about. It's finding alternatives. Living with people whom I wouldn't have otherwise gotten to know. And even at MCC orientation, [I was] experiencing all these people that were wanting to go out and spread the Word and reach out and share God's love with people."

Alisa recalls that even though missions and service were highly valued in her hometown, "it was only a small pocket who would go out."

Regarding what the stories in her life have taught her about God, she said: "God cares for us and loves us and embraces us, no matter what's going on. He's not going to leave us. There are going to be tough times, but he still holds us near. The poem 'Footprints' has always been meaningful to me—when there's only one set of footprints, it means [God is] carrying you!"

Alisa felt the presence of God during her mother's illness: "None of us kids ever got into trouble. That's a testament to God watching over us."

She understands herself as a conduit of God's love. "We need to reach out to others. We have experienced that love, and it's such a great love, so we need to share it. Not necessarily by preaching at them or giving them tracts, but by bringing people into your heart and loving them wherever they are."

Alisa has membership in two different churches—her home church and her urban church. She wishes her peers were better at "recognizing what the church is already doing. So often we get caught up in saying 'Oh, we should be doing all these things,' not recognizing that the Neighborhood Learning Center is already a ministry. Yes, we are doing stuff in the community, and we are reaching out in the community! People should be plugging into that. Let's look at the wisdom that's already been put into things. I think there's sometimes a lack of recognizing history. [Do you] think you're thinking of something new? It's been done before!"

Journal Comments

Alisa is incredibly loyal. Attending the same camp for thirteen years in a row amazes me. In the interview, she praised her family, her community, her college, her church, and MCC—and passionately defended the work of the Neighborhood Learning Center (NLC) against those who overlook its place in the church. Alisa is loyal also to God, to her faith, and to the church. I couldn't detect a hint of the cynicism, irony, or doubt that's present to some degree in all my other interviews.

In addition, Alisa is very practical. Questions about the Bible or the Jesus story eventually led to her everyday struggles with what to do for the homeless men at 7-Eleven, or how to discipline kids at the NLC, or how much TV to watch. For Alisa, faith means loving others. The mystical and theoretical don't figure much in her journey.

—Bethany Spicher

Group Interview Questions

Do you want to belong to and participate in a Mennonite church? Why or why not?

Ellen: "Yes, and participate in making it better."

Ken: "Yes. In college, I didn't think I'd belong to the church. It wasn't until I went to Guatemala after graduation that I saw religious community acted out in really powerful ways. That's when I decided to be involved."

Jennifer: "Yes, I think so. At least in the congregation I'm in right now. I have been fed by the teachings and people there, and the ways they're working in and around Philadelphia, offering another way of being in the world. And I have something to offer to it as well. It's hard for me to think about being involved in the larger Mennonite church, although I know it's important to me that the larger church is there."

Lisa: "I don't know when or if I'll ever become a member. I have stopped throwing stones from the outside. Now I've just turned and started throwing stones at the rest of the world. In other words, I'm not as focused even on critiquing the church anymore. I have a lot of respect and appreciation for the Mennonite church, but I have found there are other communities and groups that do a better job at being active in bringing positive change in the world."

భ భ భ

Anita: "I grew up Menno, but in a completely different context, so what is here I don't identify with so much. It's not where I find my strength and my faith right now."

Derek: "I want to be a part of an Anabaptist community, but I'm not necessarily attached to the name 'Mennonite.' I spent a year in Mexico, and people there had a problem with calling themselves Mennonite. Why be called by the name of a man, when we are following Jesus Christ? It makes the emphasis too ethnic."

Phil: "I want to be part of the Mennonite church, but I don't want to be restricted to only that view of who Jesus is. I believe in all that 'Mennonitism' is about, but there is potential for it to become inwardly focused, a community that exists in the world with no other focus than on itself. [If it has] an arrogant attitude, separated from the world, I don't want to be a part of that. We need to be open to God moving in other [Christian] traditions. I don't want it to become a static thing, but dynamic."

Rose: "I almost think that I took the Mennonite church too seriously when they preached the whole idea of missions. So now I want to do it, but I'm not sure how it will work out being Menno and teaching peace in so many other contexts where things are so different."

∽ ∽ ∽

Beth: "Familiarity is what I like. I don't mind other churches, but [there's] something about singing the hymns that I recognize, that I appreciate. I would lean toward attending a Mennonite church."

Tim: "Yeah, I would too. I am now, and that's what I'm familiar with—what's taught and preached. But I'm not averse to visiting other churches. I know others have good things to say. I don't want my fellowship to just be with the Mennonite church; I want to fellowship with others."

Michelle: "Yes, I want to belong to a Mennonite church. But if there was another church I liked better and agreed with the teaching, I would go there."

James: "Yes, I want to participate. It would be nice, but not essential. It really depends on what's around me. If there's a real [lousy] Mennonite church, I wouldn't go there."

∽ ∽ ∽

Tara: "Right now, yes. But I don't want to be in just any Mennonite church. I feel like I have found one right now, but if I didn't have one that fit, I would leave the denomination and find another one. I could go either way. I wouldn't go anywhere far outside the Mennonite circles. I wouldn't be Catholic or Baptist, but I would consider Presbyterian or a nondenominational church."

Linda: "A part of me says 'no.' I would love to get out and connect with something else. But the Mennonite church is very safe. Something keeps me in it. I've had a lot of questions about what keeps me in the Mennonite church. I would probably drive forty-five minutes to go to a Mennonite church, even if it wasn't as good as another church. I don't know why. Sometime I would want to be rebellious and break out, but the Mennonite church is so safe and familiar."

Tony: "I switched from Catholic to Mennonite, and back and forth. I've wanted to trash all the denominations. Going to a Mennonite college, I've seen how much people have hated Catholics. I see pride on both sides, but no pride about being Christian. I think denominations get in the way, get in the middle of stuff. This morning I participated in an ecumenical service. It was awesome.

"Is it kosher to belong to more than one church? I'm somewhere in between Catholic and Mennonite. I'm not totally Catholic. I don't know what is going on in the Catholic church. It's hard to find community in the Catholic church. All my church friends are my parents' age. If the Mennonite church would offer answers to questions I have, I would come. I don't have a nonviolent outlook, for example. I would want to go to a bunch of churches and combine these perspectives. I would want to share my music with a number of denominations. A Mennonite church is too limiting."

Ray: "If I would move to a different city, I would look for a Mennonite church, but I wouldn't limit myself to that. Being Mennonite isn't absolute for me, though there's a lot of power in growing up in that church, knowing the language, what the symbols mean, the connection."

෴෴෴

Sarah: A lot of other religions have the same beliefs we do. Since living here in Philadelphia, I've found that the cultural elements are what I'm drawn to in the Mennonite church. In my workplace where everyone comes from different backgrounds, it's really comforting to belong to a church of people of common backgrounds. I sing the same songs I sang growing up; some people there quilt; we eat together. I need to balance out the diversity of the city with the culture I grew up in.

Andy: "Yes, I'd like to belong and participate. For seven years of my life, my family left the Mennonite church for the Brethren in Christ. We were hurt by the [Mennonite] church. But now I'm back. My current church is not culturally Mennonite at all, but I go there because I believe God is there."

Conrad: "Yes. My core beliefs are directly in line with those of the Mennonite church or as close as they're going to get to any religion. The cultural things are also what pull me in. I've grown up in it, gone to school in it. Something would really have to happen to take me away from that."

Aaron: "No, not right now, at this point in my life. For one, the faith connection isn't there right now. Also, my group of friends, Mennonite college grads, mostly, all hold the same beliefs that the church holds—nonviolence, community, and so on—and we all hang out a lot and are very supportive to each other. We have the same beliefs about how the world should work and come from similar cultural backgrounds. We get together a lot, just not necessarily on Sunday mornings. That's enough for me right now."

Ann: "Yes, I'd like to belong and participate. I've been in many churches, and we have that privilege of a small faith community in which you can always play the Mennonite game, always find someone you know or someone who knows my grandmother. I've been in communities that have experienced a lot of pain. I spent time on the Hopi reservation, for example. But I saw a Mennonite community there that tried to work through that."

What I Hear

Clearly, most of the above young adults do want to belong to and participate in the Mennonite church family in one form or another, but for a variety of reasons and with a number of qualifications. For various reasons a few don't want to participate, acknowledging a lack of faith commitment or the sense that other groups are doing a better job at bringing positive change. Some of those who want to belong put the emphasis on wanting to get involved because of what the church is about, what it is doing, and its way of being in the world.

Others put the emphasis on their own comfort with the familiar, in terms of both people and culture. They tend to focus on what the church offers them, and on the safety and commonality they feel among fellow Mennonites.

Alisa's invitation to her peers seems appropriate: to recognize what the church is already doing and plug into that; to acknowledge the wisdom that is already present; to reach out and share the love we ourselves have received; and to be changed in the process, learning that not all Mennonites think (or act) in the same way.

Part 5

Conclusions

Chapter 27
What I'm Hearing—in Broad Strokes

"So what are young adults telling us?"

The wisdom, creativity, soulfulness, and dreams of these young adults speak for themselves. There is no need to further summarize or blend the magnificent richness of these stories into a tidy final word. I like what Brian McLaren says about the journey of faith so many of us are on: It's not life lived within a "static system of belief, an interlocking wall of cemented-in certainties." Rather, it's more like "a passion, an adventure, a discovery, a wild wonder."

But acknowledging the "discovery and wild wonder" of the young-adult stage doesn't deny that they are also "crucible" years of concentrated and challenging change and development. They are crucial years for connecting what we value from our formative and re-formed narratives with how we will live in the world. They are crucial years for helping each other put together "a worldview, a web or mosaic of belief, a pattern that makes sense"—as well as critiquing, adjusting, and recalibrating it as we test it out in day-to-day life.

In *The Fabric of Faithfulness*, Steven Garber describes the far-ranging conversations he's had with many young adults during and after the "crucible" years. He observes that young adults who make it into mature adulthood with a coherent faith and an integrity of being have three things in common. They each had (1) formed a worldview, presumably out of primary narratives, that was sufficient for the questions and crises of the next twenty years. (2) They met a teacher who incarnated in practice the worldview that they were coming to consciously identify as their own, thus seeing that it was possible to reside within that worldview themselves. And (3) they lived out their worldview in the company of mutually committed folk who provided a network of friendship, stimulation, and support, showing that the ideas could be coherent across their whole life. There were no exceptions, he said.

Taking what Garber suggests as essential components for moving into mature adulthood and reframing them somewhat, we ask: What have we learned from these young adults about how well their formative narratives are equipping them with a worldview sufficient for the questions and crises they face? How well are the practices they have seen modeled and also chosen for their own way of life serving them? And how do they regard the possibility that a faith community and significant mentors can help to challenge and sustain them over the long haul?

Today's Young Adults

One of the research team interviewed a young adult I'll call Zach. The researcher suggested that Zach embodies an intellectual mentality characterizing many of today's young adults. It is a mentality that discards rules and doctrine and anything universal. It recognizes validity in many different voices and lifestyles. It deplores righteousness, judgment, black-and-white morality, heaven and hell. And it describes all truths, narratives, and ethical norms as specific to certain cultural contexts. God's existence is moot. There may be a God, but he/she is mostly our construction and is probably quite distant and uninvolved in our day-to-day lives. And regardless of what any one person thinks of God, another's construction is equally valid. The interview with Zach reminded the researcher of many conversations she had in college.

If on target, the comments about Zach may set off alarms, for they appear, on first blush, to threaten what a lot of us hold dear. We may quickly become defensive, taking issue with this or that with a strong counterargument.

I include these comments here not as a way of caricaturing "many of today's young adults" but to invite us into conversation about the questions underlying Zach's outlook on the world. These questions about how we regard rules, doctrine, universality, morality, and God do not come from nowhere. They signal to me the inadequacy of an inherited worldview for dealing with present realities, and an honest wrestling with how to weave a more adequate canopy of meaning. Rather than becoming defensive and excluding Zach and others like him from our tables, how can we welcome him to the table and together find our way in the uncharted waters of an age many describe as "postmodern"?

The stories in this book are exemplary as illustrations of young adults who are drawing many vibrant threads from the wonderful but somewhat frayed heritage they've been given. They are working hard, with imagination, longing, and love, to weave those threads into an adequate, coherent faith and an integrity of being for their own generation. What are they telling us about what endures and what needs to change for moving into the future?

Formative Narratives

Scripture

Conflicted feelings about their experience with the biblical narrative show up prominently for these young adults, yet most of them also talk about a desire to know more about the Bible. They lament their lack of Bible literacy and wish to make the Bible more relevant and enjoyable, despite its seeming inaccessibility and complexity.

I think young adults have a tough time relating to the Bible because many of us who are their pastors, teachers, parents are conflicted in our relationship with it. Many of us were taught to take every last bit of it literally, and we are nervous about defending its accuracy and reliability. We've thought of the Bible, as Bruce Feiler suggests, as "a kind of machine; if you prove that two of the screws really existed, then the whole machine existed, and if you take *out* two of the screws, the whole thing collapses. But the Bible is not a machine. It doesn't have screws."

We've sometimes used the Bible to trump arguments, to add "authority" to a personal agenda, and even to inflict harm on opponents. Too often we have been deadly serious when we ponder its depths, and we almost always read it as merely words on a page rather than the most remarkable literary classic of all time—not to mention the Word of God, a concept most adults don't begin to understand.

What amazes me in what I hear from these young adults is that they don't use jargon or clichés in how they speak about the Bible. Rather, there is a longing, a confessional genuineness about wanting to have an honest relationship with the Bible. They wrestle with how to think of it as a source of truth in relation to other "truths," part of a conversation with God, something we should eat up "like a good feast."

A theme that shows up again and again is how much more interesting Scripture becomes when one learns the context behind it. This makes it possible to relate to the Bible in ways that make more sense. We are invited into active deliberation about its many-layered meanings, and it is energizing and liberating for young adults to view Scripture as open to interpretation.

Most young adults talked about their desire to engage the Bible in the company of others. They spoke of how confusing Scripture is to read alone and of wishing to "hash it out" in community, in a group study, with friends, in class, or with trusted others who can help to interpret and even challenge them. It sounds as though it is high time to recover a time-honored Anabaptist ideal—that we encounter the Bible in a gathered circle of people who discern its meaning together.

We as conflicted adults can learn to lighten up a bit in our own relationship with the Scripture. As we sit with young adults, using imagination and wise discernment to engage the Scripture in playful dialogue, it will come to life for us. Spaces will open for us to glimpse our common humanity, our common longing with folks from millennia ago to understand God, and our place in the cosmic scheme of things.

The Jesus Narrative

When asked what they think about Jesus, these young adults show none of the conflict described above with Scripture. I think it's safe to say that all of them spoke with admiration for Jesus. Even those who don't claim to be Christian think that Jesus is okay. Repeatedly they spoke of how they see Jesus as a provocative, daring young man. While they are ambivalent about how pieces of the Jesus story were used in their childhood, they're astonished as they discover the fuller story for themselves. Here is a gritty and magnificent story of a down-to-earth human being with whom they can identify.

The young adults with whom we spoke seem to relate to Jesus in at least three ways. Many see Jesus as a model or a pattern for their own lives. They put an emphasis on the radical, courageous business of fashioning one's life after the teachings and example of Jesus's life. And those who put the emphasis here tended to focus on Jesus's life rather than his death and resurrection. But in nearly equal proportions during group interviews, they referred to Jesus as "salvation for us," as one whose death and resurrection are vitally important. Jesus is the one "God sent to save us from ourselves." And many referred to Jesus as a personal friend and mysterious presence "within me."

The primary dilemma that seems to emerge for many is the standard Christian teaching about the exclusivity of Jesus as the only way to God. They clearly see Jesus as "unique and special," and yet they have misgivings about an expectation that he is "*the* way" in an exclusive sense (cf. John 14:6). By the frequency with which this question comes up, young adults seem to be saying that we must together do some significant theological work. We need to find a more dynamic theological vision that calls us to honor what is "unique and special" about Jesus, even as we honor "that of God" in people of other faiths.

Following her interviews and extensive contact with young adults in many settings, one of our research team commented, "My peers desire something in the middle between exclusivity and universal salvation, but there doesn't seem to be a satisfactory middle, so we search and search." She also suggested that her peers are reluctant to talk about the implications of Jesus's death and resurrection for personal salvation, because they don't want to draw distinctions between "who's in and who's out." She doesn't hear concerns from her peers about whether they are "saved" or not. "We don't talk about it," she said. "I, for one, never have really asked myself that question."

So while all these young adults admire Jesus, many of them are deeply ambivalent about who Jesus should be for others. This, I suggest, is where the faith community and young adults should be putting significant energy. Together we must construct a more viable theological framework that will free us all both to follow Jesus wholeheartedly and to truly honor and love our neighbors.

Relating to Persons of Other Faith Narratives

As recognized above, on one level many young adults are finding standard theological assertions about the exclusivity of Jesus inadequate. Yet they are, in practical ways, providing us with a way forward.

I see their comments clustering around two somewhat different emphases on how to relate to people of other faith narratives and practices. The first cluster I characterize as being " open" but also owning a particular "truth." This stance is perhaps characterized best by a comment: "I'm totally open to and genuinely interested in talking to people of other worldviews, but if I lack the ability to claim my own truth, I render myself useless in that conversation. Christ is my truth, so when I am in conversations with people, I have to be unabashedly open about that."

The other cluster places the emphasis less on the specific truth that one is owning and more on the process of listening to the other's "truth." This stance is characterized by another comment: "You have to approach them with an attitude of not trying to impose beliefs on them, not just assuming you are right. For these conversations to work and be productive, the approach has to be that your truth is not necessarily the only truth."

I would identify a third and somewhat smaller cluster of comments converging around the emphasis on living out one's faith rather than pushing it on others. This means being a good example and walking consistently with people, doing rather than talking, and living in ways that are observable and may become compelling in and of themselves.

The young adults with whom we spoke seem humbly sensitive to the need to do damage control for other Christians who have forcefully insisted that there is one right way, or "this is the only way." They seek a middle ground between extremes: one extreme suggests that all truth is relative; the other operates with dogmatism about Christian truth. Rather than taking one of these two easy ways out, they are modeling how to both respectfully listen and honestly speak about their loyalty to the truth they have found in Jesus.

Formative Practices

Typical Faith Community Practices

The young adults we spoke with brought a lot of energy to our questions about practices they consider important. By the kinds of answers they gave, it seems clear to me that it is high time to engage in more frequent conversations about practices we think should characterize our life together as communities of faith. Those of us who are middle-aged and older remember a time not so long ago when church leaders, in ways that often felt heavy-handed, tried to enforce practices related to dress code, TV watching, lifestyle choices, and more. As we came of age, we took issue with expressions of faith that seemed too legalistic. But any community that hopes to counter mass culture with deeper and richer values will need to think intentionally about the practices that characterize our life individually and together. I sense that young adults are ready for more of those kinds of conversations.

The young adults we questioned affirmed many of the practices on the lists we used for our group interviews. But as they shape their own way of life, many raise questions and seek more conversation about the meaning and motivation of many of the practices.

About "simplicity of lifestyle," for example, they wondered what the simple life really is, what it means in different contexts, how to come to terms with our many possessions and exercise good stewardship, experiencing "more with less." There was a strong call for more discussion about this practice, without resorting to "rules."

The practice that received the highest number of qualifying and objecting comments, according to my calculation, was "testifying or speaking publicly about one's faith experience." Comments clearly indicated that a fair number of young adults have "baggage" with this practice. They have seen it mishandled and used in harmful ways.

"Cross-cultural mission and service" also received a high number of comments, suggesting significant ambivalence about mission as it's been "historically defined." And several suggest that mission and service in one's local community, right outside one's door, are as important or more important than mission or service in other countries.

On "Sabbath-keeping," people talked mostly about not knowing what it means and about concern that it not be interpreted legalistically, while acknowledging that "rest" is important.

"Group discernment/listening to each other and the Spirit" provoked some significant interest and a desire to know more of what this might be about. Some carried negative connotations about it, but several others mentioned how they connect this with "engaging the Bible" and would welcome the church talking more about how together we discern the meaning of the Scriptures.

There were also frequent comments about "modest" or "nonprovocative attire," asking for more definition, for contextual sensitivity, and suggesting that we not think about it in the traditional Mennonite way. And a fair number mentioned "nonswearing of oaths," mostly indicating that it isn't important, or at least not in the way often assumed.

One of our research team aptly commented: "I hear a desire among the young adults I know to model a way of life that is different from the mainstream. But they don't want practices like dress to be the distinguishing factor."

Sex

Some on the research team were surprised to see "sexual fidelity" come in as the most frequently rated "very important" practice. One team member commented to me in private that the findings on sexual fidelity are difficult for her to believe because they don't match her experience. She said that many of her peers, Mennonite and not, are sexually active before marriage. Perhaps those interviewed understood "sexual infidelity" only to mean extramarital sex, not premarital. Or maybe, she acknowledged, her perceptions of her age-group are off.

As we saw in chapter 19, "sexual integrity and fidelity" pose a "huge question" for many young adults who are not sure what it means. They call for more open talk about a subject that has been taught so prudishly and simplistically that it's difficult to navigate the variety of scenarios they encounter.

Many regret a lack of openness in discussing sex among their peers and want more guidance from the church. Several spoke in confessional ways about a desire to avoid inappropriate thoughts and behaviors, and about how important it is to be around others who share a commitment in this area. Uncertainty about a biblical basis for sexual fidelity came up a couple times. A few expressed reservations about the implications of sexual fidelity for gay and lesbian friends in the church. Some were distressed that concern about sexual practice is all they see in the church.

What I hear over and over is a call from these young adults for us to talk in the church more often and more honestly about sexual practice.

Prayer

Many young adults spoke about prayer as part of their daily lives. They placed it among the practices most important to them. They often expressed a desire for regular prayer, and to see it as a continuous flow of conversation with God. There seems to be a shift away from thinking of prayer as "asking for stuff" to prayer as "listening." Most referred to prayer as occurring during times of solace and solitude, during personal time.

Spirituality

Throughout these narrative responses flows a desire for a spirituality that embraces all of life, that is able to see God as active in all things, as the undercurrent and overarching life source of all we are and do. The "whole" spirituality these young adults long for seems to be related to a desire for more silence, more of the "contemplative stuff," more contact with nature, and a slower pace of life—a life in which we can stop and listen to God and to others. This longing is also related to concrete expressions such as war-tax resistance, care for neighbors, energetic singing, and even composting. In fact, "balance" is most often called for—balance between a "spiritual relationship" and "social activism," between "contemplation" and "expressive faith," between self-confidence and acknowledged doubt.

Many want their peers to take the corporate side of worship more seriously and be more involved in local congregations. Many would like more opportunity to pray with each other and to discuss things close to the heart. And they wish more of their peers would learn to simplify their lives.

A longing for more purposeful interpersonal relationships is apparent. Young adults wish to spend more time with people in a free and unhurried way. They want to be more hospitable and to show respect for people regardless of background. They want to be more encouraging in nonjudgmental ways and to be part of communities that are open to questions, communities that are malleable and nondogmatic.

The Future Church

Most of the young adults who talked with us about the future of the church are calling for significant changes. They want the church to continue because of all the "good stuff," but it must be open to change.

Welcoming Young-Adult Questions

These young adults spoke often about their longing that the church become the kind of place where we can acknowledge the complexity of the world, and faith, and ask the very questions many of us are afraid to ask "in church" lest we "turn everything upside down." Authenticity is a big word with them. The longing is for the church to be the place where we can talk about the difficulty of the journey and even about the absence of God; where there is more vulnerability and transparency both about our differences and what we have in common.

Offering Accountability

Many young adults spoke of wanting more accountability. They want to be around others who will ask them hard questions and support them in living responsibly and ethically. Frequently they spoke of wanting a church that doesn't let them be a passive member, a church that is watching out for them and willing to confront them in healthy ways.

Mentoring Each Other

The desire for more accountability is often linked to mentoring. I hear a strong call from many young adults for "more people who will walk along side us" and serve as mentors and spiritual directors. "I don't want to do this on my own. I need direction." And yet, there was also the wonderful acknowledgement that mentoring should be a mutual process in which the young adult assists the older person in his/her journey as well.

Meeting in Small, Friendly Circles

Young adults described a desire for small close-knit, friendly circles in which they would feel free to establish deep, trusting relationships and in which they can be themselves, with all of their questions, failures, and love for fun. "How can we become more candid about the reality of our lives and the questions we face instead of going along 'in a parallel fashion?'" they are asking. There are no simple answers here.

Nevertheless, many of them talked about small groups, smaller congregations, meeting more times during the week, having deeper discussions about faith and the world, studying the Bible, more potlucks, hymn singing, and going on retreats together. They repeatedly spoke of wishing more of their peers would get involved in church, but also about a desire for the church to be a diverse community—intergenerational, as well as racially, socioeconomically and culturally diverse.

Worshiping and Serving Together

Many of these young adults expressed a vision for the church that emphasizes service over doctrine, with "more grace" and "less drawing of lines." They envision the church learning to live with more diverse viewpoints and less bickering, and incorporating more use of liturgy and rituals, including frequent "breaking of bread" and foot washing. They wish that our worship would often include a Taizé-type service, mixing silence and corporate worship, with more storytelling about "what's really going on" and more hymn singing.

Should the Mennonite Church Continue to Exist?

The direct answer from most of the young adults with whom we spoke was a strong yes. For some, the yes is emphatic; for others, there's a qualified "but" or "if" attached.

A lot of young adults truly believe the Mennonite church has a distinct and vital role to play in today's world. With its social conscience, commitment to peacemaking, and call to discipleship, it offers a unique alternative to standard American evangelical "pop" Christianity. There is a great appreciation for Mennonites' rich community life and the sense of identity it provides.

Many of the qualifications coalesced around the suggestion that while the Mennonite church should continue because of all the "good stuff," it needs to acknowledge the "negative stuff" and the terrible things that have happened. It must be open to change and to expanding its borders lest we become arrogant and imagine we are "the best" or "the only way." Young adults showed a great appreciation for the rich diversity of other denominations, for their beauty and variety.

Other qualifications clustered around a caution that Mennonite heritage must be kept in a healthy relationship to the "religious" aspects of faith. Young adults were concerned about the polarities that seem so prevalent in our faith communities. They described those polarities in various ways: cultural versus religious, horizontal versus vertical, Mennonite but not Christian, a church about Jesus versus a church about peace, secular versus spiritual.

Yet, there was much encouragement to keep our focus on Jesus Christ as the foundation of our faith, that our core identity is grounded in Scripture and love for Jesus. They hope that being Mennonite is more than ethnicity, that it isn't reduced to mere culture. In my view, many of these young adults maintained a dynamic tension between valuing treasured cultural practices and acknowledging the need to keep them rooted in Christ-centered faith. After all, if "the church becomes your family," as Miguel suggests, there is no easy bifurcation of culture and faith, secular and sacred. If it's like many families I know, it's all of one piece in the truest sense of being holistic.

Do You Want to Be Part of the Mennonite Church?

Most of the young adults we spoke with definitely want to belong to and participate in the Mennonite church in one form or another. Some acknowledge that the Mennonite church is where they feel most at home. But many say they believe the Mennonite church has a unique calling in the world of which they want to be part.

Those who for various reasons don't want to participate talked about their own lack of a faith commitment or the sense that other groups are doing a better job at bringing positive change.

Most of the "yes, buts" refer in some way to preferring affiliation with Mennonites, because "I want to fellowship with others," but "it really depends" on what is available. Perhaps more to the point, many wanted to highlight their belief that God is also moving in other traditions/churches/communities and that in order for the Mennonite church to stay dynamic, we must be open to the movement of God among others.

In Conclusion: Young Adults and A. D. Wenger's Core Vision

I remarked early on how surprised I was that a hundred years later, A. D.'s core vision, at least as I understand it, continues to ring true throughout most of these young adults' stories. Today's Mennonite-affiliated young adults use different language, have worldviews that allow for more complexity, talk more about contextualization than universality, don't generally relate well to abstract and doctrinal "truths," speak in humble and confessional ways about their understanding of God, are embarrassed about how the United States dominates the rest of the world, and are more circumspect about how they use the biblical meta-narrative to make sense of their world. However, I think it is fair to say that almost all of them would agree with the young-adult globe-trotter from a century ago: A few faithful Mennonites could "wield a wonderful influence for the betterment of the human race" if they remain true to "the humble teachings of Jesus, and thus be a great power for good to the world."

Across the board, these young adults found the Jesus story the most compelling narrative for informing a way of life and a worldview that is sufficient for the questions and crises of this time and place. Most of them want to belong to communities of faith that welcome and challenge them.

I hope the stories from these bright, thoughtful, activist young adults will stir our faith communities to tap their insights and gifts out of our mutual need and benefit. Many young adults long to be a part of "mentoring communities." And the rest of us need their questions, discerning minds, and creative energy so that together, younger and older, we can do the theological reflection required to realistically engage the complexities of our day and to shape a sustainable way of life before God.

Afterword

"Thank You for Asking"

Which stories and practices will the young adults whose voices fill this book find sufficient for the questions and crises of the coming years? What mentors, teachers, and friends are "living the narrative" in ways that are delightful, wholesome, and downright good? Who are the friends with whom they'll forge an enduring network of support and camaraderie?

Journal reflections from members of the research team provide some answers to questions of how we are sustained on the journey. The researchers reported how energizing the conversations with their peers were, how it often stirred their own questions, and how pleased the interview subjects were to reflect with a peer about things that matter and yet are rarely talked about.

Here are some excerpts from the interviewers. The names of the subjects being discussed in these entries have been left out.

"After this first interview I am excited about all there is to learn from each individual to be interviewed. It is exciting, too, to hear the interviewee respond with such gratitude and a certain sense of awe after we are done. The gratitude is for the chance to think about and articulate such matters on a personal level; the awe comes in finding how easy and natural it is to converse about them out loud with a peer. We discussed how important these discussions are for finding a place in the church and the broader world, for naming certain aspects of spirituality that we would like to call our own."
—Melody King

"I've gained so much insight from just these two interviews that I want to use this information to strengthen the young adults in my congregation. How can we move them to the point where they feel they have a voice? How can we encourage them through times when they feel the church is just floating by instead of being actively involved in the day-to-day life of the body? These are questions I want to get to the bottom of."

—*Nate Barker*

"_____ stayed afterward and, as soon as the tape stopped, began talking on a more personal level about the struggles he is facing in his faith journey. It looks like I will meet with him periodically for discipleship or spiritual direction of some sort. I am grateful for that opportunity!"

—*Aram DiGennaro*

"Wow. This was fun but long. I heard a lot of myself in _____. I think she shares some of the same values, commitments, and points of tension with the church and the world that I and others I know do. I think much of this would be common to most college-educated Mennonites: We value dialogue over laws. We value Jesus's life more than his death. We hate altar calls, are slow to evangelize, and aren't even sure we have the right answer any more than the next guy—but this is hard to reconcile with a commitment to the Christian story. We want to be all-inclusive, but what do we do about the guy down the pew who is doing something *wrong*? I also saw myself in _____ in the somewhat contemplative stream she falls into. Time alone is important. God is found in silence and in sorting through the day's thoughts and happenings."

—*Deborah Good*

"_____ has an extroverted, dynamic personality, so the entire interview was full of vigor and life. His passion for life emerged throughout the interview, and he has a zeal that I found refreshing in comparison to some other more apathetic responses. He is on the upper end of young adulthood, and his current urban lifestyle spoke loudly through his practices and narratives. He seems to be a very self-confident, assured, independent individual with a can-do attitude typical of the urban pace of life. He has the idealism of youth in his perspectives on current trends in the world and in his views of the future. He also has strong leadership skills that he carries with ease and assertiveness."

—*Annie Lengacher*

"_____ struggled with the concept of narrative or story, but as we talked further, I heard narratives seeping out. It makes me wonder at what point we begin to objectively view pieces of our life as shaping realities. I'm so glad for the opportunity we as interviewers had when we met together as a group at the beginning of this project to share our own forming stories. At that time I also struggled to know what those pieces of my life were. But as I sat and listened to others in the circle that evening, and as I continue to listen to those I interview, I came to believe that narratives have many origins, take many forms, carry many different weights. We do not have tangible pictures of our lives carved into cave walls somewhere. What we have are experiences that we hold alone or with a group of people. [We] long to [name our experiences] as shaping narratives. In doing so, they grow roots, and the individuals that carry them gain a sense of self that is refreshing and sometimes surprising."   —*Melody King*

"_____ struggled with the story theme. He doesn't think about his life in stories. He remembers more about the values and principles he was taught than stories he was told. He thinks more about what beliefs to embrace today than about the stories that give meaning to his life. But as we stumbled through the interview, he had more stories to tell than he first realized."   —*Deborah Good*

"_____ had an unpretentiousness that was inviting and comfortable. Throughout the interview his apparent honesty was consistent, and he had a humility and openness that made the interview feel at ease and natural. He made no attempt to find the 'right words' or put up any pretense about his faith. He had an innocence in his faith that seemed almost childlike at times, in a trusting, accepting way. I appreciated the self-awareness and self-acceptance that he projected in his responses. Within that self-awareness, he also had a genuine deep desire for personal growth."   —*Annie Lengacher*

"I wonder how similar _____'s story and experiences are to others. He is really cutting out all pop culture and trying instead to write his own history and story. I think this is a noble thing and a way to nurture a faith that is fresh and alive. It seems that too much of our world as young adults revolves around quoting movies or using slogans of the mass media."   —*Nate Barker*

"The interview lasted for almost three hours over the phone, and I had seven pages of typed notes at the end, mostly because I couldn't ask one question, tug at one strand, without pulling the whole web. When I asked for _____'s 'thumbnail autobiography' at the outset, I listened to the descriptions and ages of almost his entire extended family and the stories of his mother's and father's lives before he launched into his own story. And 'one's own story' doesn't fit with _____'s understanding anyhow; he very much sees himself in the church, in a family, in a 'people.' The written narrative is somewhat deceiving. Nothing was in chronological order. I moved things to fit that way, but one story led to another and always back around to the themes of community and heritage."   *—Bethany Spicher*

"_____ reminded me of myself and a lot of my friends in that she was very slow to say much of anything for sure whenever we got into 'God territory.' She often said, 'I don't know,' or 'I don't understand God/Jesus.'"   *—Deborah Good*

"At the end of the interview, the post taping dialogue is again revealing in and of itself. _____ discusses the rarity of discussing such things with a peer and feeling as though the conversation takes a bit of a forward motion. Thoughts are nurtured a bit. She apologizes for long-windedness. I am blessed by the elaboration of yet another story of struggle, desire, pain, and stubborn idealism. She wants now to hear my story. I'm pleased for the deepening level of relating."   *—Melody King*

"I enjoyed the honesty of the young woman in this interview, and yet I was also aware that the wording and focus of the interview caters toward young adults who have experience with higher education. The nature of the questions requires a different kind of thinking and a lot of self-analysis. In the case of this young woman, I found that many of the concepts were completely new to her or ones that she didn't fully comprehend."   *—Annie Lengacher*

"_____ is an intellectual. Very thoughtful, very well-read, very postmodern, very agnostic. But what struck me about this interview was the apparent disconnect between his head and his practice. I now wish I had pushed him more on one interview question: 'Looking back at the practices you mentioned that are typical for your life as a young adult, what do you think they indicate about what you most value?' _____ had very little to say in response."   *—Deborah Good*

"I have begun to use the concept of practices in my ministry with young adults at my church. It remains to be seen how long I will continue in this vein, but the first session went very well. I felt that the students grasped and appreciated the concept and significance of Christian practices, and that we will be able to use that as a platform for learning and reflection on our faith journeys."   *—Aram DiGennaro*

"If the three I have interviewed thus far are any indication of a broader whole, young people today, semi-affiliated with the Mennonite church past or present, are constantly wondering where God fits into this picture. There are questions that cry for answers. Souls seek an intimate, safe setting in which to explore how their story fits into this web of others that constitute the community around them and then the broader world. A desire for ritual and traditionalism emerges, wed with a steadfastness to pluralism."   *—Melody King*

"_____'s immersion in a farming environment has limited her exposure to some of the ideas asked about in the interview. I found that she easily answered the first section of a question; she quickly answered the parts that asked her for quantitative information, like the number of times she performed an activity. When I asked her to explain the connection between why she had certain practices and what she values, it was more difficult for her to understand. Often, she looked at me quizzically or answered, 'I don't know.' I realized that some vocabulary, like 'spirituality,' or the more abstract ideas, like 'a sense of identity,' were not part of her everyday thoughts and words."   *—Annie Lengacher*

"I walked away from my group interview really pumped up, thinking about many of the responses that had just been offered. The interaction with the questions and between the participants had been exceptionally honest and genuine. What struck me the most was not just their willingness to discuss these questions together, but also the eagerness with which they did so. One of the group commented about how much fun the group conversation was for her, admitting how rarely she gets to talk about those types of questions with a group her age. 'We need to do that more often,' she said. I hope the interaction that happens through this project will encourage and empower young adults to continue the conversation."   *—Chet Denlinger*

"If I could sum up the interview in one word, it would be 'earnest.' As _____ told me about God calling her to missions or talked about her work with the kids in the after-school program, her face gleamed (seriously). And as she spoke about the community surrounding her family during her mother's illness or elaborated on the "Footprints" poem, her voice broke and her eyes teared. I even cried a couple tears while listening to the interview again. _____'s a rare one."   *—Bethany Spicher*

"Another interview completed, and with it another intimate glimpse permitted into an individual's life. The last two interviews now have given me the sense that the interviewee is unloading and reorganizing the bags that are their stories, their beliefs, their selves. Multiple times throughout these interviews there is the comment, 'Well, I hadn't really thought about it in this sense until you asked the question, but I guess . . . ,' and they go on to tell me why they believe something, why they hold to a certain practice, or why they don't."   *—Melody King*

"_____ has not yet graduated from college. She went to public schools through high school and then to YES, and is now taking classes toward a degree at a community college. And partly as a result of this, I think, I found _____ was much less prone to critical thinking and reflection. In earlier interviews, I would ask what persons would like to change about their childhood or about the church, and they would sit pensively for a moment, and then spill thought after thought. But _____ was usually content, after a moment's silence, to say, 'No, not really. There's noth -ing I would change.'"

—Deborah Good

"I will want to continue parts of this conversation with _____ at a further point or even have all of the people I interview sit down and talk together about this expe-rience. _____ said to me at the end of the interview that this was a good experi-ence and that he had reflected more in the one-and-a-half hours that we had together than in his whole life."

—Nate Barker

"I struggled a little more with this interview, because I felt like _____ never dropped his guard with me and only gave me the answers he assumed I wanted. _____'s com-ments reflected his upbringing in a very nontraditional Mennonite church. Many times, I needed to explain some question and how it related to being Mennonite. He didn't seem to have much connection with his Mennonite heritage or an affinity with the present-day Mennonite church. He demonstrated close ties with his current con-gregation but had no concept of the larger church. This seemed in line with his choice of a local college, his decision to live at home, and his commitment to the same con-gregation for an extended period of time."

—Annie Lengacher

"Interviewing _____ was a somewhat different experience. From what I knew of him previously, I doubted that he would be either very adept at expressing inner workings of his faith or very interested in the abstractions to describe them. I also knew he was pressed for time. It turned out that things went very well. While he was not abstract, and his not-so-smooth flow of thought made it difficult to find usable quotes, he really gave me some high-quality stuff by keeping things very concrete."

—Aram DiGennaro

"I found this interview extremely rewarding. I had predicted that this person's faith would provide an interesting interview. Throughout the interview, I found _____'s candor refreshing. He carried an ease about him that quickly diminished the 'formal' setting of an interview. I could also tell that he gave very heartfelt, honest answers and had spent time reviewing and analyzing his life before he came to the interview."

—Annie Lengacher

"As in my other interviews, I once again heard _____ wrestling with the relativism dilemma. I'm not sure if this really is a core question of our generation, or whether it is just *my* core question, so I pay attention to it in my interviewees. He said he didn't like to exclude people and therefore sees his belief in God as an individual reality, not a universal truth. But he also talked about it being important that the church draw lines—but he doesn't know where."   —*Deborah Good*

"Everyone commented that they were happy to have taken part in the discussion. I was glad to hear _____ say that taking part in the discussion made her realize how passionate she really is for the church. To know that the discussion was able to bring that out was a good feeling for me. She had been quite hesitant about the interview in the first place because of some serious time constraints, but I had told her that she would be glad if she participated, so that made me feel better to hear her say that. The conversation could have continued for hours and hours, but we kept it to about one-and-a-half hours since the participants were all busy. By the time it was over, I could tell that they would have been happy to stay and keep talking."   —*Allan Reesor-McDowell*

"In the last couple of weeks I have observed that I have a strong interest in young-adult faith development. I feel there is so much potential for us to 'do the works of the kingdom' as well as to have our lifestyles and values shaped as distinctly Christian. Our choices in this stage set a precedent for how much our generation will conform to cultural pressures vis-à-vis Christian values in areas such as career choice, use of money, sexuality, upward mobility, need for security. Can we effectively capture the exploration and experimentation inherent in this stage, in a way that leaves us bold people of faith? Is it necessary to assume that 'antistructure' or 'questioning faith' must be expressed outside the domain of the faith community?"
—*Aram DiGennaro*

To conclude, I think Rose said it so well in chapter 25: "This kind of discussion makes me realize that I really do care about the church. It makes me want to go out and change things. A hundred years ago, the people running the church were our age. It makes me want to mobilize people. There are so many people my age that care about these things. So why don't we get together and talk about this kind of thing? That's why I love my church in D.C. so much, because each week people get together and talk about their faith while they are cooking and doing other things."

I hear: "Thank you for asking. I'm so glad you did." What do you hear?

Appendix 1
Research Project Methodology

Purpose

The primary purpose of this project was to invite Mennonite-affiliated young adults

- to become critically aware of the narratives and practices that currently give meaning and identity to their lives;
- to actively deliberate about what narratives and practices most readily enable them to live in response to God's presence in the world, particularly as they have seen it modeled in Jesus Christ; and
- to imagine the future narratives and practices that should characterize communities of faith to which they might want to belong, thus showing the way into the emerging church of the future.

Process

The research team consisted of eight young-adult research assistants, myself, and one faculty colleague, with whom I consulted before and throughout the duration of the project. The team met initially for an evening, then a day of orientation, reflection, and training in ethnographic research. Several other faculty colleagues joined us for portions of the day, serving to resource different aspects of the event.

Following our intense work together, I finalized the interview materials and sent them to the research assistants. (For more information on this, see Interview Protocol and Interview Guide on the web site).[3]

In the following four months, the assistants engaged in one-on-one interviews with twenty-eight of their peers. Our approach to this research was primarily qualitative rather than quantitative. We kept a focus on narratives that tell stories of different aspects of young-adult experience, rather than expecting to make numerical calculations—such as claiming that 90 percent of young adults do this, or 50 percent do that.

After editing the field notes and journals from the twenty-eight interviews, I sent them to the research assistants and to Lonnie Yoder, faculty colleague and consultant. They read and reflected on all of the interviews in preparation for

---

3. Online: www.heraldpress.com

further consultation and discussion on what we had learned. Though some of us felt that not all young adults we know of are adequately represented, we were pleased with the diversity of voices. They speak powerfully about a reality that is characteristic of others somewhat like them. Some of us were struck more by the diversity than the commonality and wondered if anything meaningful can be said about young adults *in general*. We agreed that we didn't want to reduce the rich diversity of experience to generalizations that are unhelpful and unreflective of the complexity of young-adult life, yet we did pay attention to the themes that repeatedly show up.

I re-formed the team of researchers. We met for a day to discuss what we were hearing from the individual interviews and which of the findings we want to follow up, clarify, confirm, and deepen in group interviews. We drafted questions drawing on multiple quotes from the earlier interviews to serve as illustrations for evoking responses from the group. Our intention was that the group interviews would enlarge on and deepen themes that we were already hearing. We feel the group interviews succeeded in this. (See Group Interview Protocol and Questions for Group Interview on the web site.)[4]

Demographics

As we selected persons to interview, as individuals and in groups, we agreed to include some diversity among these various categories:

- age (young adults ages 20-29)
- affiliation (as self-defined) with Mennonite Church USA, either past or present church involvement—a spectrum of marginal to high
- educational levels (noncollege, college, graduates)
- ethnicity
- marital status—married, single, other (without children)
- gender
- theological orientation
- geography

Below are some of demographics of the fifty-six young adults we interviewed individually and in groups:

- Thirty subjects were males and 26 were females.
- Ten were persons of color, including three of international origin.

---

4. Online: www.heraldpress.com

•Ages ranged from 19 to 31, with the average age being about 24. Two people didn't list their date of birth.

•Twenty-four were current college students, many finishing degrees within weeks of the interviews; 22 had completed their college degree and were currently working or looking for work. Four were currently graduate students, and four had completed a graduate degree. Of those interviewed, 43 attended (at least a year) or were attending a Mennonite college. Two had a high school education only.

•Forty-five persons were single, at least two were engaged, six were married, and three were cohabiting.

•Of those who answered the question on church attendance, two said they attend from eight to ten times a month, 20 said they attend church about four times a month, 16 said about three times a month, ten about two times a month. Five indicated that they don't attend, and three didn't respond to the question.

•At least seven interviewees were not raised Mennonite but came to identify themselves as Mennonites as young adults.

•Places of birth include 15 different states and seven foreign countries, including Canada and Puerto Rico.

Appendix 2
Research Assistants

Nate Barker (29). Nate works as a youth and young-adult pastor at Weavers Mennonite Church near Harrisonburg, Virginia. He has an MDiv degree from Eastern Mennonite Seminary. For several years he worked as a video producer and editor at Mennonite Media. Nate grew up in Connecticut as a Baptist and joined the Mennonite church during his college years. He is married to Denise, and they have one son.

Deborah Good (24). After a year as an editor at *The Other Side* magazine, Deborah is working on writing projects and odd jobs, including trying to write her grandparents' memoirs. She lives in Philadelphia and has a BA degree from Eastern Mennonite University in sociology and justice, peace, and conflict studies, with a minor in Spanish. She attends West Philadelphia Mennonite Fellowship. Deborah grew up in Washington (DC), where she attended city public schools and a Mennonite-affiliated house church.

Chet Denlinger (23). Chet is a second-year MDiv student at Eastern Mennonite Seminary. He completed a BS in Business Administration at the University of Florida, where he was also extensively involved in a campus-based Christian student organization. Chet was born in Lancaster, Pennsylvania, but spent most of his growing-up years in Sarasota, Florida, where his family attended Bahia Vista Mennonite Church. Currently he is interning in a United Methodist church, though his long term ministry interests are with the Mennonites.

Bethany Spicher (26). Bethany currently works at the Mennonite Central Committee Washington Office, educating MCC constituents (and herself) about U.S. welfare, healthcare, and immigration policy. Before joining MCC, Bethany gardened in Topeka, Kansas, with Mennonite Voluntary Service, studied agriculture at Eastern Mennonite University, and worked for a year with *Sojourners* magazine. Bethany was born in Phoenix, but grew up near a Mennonite community in rural central Pennsylvania. She attends Community House Church in Washington (DC).

Aram DiGennaro (26). Aram attends Eastern Mennonite Seminary as a third-year MDiv student concentrating in church history. He did his undergraduate work in psychology with a minor in Spanish literature at the University of Missouri-Rolla. Currently he and his wife, Debbie, participate in various ministries at Immanuel Mennonite Church in Harrisonburg, Virginia. His passion for ministry extends especially to multicultural and international settings. Aram, who as a boy lived in Maryland and Missouri, did not grow up Mennonite. He began relating closely to Mennonites in various missions contexts during his high-school years.

Melody King (24). Melody works as a nurse on the oncology floor of the Hospital of the University of Pennsylvania in Philadelphia. She attended Goshen College and Eastern Mennonite University, graduating with a BS in nursing. She participates in the West Philadelphia Mennonite Fellowship. Melody grew up in Walnut Creek, Ohio, where her family attended a local Mennonite church.

Annie Lengacher (25). Annie lives in Denver, Colorado, where she is completing an MDiv with a special interest in spiritual formation at Iliff School of Theology. She has a BA degree in culture, religion, and mission from Eastern Mennonite University. Annie grew up attending a local Mennonite church near her family farm in the southern part of Lancaster County, Pennsylvania.

Allan Reesor-McDowell (22). Allan works as a Teacher's Assistant at Rockway Mennonite Collegiate in Kitchener, Ontario. He is also currently working on a history of Fraser Lake Camp for its fiftieth anniversary. Allan has a BA degree in history from Eastern Mennonite University. He currently attends First Mennonite Church in Kitchener. Allan has traveled abroad extensively, including a year in Haiti. He grew up in Ontario, attending a local Mennonite church.

Bibliography

Bass, Dorothy, ed. *Practicing Our Faith: A Way of Life for a Searching People.* Jossey-Bass, 1997.

Bruner, Jerome. "Narrative and Paradigmatic Modes of Thought." In *Learning and Teaching the Ways of Knowing.* Edited by Elliot Eisner. National Society for the Study of Education, University of Chicago Press, 1985,

Feiler, Bruce. *Walking the Bible: A Journey by Land Through the Five Books of Moses.* Morrow, 2001.

Garber, Steven. *The Fabric of Faithfulness: Weaving Together Belief and Behavior During the University Years.* InterVarsity, 1996.

MacIntyre, Alasdair. *After Virtue.* University of Notre Dame Press, 1981.

McLaren, Brian D. *More Ready Than You Realize: Evangelism as Dance in the Postmodern Matrix.* Zondervan, 2002.

———. *A New Kind of Christian: A Tale of Two Friends on a Spiritual Journey.* Jossey-Bass, 2001.

———. *The Story We Find Ourselves in: Further Adventures of a New Kind of Christian.* Jossey-Bass, 2003.

Murphy, Nancey. *Reconciling Theology and Science: A Radical Reformation Perspective.* Pandora, 1997.

Parks, Sharon Daloz. *Big Questions, Worthy Dreams: Mentoring Young Adults in Their Search for Meaning, Purpose, and Faith.* Jossey-Bass, 2000.

Roxburgh, Alan J. *Crossing the Bridge: Church Leadership in a Time of Change.* Precept Group, 2000.

———. *Reaching a New Generation: Strategies for Tomorrow's Church.* InterVarsity, 1993.

Shenk, Sara Wenger. *Anabaptist Ways of Knowing: A Conversation about Tradition-Based, Critical Education.* Cascadia, 2003.

Index of Interviews

Below is an index of young-adult interviews. A boldface page number indicates the beginning of the main interview(s) with each subject. To protect confidentiality, all names have been changed.

Group Interviews

Phil, Rose, Derek, Anita: 82-83, 105, 121, 183-84, 222-23, 238-39, 244-45

Ken, Jennifer, Karla, Ellen, Lisa: 83-84, 121-23, 182, 223-24, 232-35, 244

Josh, Greta, Don, Margo, Al, Curt: 84-86, 105-07, 123-24, 224-26, 235-36

Tara, Tony, Linda, Ray: 86-87, 107, 124-25, 184-85, 226-27, 236-37, 245-46

Beth, Tim, Michelle, James: 87-88, 108, 125-26, 185-86, 227, 237, 245

Andy, Conrad, Aaron, Ann, Sarah: 108, 126-27, 183, 227-28, 237-38, 246-47

The Author

Sara Wenger Shenk is Associate Dean and Associate Professor of Christian Education at Eastern Mennonite Seminary, Harrisonburg, Virginia. She holds an EdD degree from Union Theological Seminary in Richmond. She is the author of five books on themes related to family culture, everyday spirituality, changing family dynamics, Anabaptist educational theory and practice and a frequent speaker on formational and educational themes. Sara and her husband are parents of two sons and a daughter.